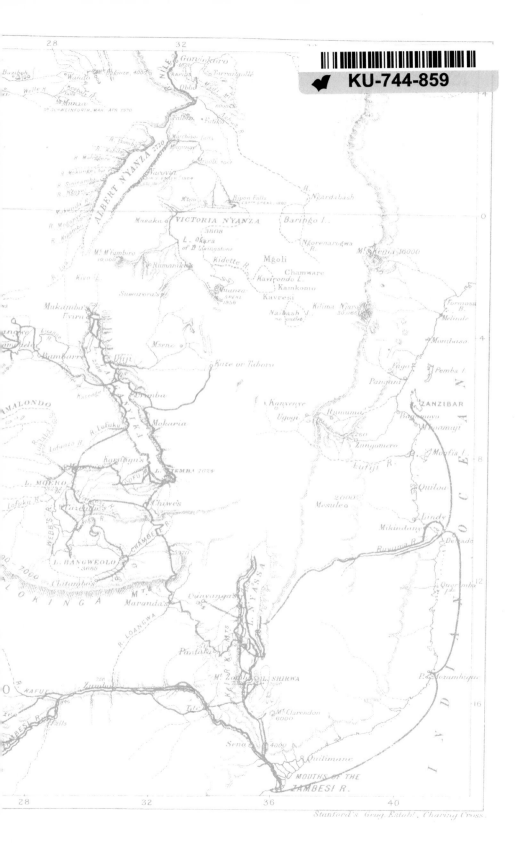

ALBERT NYANZA

VICTORIA NYANZA

Baringo L.

Mt. Kenia 18000

Masaka

L. Okara
or D. Livingstone

Kidette R.

Mgoli

Chamware

Kavirondo L.

Kaimkomo

Kavresi

Kilima Njaro 20,060

Naibash

Formosa B.

Melinde

Mukambar

Mombasa

Uvira

Mseno

Kaze or Tabora

Fuga

Pemba I.

Bambarre

Ujiji

Urumbu

Mekaria

Kanyenye

Ugogi

Runuma

Panguni

ZANZIBAR

Bagamoyo

Minamayi

MALONDO

Zungomero

Mofia I.

Lufiji R.

L. MOERO

Karungu's

L. TEMBA 2674

Chiwe's

2000

Mesule

Quiloa

Linde

Mikindany

L. BANGWEOLO
3688

Chitambo's

Ruvuma R.

Deloada

Querimba

LOKINGA

Maranda's

Uonvanga's

NYASSA

Pantuka

R. LOANGWA

Zumbo

Mt. Zomba

L. SHIRWA

R. Mozambique

KAFUE

Mt. Clarendon
6000

Falls

Senu

4000

Quilimane

MOUTHS OF THE
ZAMBESI R.

INTO AFRICA

INTO AFRICA

THE DRAMATIC RETELLING OF THE
STANLEY–LIVINGSTONE STORY

MARTIN DUGARD

BANTAM PRESS

LONDON · NEW YORK · TORONTO · SYDNEY · AUCKLAND

TRANSWORLD PUBLISHERS
61–63 Uxbridge Road, London W5 5SA
a division of The Random House Group Ltd

RANDOM HOUSE AUSTRALIA (PTY) LTD
20 Alfred Street, Milsons Point, Sydney,
New South Wales 2061, Australia

RANDOM HOUSE NEW ZEALAND LTD
18 Poland Road, Glenfield, Auckland 10, New Zealand

RANDOM HOUSE SOUTH AFRICA (PTY) LTD
Endulini, 5a Jubilee Road, Parktown 2193, South Africa

Published 2003 by Bantam Press
a division of Transworld Publishers

The right of Martin Dugard to be identified as the author of this work has been asserted in
accordance with sections 77 and 78 of the Copyright, Designs and Patents Act 1988.

Endpaper map: 'A map of the forest plateau of Africa . . . discovered and explored by
Dr Livingstone . . .' from volume I *The Last Journals of David Livingstone*,
edited by Dr Horace Waller, 1874.

A catalogue record for this book is available from the British Library.
ISBN 0593 04956X

Typeset in 10/13pt Sabon by
Falcon Oast Graphic Art Ltd.

Printed in Great Britain by
Mackays plc, Chatham, Kent

1 3 5 7 9 10 8 6 4 2

To Calene with Love

We also rejoice in our sufferings, because we know
that suffering produces perseverance; perseverance, character;
and character, hope – and hope does not disappoint us.

ROMANS 5:3–5

CONTENTS

CONTENTS

PROLOGUE

Henry Morton Stanley, 1866
© Bettmann/CORBIS

Dr David Livingstone with his daughter,
Anna, before leaving England to search
for the source of the Nile
© CORBIS

PROLOGUE

LIVINGSTONE

15 MARCH 1866
Zanzibar

TWENTY-FIVE YEARS TO THE DAY AFTER FIRST SETTING FOOT IN AFRICA, AND just four days before his fifty-third birthday, David Livingstone was holed up in a small house on the island of Zanzibar, waiting for a ship to take him back to his beloved continent. He had been away nearly three years and was impatient to return. The mere thought of mingling with African villagers, tramping through pristine wilderness, and 'the stimulus of remote chances of danger either from beasts or men' exhilarated him.

Livingstone had been stuck on the small island, just twenty miles off the coast of East Africa, since January. With every day that passed, he grew more disgusted by it. Zanzibar had once been a tropical paradise, lush with palm and mango trees, swept by sensual trade winds. But now the island was choked with people. Piles of human excrement and trash were stacked on the sandy beaches and the air smelled putrid at low tide. In the largest city, also Zanzibar, diplomats and merchants from the United States, Great Britain and the European continent battled for control of East Africa's expanding regional economy, even as they turned a blind eye to the slave trade Livingstone had fought so hard to end. Newly captured African men, women and children, still wearing the manacles and dog collars from their long march out of the African interior, were imprisoned in caves beneath the island, waiting for the day they would be sold in the city market.

The mood throughout Zanzibar was menacing, transient, bristling with compromise. Livingstone ached to be away from the chaos, in the wilds of Africa, alone.

Zanzibar, however, was also where European explorers bought their supplies and began their journeys into Africa's unknown heart. Livingstone was one of those men. Many said he was the best – or had been, in his prime. Now, in his fifties, Livingstone was about to begin the most ambitious expedition of his career. His goal was to achieve the Holy Grail of discovery: to determine once and for all the Source of the Nile River – a challenge that had eluded scores of worthy explorers through the centuries. And while there was a time when his prowess was so esteemed, and his expeditions imbued with such moral purpose, that finding the Source was almost beneath him, now he needed this accomplishment desperately. It would not only seal his legacy – it would restore him to the pinnacle of world exploration.

Before leaving England he'd assured his children and friends the journey would take just two years – an uncharacteristically brief sojourn for Livingstone. He would breach the African continent on its eastern shore, then travel west into the interior with the assurance of a man who had been there before. Livingstone knew the land, knew where he was going and knew where he would likely find the Source. Two years seemed an accurate prediction.

At first glance Livingstone seemed too benign and diminutive – too *religious* – to pursue such an epic undertaking. His spiritual aura was so great that even the Arab slave raiders against whom he battled so vehemently said he possessed the intangible known as *baraka*, uplifting and blessing all who came into contact with him. But within Livingstone were also limitless reserves of bravery and perseverance. The thin man with the stutter, crooked left arm and brown walrus moustache had walked across the Kalahari Desert, traced the path of the Zambezi River and, in the journey that made him famous, ambled from one side of Africa to the other. Although the London papers reported his death on more than one occasion, Livingstone was never actually lost, just overdue, for the very nature of exploration meant walking through spaces without the benefit of a map. His treks were rambling, circuitous wanders through jungles, swamp and savannah lasting years and years.

Throughout his travels, Livingstone scrawled copious daily notes. His handwriting had presence – big loops in his lower-case l's, no slant to his cursive, pithy phrasing – and the journal pages were often flecked with blood or stained by drops of sweat falling from his brow. Those simple words, often written by firelight with mosquito netting draped over his head, were published when his wanders were through. His books became bestsellers. The world learned about Africa through Livingstone's eyes. Unlocking its greatest mystery was a fitting career summation.

Before Livingstone's discoveries, geographers surmised that a vast desert lay in the middle of Africa. But as Livingstone travelled between 1841 and 1863 further into that blank section of the map, he saw for himself that Africa's interior was a marvellous mosaic of highlands, light woodlands, tropical rainforest, plateaus, mountain ranges, coastal wet-lands, river deltas, deserts and thick forests. Just like Egypt and the rest of Northern Africa, civilizations had thrived in Southern and Central Africa for millennia. An estimated twenty million people inhabited the interior when Livingstone first arrived. The tribes lived in villages, great and small. Their mud and grass huts with a single low doorway would be clustered within a protective fence of thorn bushes or sharpened stakes. Entire families shared a hut, and entire villages worked together to cultivate the surrounding fields and, if necessary, wage war. They understood metallurgy, and made spears from iron and copper. Artisans wove fine cloths, baskets and other functional *objets d'art*. Beer was brewed from bananas or grain. Fish and game were plentiful. Coffee was indigenous. Communication between villages and kingdoms was accomplished through a relay of swift runners. This 'bush telegraph' allowed information to travel quickly over thousands of miles.

The common root language, which Livingstone quickly learned, was Bantu. An amazing six hundred dialects had spun from that tongue as tribes spread out across the continent over thousands of years. Through the insular nature of Africa's geography, and the fact that people from other continents were terrified of exploring its interior, Africa's hidden civilizations had flourished.

One of the primary reasons Europeans stayed away so long dated back to the fifth century BC. While attempting an anti-clockwise circumnavigation of Africa, the Carthaginian explorer Hanno the Navigator dropped anchor on the west coast of Africa, near the equator. He and his men went ashore to hunt game and find fresh water. Slogging into a tropical rainforest, the music of drums and bamboo flutes wafted through the jungle from somewhere not too far off. Hanno and his men were scared, but they stayed the course. Then an enormous black man attacked them. The Carthaginians were in awe of his rippling muscles, great white teeth and full body hair. Fearing for their lives, the Carthaginians killed him. To prove to the world that such a man existed, he was skinned then brought back to Carthage. This 'gorilla', as Hanno's translators called him, terrified all who saw it. That display, plus Hanno's written account of the voyage, later translated into Greek and distributed throughout the known world, established Africa's reputation as a savage land. It would be twelve hundred years before Equatorial Africa was penetrated again.

Livingstone was the man who did it. Even more than the Arabs and Portuguese who went into Africa seeking ivory and slaves, he traversed the continent's unknown sub-Saharan region. Between 1841 and 1851 he explored the deserts, rivers and lakes of Southern Africa in a series of journeys lasting weeks and months. From 1852 to 1856 he walked from east to west across South-Central Africa along the course of the Zambezi. Then, after returning from his first visit to England since 1840, he explored the Zambezi and the area to its north more thoroughly. This single expedition lasted from 1858 to 1863.

Livingstone didn't emerge unscathed. The continent had insinuated itself into his appearance, given him bearing and presence, set him apart from other men. The narrow face with the hound-dog eyes had become taut, furrowed and tanned from day after day squinting into the sun. His Scottish burr had an African inflection and his lips struggled to form English sentences after years of wrapping themselves around Bantu's many dialects. Hookworm thrived in his belly. He was chronically anaemic. And of course, there was the famous left arm, permanently crooked after a lion bit deep and shook Livingstone like a rag doll. Not only did Livingstone survive the mauling with a preternatural calm, but also set the bone and sutured the eleven puncture wounds himself, without anaesthetic. Later he said that his time in the lion's jaws was an epiphany. He'd learned a secret that made him unafraid of death.

Livingstone was, then, the perfect man to venture into Africa to find the Source of the Nile. The explorer left England in August of 1865. Travelling via Bombay, he arrived in Zanzibar on 28 January 1866. There he purchased supplies, including the cloth and beads that functioned as currency for buying food in villages along the way and paying his porters. He also arranged for a second, crucial shipment of relief provisions to be sent overland to the village of Ujiji. Ujiji lay almost due west from Zanzibar, in the very centre of Africa. It was a primary Arab slave-trading outpost on the eastern shore of Lake Tanganyika. The relief supplies, so vital to an extended expedition, would be waiting when Livingstone reached Ujiji. In the event of a calamity such as theft or medical emergency, Livingstone would have peace of mind, knowing that his problems would be solved – as long as he could navigate to Ujiji. Despite his sworn opposition to the slave trade and disdain for the heathen Arabs who played such a pivotal role, he was depending upon them to carry these vital supplies to Ujiji and store them until he arrived. The success of Livingstone's entire expedition depended upon this act of trust.

Livingstone would lead an unlikely caravan. 'I have thirteen sepoys, ten Johanna men, nine Nassick boys, two Shupanga men, and two Waiyaus, Wakatini and Chuma,' Livingstone wrote in his journal. The sepoys were Indian marines assigned to Livingstone by Sir Bartle Frere, the Governor of Bombay. They carried rifles instead of a porter's load, and would serve as bodyguards. The Nassick boys also signed on in India, and would serve as porters. The Johanna men were from the Comoros Island of the same name, and many had served with Livingstone on his previous expedition. Most notable of all the men were the Waiyau lad named James Chuma, who had been a slave until Livingstone arranged his freedom in 1861, who could read and write English and would begin the journey as Livingstone's cook; and the Shupanga man named David Susi. Their deep loyalty to Livingstone would be vital in training the newcomers in the ways of an African expedition.

Those loads not carried by human beings would be lashed to an odd-ball menagerie of experimental pack animals: six camels, three buffalo, a calf, two mules and four donkeys.

Most important of all, there were no other Britons, Europeans or other white men making the journey. Livingstone had no peer, no confidant. He was ostensibly alone, which was as he liked it.

So it was that on the twenty-fifth anniversary of Livingstone's first arrival in Africa, HMS *Penguin* docked in Zanzibar to take him there again. Over the next few days the supplies and animals were loaded. Then, at 10 a.m. on 19 March 1866 – Livingstone's birthday – *Penguin* sailed from Zanzibar harbour under the command of a British officer named Lieutenant Garforth. They would steam three hundred miles south before putting ashore at the mouth of the jungle-clotted Rovuma River. From there Livingstone would push inland. He believed the Source of the Nile flowed into the Zambezi, and maybe even into West Africa's Congo. In Livingstone's mind, fountains south of the equator thrust these great rivers from the ground. Livingstone would travel west into Africa to find those fountains, and find his destiny.

Livingstone's journal entry practically sang as the trip got under way. 'Now that I am on the point of starting another trip into Africa I feel quite exhilarated,' he wrote. 'The effect of travel on a man whose heart is in the right place is that the mind is made more self-reliant: it becomes more confident of its own resources – there is greater presence of mind. The body is soon well knit; the muscles of the limbs grow hard as a board and seem to have no fat. The countenance is bronzed, and there is no dyspepsia. Africa is a most wonderful country for appetite, and it is only when one gloats over marrow bones or elephant feet that indigestion is possible. No doubt much toil is involved, and fatigue of which travellers in the more temperate climes can form but a faint conception. But the sweat of one's brow is no longer a curse when one works for God. It proves a tonic to the system, and is actually a blessing. No one can truly appreciate the charm of repose unless he has undergone severe exertion.'

On 24 March 1866, Lieutenant Garforth unloaded Livingstone's men and animals at the sweltering port of Mikindany, twenty-five miles north of the swampy, hippo-infested Rovuma. Livingstone planned to hire additional porters there before setting out. That evening, Livingstone shook Garforth's hand, thanked him, then went ashore. 'The *Penguin*,' Livingstone wrote simply of the last Englishmen who would see him alive, 'then left.'

On 4 April 1866, the explorer marched his caravan into Africa. As if the continent was swallowing him whole, Livingstone's entry into the jungle marked his disappearance from the outside world.

STANLEY

6 MAY 1866
Denver, Colorado
9,200 miles from Livingstone

ONE MONTH LATER, AND HALFWAY AROUND THE WORLD, HENRY MORTON Stanley unknowingly began a journey towards David Livingstone. He was twenty-five years old, a squat, dogged Civil War vet who fought for the blue *and* the grey, but had otherwise achieved nothing remarkable in his lifetime. In fact, Stanley's life to that point was notable only for its mediocrity. He had tried and been found wanting as a soldier, sailor, gold miner, son and lover. Yet there seemed no limit to the endeavours he was willing to attempt, then abruptly discard, without noteworthy accomplishment. He did, however, possess a natural flair for writing. He had already published several freelance newspaper pieces and had vague plans to become a success through a career in journalism.

The Front Range of the Rocky Mountains burst with wildflowers and the air smelled of budding green buffalo grass as Stanley stood on the banks of the South Platte River. A prairie wind, hard and cool, slapped Stanley's clean-shaven cheeks and blew back his brown hair. At his feet lay a collection of logs and planks bound together into a flat-bottomed raft drawing just eight inches of water.

Beside him was his friend and fellow would-be journalist, William Harlow Cook. They had met in Black Hawk City, Colorado, the previous year. Stanley was working in a smelting plant and sent Cook a congratulatory letter about a story the other man had written for a local paper. Cook was a meek individual, the perfect foil to Stanley's bluster. When Stanley made plans to travel from Colorado by rafting down the South Platte at flood stage, Cook didn't so much agree as follow timidly in his wake. It was of little consequence that the journey was potentially suicidal. What was important was that both could swim, for neither man had river-rafting experience and melting snow had engorged the otherwise lazy Platte. Stanley and Cook planned on riding those newly cut tree trunks for hundreds of miles down the ripping, snorting river until they reached an even broader and more swollen flow, the Missouri. The two freelance writers had had their fill of the west. They were off to points east, maybe all the way to China – wherever they might find an adventurous story to sell. Rafting the Platte would be a much quicker and easier method of crossing America's Great Plains, their first major geographical barrier, than walking.

'Stanley,' Cook noted, 'is short and quick and not easy to forget an enemy, but he is also firm and true as a friend.' Stanley was thick around the middle but otherwise muscular. He wore his moustache neatly trimmed and his hair combed straight back. His accent was a curious composition of a Louisiana drawl and a singsong lilt that overtook him when he became excited. He was fond of tall tales, but there was just enough truth in his stories to make them entirely believable. He was tight with a dollar and a prodigious saver, yet was always telling new acquaintances about one lavish scheme or another: gold mining in Alaska, grand adventures in Asia Minor, going to New York to become a real newspaper writer. Like his tall tales, there was just enough truth and ambition behind Stanley's schemes to make people believe he meant to accomplish them.

Key pieces of Stanley's character had been shaped in recent years. The Civil War, of all things, had been a positive experience for him. He had begun the war as a dry-goods salesman in an Arkansas backwater and come out of the war physically and emotionally equipped for a life of adventure. He had seen combat. He had become an expert marksman. He had endured the blisters, exhaustion and muscle pain of forced marches and seen first-hand the logistics of moving men and material over great distances, rapidly.

Stanley learned something else in the war – that he had a way with the written word. While serving as a clerk in the Union Navy he began writing newspaper stories on the side, detailing his battle experiences. He also began expressing his thoughts in a journal, revealing both surprising depth and moments of great melancholy.

When the war ended Stanley joined the scores of Civil War vets who were travelling into the American West to make their fortune. He made his way to the California gold fields and then to Colorado's silver mines, selling the odd freelance story to the Missouri *Democrat* about life on the authentic frontier. For the most part, however, Stanley was a drifter. In January 1866, frustrated with shovelling quartz in the Black Hawk City smelting works, Stanley moved two miles west to Central City and found employment as an apprentice printer with the town newspaper. The *Miner's Daily Register* wasn't glamorous (he had to moonlight by prospecting for gold to make ends meet) but it was regular work. After four months, however, Central City became tedious and Stanley hatched his plan to travel to New York then Asia Minor to assemble stories for a proposed book. With Cook, Stanley began his journey by taking the stagecoach from Central City into Denver, and it was there that they built their raft.

On 6 May, the two men carefully dragged it down the banks of the South Platte and scampered aboard. Stanley carried a pistol and rifle to hunt game for dinner, and each man had a bedroll, but otherwise their gear and provisions were minimal. They poled the raft into the swift, swirling current. The river carried them through Colorado towards Nebraska.

Stanley and Cook kept a sharp eye for Indians along the banks at all times. The Cheyenne and Pawnee were ostensibly peaceful, but rogue bands of braves still attacked travellers. The American Indians had had their lands to themselves until European powers and their colonial offspring grew interested in the vast region's commercial possibilities. Everything west of the Missouri River had been a blank spot on the map a mere sixty years earlier, when Lewis and Clark marched westwards for a definitive reconnaissance in 1804. The Indians were forced off the prime agricultural and pasture lands onto desolate reservations that served as open-air prisons. Now, Stanley and Cook's river ride allowed them to bear witness to what remained of the American frontier. The miles passed quickly. The prairie was beautiful and pure, awash in the renewal of spring.

A week into the journey the raft flipped. Stanley and Cook escaped by swimming to shore, then ran hard along the banks trying to catch up with their craft as it bobbed downstream. Stanley finally dived back in and swam towards it. The muddy water swirled about him, threatening to suck him under. But Stanley was persistent, if nothing else, and finally he caught the raft and guided it back to shore.

The next day, he and Cook floated downriver to Platte City, a small town at the convergence of the North and South Forks of the Platte. They were chilled from a night spent trying to sleep in wet clothes, and limped into town after carefully hiding their raft by the river. The town consisted of a dozen houses, some made of wood and some of sod. There was a small hotel, assorted saloons, a dry goods store and a few stray goats and mules. It was a town, however, with a reputation for vigilante violence. There were few trees in the area, so the bodies of horse thieves and murderers could be seen dangling from telegraph poles. One visitor to Platte City wrote that the telegraph poles served as 'a line of gallows, twenty to the mile'. Stanley and Cook took a room.

Platte City was just eighteen miles down a dirt road from Fort McPherson, headquarters of the US Army's 5th Cavalry. A captain of the cavalry was in town when Stanley and Cook checked into their hotel. Taking one look at the bedraggled travellers, the captain accused Stanley and Cook of being deserters from the army post at Fort Laramie, up the North Fork of the Platte. He ordered them not to leave Platte City until he could check their status. Just to make sure they stayed in town, the captain ordered two of his soldiers to keep Stanley and Cook under surveillance.

Not only did Stanley refuse to be intimidated, he seemed to revel in disregarding authority. He calmly went about his business, eating a meal in the small hotel and stocking up on food and ammunition for the remaining few hundred miles to Omaha, where the Platte and Missouri combined. The fact that his every movement was being watched didn't fluster Stanley.

After spending the night in town, Stanley and Cook paid their hotel bill and made to leave. The captain had been warned by his men, and was waiting for the erstwhile journalists. 'Shall I put you under arrest?' he said, squaring off in front of Stanley.

There was little about Stanley that was physically intimidating. His nose was unbroken. His ears lacked a fighter's cauliflower. He had no visible scars. His hands ran to small and had a curiously reddish tint. There was an omnipresent look of childlike confusion in his eyes. Yet Stanley glared at the captain with a menace Cook had never witnessed before. Placing one hand on his revolver, Stanley calmly agreed with the captain. 'Yes,' he said, clearly willing to shoot. 'If you have men enough to do it.'

The captain let them pass.

On 12 June 1866 Stanley arrived in New York City. His ungainly search for success was under way. More important, Stanley had begun travelling east as Livingstone worked his way west. As the miles between them decreased, the adventures that would ensue – random and whimsical at first, then linear and relentless – had begun, as well. Not even Stanley, with his enormous capacity for bluster and outlandish dreams, could imagine all that lay ahead.

I

THE SEARCHERS

Sir Richard Francis Burton

John Hanning Speke

ONE

THE NILE DUEL

16 SEPTEMBER 1864
Two Years Earlier
Bath, England

THE CATALYST FOR THE SAGA OF DARING TOOK PLACE SHORTLY AFTER eleven in the morning on Friday, 16 September 1864. Richard Francis Burton stood alone on the wooden speaker's platform at the British Association for the Advancement of Science's annual convention, awaiting his debate opponent. His wife Isabel sat a few feet behind. He clutched a sheaf of arguments. He was strong but narrow in the shoulders and hips, like a matador. His eyes were so dark brown they were often described as black. His moustache, truly black, flowed over and around his lips to his chin. The legendary Somali scars ran up his cheeks like slender compass arrows pointing north. He remained calm as he watched the doors for John Hanning Speke's entrance. The fair-haired geographical hero with the cold blue eyes was Burton's opposite, and Burton had waited six years to settle their rivalry. A few minutes more meant little.

The audience felt differently. It had been a wet, cramped morning and they were lathering up into a righteous fury. There had been rumours of a cancellation due to some sort of injury to Speke, but the almost two thousand adventurers, dignitaries, journalists and celebrity gazers came anyway. They braved a howling rain to get seats for what the newspapers were calling the Nile Duel, as if the debate was a bare-knuckle prizefight instead of a defining moment in history. Burton and Speke would argue who had discovered the Source of the Nile River – the most consuming geographical riddle of all time. Curiously, Burton and Speke made their conflicting Source discoveries during the same expedition. They had been partners. And even as they made plans to destroy one another, Burton and Speke suppressed deep mutual compassion.

They were former friends – lovers, some whispered – turned enemies. Theirs was a 'story of adventure, jealousy and recrimination, which painted their achievements in bright or lurid lights and tragic shades', in the words of Sir Bartle Frere, Governor of Bombay. Each man's aim was not just claiming the Nile, but destroying the other socially, professionally and financially. The winner would know a permanent spot in the history books. The loser would be labelled a delusional, presumptuous fool, with all the public ridicule that implied.

Speke was a thin loner whose family home, Jordans, was just forty miles from Bath. He was childlike, titled, wealthy, bland, deaf in one ear. At thirty-seven, he doted on his mother and had never courted any woman. Critics acknowledged his prowess as a sportsman, but puzzled over his penchant for slaughter and fondness for eating the unborn foetus of a kill. They wondered about the character of a man who once gave a rifle as a gift to an African chief fond of shooting subjects for fun, and who allowed a live human child to be steamed like a lobster during a tribal ritual in his honour. Speke felt that the ends justified the means – in his case, finding the Source was worth the inconsequential loss of African lives. The Source, Speke claimed, was a massive rectangular body of water the size of Scotland. He named it Victoria Nyanza – Lake Victoria – for the Queen.

The dark-haired Burton claimed Lake Tanganyika as the Source. That body of water lay 150 miles south-west of Victoria Nyanza, separated by mountainous, unexplored jungle. Burton did not dispute that the Nile flowed from Victoria, but he believed that another, yet undiscovered, river flowed from Tanganyika through the mountains, into Victoria.

Lake Tanganyika's shape was slender and vertical on the map, like a womb parting to give birth to the great Nile. Its choice as Burton's geographical talisman was apt, for his character tics veered towards the sensual. The accomplished linguist had a fondness for Arab prostitutes and would one day write the first English translation of the *Kama Sutra*.

In 1845, as a young army officer stationed in India, he'd been ordered to investigate Karachi's homosexual brothels. Burton's detailed reportage implicated fellow officers and gave rise to suspicion about his own sexuality – both of which combined to ruin his career. So he'd become an explorer. His knowledge of languages and Islam allowed him to infiltrate cities such as Mecca and Harar which were forbidden to non-Muslims. The resulting books about those escapades were best-sellers in the mid-1850s, earning Burton a reputation for daring while introducing Oriental thoughts and words to his readers. It was Burton who made the term *safari* – Swahili for 'journey' – familiar to the English-speaking world.

The mob packing the auditorium, so eager for spectacle and rage, knew the Burton and Speke story well. The time had come for resolution. When the eleven o'clock starting time came and passed, the crowd 'gave vent to its impatience by sounds more often heard from the audience of a theatre than a scientific meeting', sniffed the Bath *Chronicle*. The audience gossiped loudly about Speke's whereabouts and stared at the stage, scrutinizing Burton with that unflinching gaze reserved for the very famous. In an era when no occupation was more glamorous than African explorer, Burton's features were already well known through photographs and sketches from his books. But for many in the audience, seeing his face up close, in person, was why they'd come. They felt the same about Speke.

There was a third explorer many hoped to glimpse, a man whose legend was arguably greater than any living explorer. 'The room,' the *Chronicle* noted of the auditorium, 'was crowded with ladies and gentlemen who were radiant with the hope of seeing Dr Livingstone.' The British public hadn't caught a glimpse of their beloved Livingstone since the halcyon days of 1857 when he seemed to be everywhere at once. His exploits had been a balm for the wounds of the Crimean War, the ill-fated Charge of the Light Brigade and the bloody slaughter of British women and children during the Indian Mutiny. Livingstone reminded Victorian Britain of her potential for greatness. The fifty-one-year-old Scot was their hero archetype, an explorer brave, pious, and humble; so quick with a gun that Waterloo hero the Duke of Wellington nicknamed Livingstone 'the fighting parson'. Livingstone was equally at home wandering the wilds of Africa and making small talk over tea with the Queen. The public made his books bestsellers, his speeches standing-room only, his name household. Livingstone was beloved in Britain, and so famous worldwide that one poll showed that only Victoria herself was better known.

Livingstone, though, wasn't scheduled to appear at the Nile Duel. His first public appearance since returning from an exploration of Africa's Zambezi River six months earlier was officially supposed to take place the following Monday. He would lecture the British Association on the details of that journey. Ticket demand was so enormous that Livingstone, standing before a massive map of Africa, would give the speech live in one theatre as Clements Markham of the Royal Geographical Society read it concurrently to the overflow crowd in a second auditorium. The *Chronicle*'s special edition would publish the text in its entirety.

Rumours, however, said Livingstone would make an appearance at the Nile Duel as moderator. His appearance would confirm the Duel's heft, counterbalance smirks of innuendo. For celebrity gazers and scientists alike, Livingstone, Burton and Speke on the same stage would elevate the proceedings from grudge match to intellectual field day. Those three greats hurling geographical barbs would make the long hours in the rain more than worthwhile.

Ironically, the crowd was unaware that the larger-than-life Livingstone was enduring a season of tumultuous upheaval. His problems had begun with the five-year journey up the Zambezi. The expedition had accomplished a great deal. But many of his companions died during the journey – including Livingstone's wife, Mary, who had been so desperate to be with him she left the safety of England to venture into Africa to find him, then joined the expedition halfway through the journey. Because of the deaths, the failure of a highly touted project that would have established Christian missions in the African interior and reports that Livingstone was an inept leader, the British Government viewed the Zambezi expedition as a débâcle. Hence, *The Times* questioned Livingstone's judgement, he was *persona non grata* at the Foreign Office – his place of employment – and influential Christian politician William Gladstone quietly severed their relationship.

Financially, Livingstone was almost destitute. Even as friends urged him to retire and spend time with his children, he needed one last great geographical discovery so he could write the bestselling book about his travels that would provide for him and his family. 'I don't know whether I am to go on the shelf or not,' he wrote to a friend, acknowledging that the Foreign Office might never let him lead another expedition, but vowing to return to Africa nonetheless. 'If I do, I make Africa the shelf.'

Most devastating of all, however, was that Robert, his prodigal eldest son, had secretly sailed to America to fight for the Union Army in their Civil War. Robert Livingstone had been taken prisoner during the Siege of Richmond and been sent to a Confederate prisoner of war camp. There was no news of his whereabouts or physical condition. Livingstone, tragically, had castigated Robert for being aimless and base not long before the boy fled to America and enlisted.

In Bath that morning, the British public knew nothing of Livingstone's personal travails. In its eyes, Livingstone was not a legend in decline, but a luminary whose lined, tanned face they longed to glimpse. As eleven o'clock came and went, however, Livingstone, like Speke, was nowhere to be seen. Burton and the audience watched the doors, straining for a glimpse of their entrance. In fact, what would happen in the next few minutes would alter the future of exploration, Africa and the world.

Broken down to its essence, the Nile Duel was simply a search for water – two hydrogen molecules bonding with a single oxygen molecule in the bowels of the earth, then seeping forth somewhere in the heart of Africa, becoming a trickle, then a stream, then a mighty river. The Nile was longer than any other in the world, rolling effortlessly from mountains through jungle through Sahara through Cairo and into the Mediterranean. Mankind's most prolific kingdoms had risen and fallen on the Nile's shores. Moses, Cleopatra and Alexander drank her waters. The Nile never shrivelled, despite not having tributaries, substantial rainfall, or other obvious means of replenishment. She even flooded during September, the hottest month of the year in Northern Africa. Farmers planted in her fertile silt once the floods receded. Lush green fields blossomed in the desert as if the Nile was life itself.

The Nile flowed south to north into the Mediterranean, but its Source had always been a mystery. Theories ranged from the equator to the bottom of the world – or maybe from an even greater river, fed by an ocean, that sliced like an aqueduct across the entire African continent. In 460 BC, Herodotus, the Greek 'father of history', took it upon himself to find out. He pictured massive fountains spewing the Nile from the earth, and set off alone to witness the spume and mist. Six hundred miles inland from Cairo, however, the Nile turned white at the waterfalls that would someday be labelled the First Cataract. Like sentinels, they guarded the Nile's inner reaches. The desert turned to jungle. The civilized world ended and a land of cannibals began. Herodotus turned back.

The mystery was still unanswered when Ptolemy drew the first conclusive world map in AD 140. Based on African legends, he speculated that the source lay in snow-covered peaks along the equator, which he dubbed 'The Mountains of the Moon'. Critics wrongly ridiculed that idea, saying that snow couldn't possibly exist in that latitude. Neither Ptolemy nor those critics travelled up the Nile to see if he was right. Centuries passed. The Source became a force unto itself, too great for man to divine or witness. 'It is not given to us mortals,' the French author Montesquieu wrote in the eighteenth century, 'to see the Nile feeble and at its Source.'

In 1798, Source still undiscovered, Admiral Lord Nelson destroyed Napoleon's navy at the Battle of the Nile. Having established a toehold in Northern Africa, the British set to exploring their new land. The seas mapped and the continents defined, finding the Source became the new grail of international discovery. There was no pot of gold, no fountain of eternal youth at the Source, just glory – which, for most, was enough. Between 1798 and 1856 an eclectic collection of loners, thrill seekers and adventurous aristocrats trekked upriver from Cairo, chasing the Source. Most were British. A handful were female. Most died from disease, parasites, animal attack or murder. None found the Source. None came close. And with every failed attempt, Montesquieu's words rang more true.

The grail became more exalted as the failures mounted, as tackling the summit of Everest would become a century hence. Britain's growing sense of empire gave her a proprietary interest in finding the Source first. The reign of Queen Victoria, which began inauspiciously in 1837 with a botched coronation, had become a time of international expansion. Great Britain's citizens and companies controlled colonial outposts around the world, insinuating British ways and words into China, the South Pacific, South America, India, North America and Africa. The term 'the sun never sets on the British Empire' began during those heady times. No empire in history had ever been as vast, and the British were fond of comparing their empire with the Greek and Roman epochs. The Nile was a viable connection to that past. Finding the Source would heighten that connection.

'In the absence of adequate data we are not entitled to speculate too confidently on the Source,' Sir Roderick Murchison told Britain's unofficial governing body of exploration, the Royal Geographical Society, in 1852. The eminent geographer and RGS founder's attention focused on the Mountains of the Moon. 'It must be said that there is no exploration in Africa to which greater value would be attached than an ascent of these mountains from the east coast, possibly from near Mombasa. The adventurous travellers who shall first lay down the true position of these equatorial snowy mountains and who shall satisfy us that they throw off the waters of the White Nile . . . will be justly considered amongst the greatest benefactors of this age of geographical science.'

It was April of 1855 when Speke and Burton made their first Source bid. Their pairing was accidental: Speke was on leave from his regiment, the 46th Bengal Native Infantry, in India. They met in Aden, where Burton was finalizing his journey. Speke had planned to hunt big game, find the Source by himself, then float downriver to Cairo. Burton invited him to join his expedition instead. They were accompanied by a pair of British military men, Lieutenants William Stroyan and G. E. Herne, and the usual phalanx of porters vital to African travel. Instead of beginning at the mouth of the Nile in Egypt and working upriver, as explorers had done since Herodotus, Burton and Speke proposed to penetrate Africa from the east, beginning in Somalia then cutting the tangent from the Indian Ocean along the equator to the Mountains of the Moon's theoretical location. The northern regions of Africa were already mapped, as were the continent's southern and coastal fringes, but theirs would be a bold gambit through uncharted land. If the Source truly resided in the Mountains of the Moon, the shortcut would save them over two thousand miles of travel in both directions.

Burton and Speke made it to Africa but never even left the coast on that first expedition. Their forty-two-man caravan was camped along the Somali shore, waiting for the monsoon season to pass so they could move inland. Sentries were posted around the camp and a fire burned into the night to ward off Somali bandits, legendary as the 'penis-cutting people' because they emasculated vanquished enemies. When the attack came, however, the expedition was unprepared. It happened at 2 a.m. on the morning of 18 April 1855. Sentries and porters were slaughtered first by the Somalis, who wielded sabres, curved daggers, war clubs and six-foot-long spears. Burton stepped from his lean-to at the first sound of violence, brandishing a sabre. Stroyan rose to his side clutching a Colt revolver in each hand. Together they battled the Somalis, even as the remaining porters fled into the night or were butchered alive.

Speke stayed in his tent through the early part of the battle, saying later that he mistook the sounds of gunfire for warning shots fired by spooked sentries. But then the Somalis began using the British tents as snares, collapsing them on top of men and thrusting spears into the writhing piles of canvas. Speke grabbed his pistols and stepped from the solitude of his tent into the frenzy. Burton was still alive but Stroyan had run out of bullets. He was being hacked to pieces by the Somalis, even as he swung his empty pistols like clubs. Speke began fighting his way through a cloud of Somalis to rescue Burton when a warrior thrust a javelin clean through Burton's face, fleeing before Speke could shoot. The spear remained stuck in Burton's head, jabbing out at right angles. He had lost teeth and blood poured from his mouth and both cheeks. Unable to pull out the javelin and unable to link up with Speke, the would-be explorer miraculously escaped into the night before another warrior could finish him off.

Speke, however, was taken prisoner. The Somalis could have killed him quickly like Stroyan, but with the battle winding down they had the luxury of enjoying his terror. Speke's hands were tied behind his back and he was shoved to the ground. The Somalis began fondling his genitals as if debating the most wrenching means of slicing them off. His captors, though, turned their attention to looting the camp before they could finish the job. Just to make sure Speke didn't escape while they were gone, the Somalis plunged spears deep into his thighs. They narrowly missed his groin but severed the muscles of his hamstrings and quadriceps.

In his agony, Speke still managed to slip his bonds and escape without being detected. He dragged himself three miles down the beach to where a British ship was anchored. And somehow, miraculously, Herne and Burton – javelin still jutting from his face – were waiting. All three were soon on their way back to England.

Lesser men would have set aside exploration after that – G. E. Herne certainly did. But no sooner had their wounds healed than Burton and Speke, who had both been army officers before venturing into exploration during peacetime, resumed their army careers to fight Russia in the epic blunder known as the Crimean War. When the war came to an end it was back to Africa to find the Source, this time funded by the Royal Geographical Society. Burton and Speke were brave loners, a type of personality society idealizes from a polite distance but finds discomfiting up close. Speke was often blunt and inappropriate, and since childhood had fled to the hunting fields to regain his inner strength. Burton simply scared people. The facial craters from the Somali spear only made it worse.

The life of an explorer, then, was almost a mandate for both of them. Explorers, by the original Latin definition, are those who cry out. The men earning that title first were searchers for game instead of searchers for geographical features. They walked far ahead of hunting parties, shouting out the locations of animals they discovered. As tribes became kingdoms and kingdoms became countries, the searchers were called on to look for new lands instead of game. They returned home to cry out what they saw so that civilization might follow in their wake. Then, because a searcher's special talent belonged to the wilds, not cities, they went back again. And again.

Burton and Speke fit this description. Neither man was suited to holding down a steady job. Both their childhoods had been marked by loving mothers and diffident fathers. In the absence of paternal guidance, Burton and Speke had navigated their own paths through life, making up the rules as they went along. The chip on each man's shoulder was prohibitive, diminished for brief periods by the euphoria of achievement. Africa, or some other land without limitations, was where they belonged.

Their second Source attempt began two years later, in the spring of 1857. It was a smaller expedition – just Burton and Speke and their porters this time, no other Englishmen. As expedition leader, Burton made the decision to start further south, in an area where tribes were less hostile and where Arab traders had been penetrating inland for centuries. After purchasing supplies on Zanzibar, where 'gonorrhoea is so common it is hardly considered a disease', according to Burton, and corpses floated in the city harbour, Burton and Speke sailed for the mainland. They put ashore just north of the port of Bagamoyo. If the shape of the African continent is an east-facing skull, their landfall was a point somewhere just below the nose. That region would become the pivotal jumping-off point for African exploration over the next half-century. In Burton and Speke's case, the proposed journey was an eight-hundred-mile trek through swamps, savannah and forest to a village known as Ujiji, on the eastern shores of Lake Tanganyika. Arab traders had been going there for over three decades. En route, Burton and Speke would seek information about the Source's location.

In early June the monsoon season ended. Burton and Speke bored inland leading a column of thirty-six porters and thirty pack animals. They were an odd-looking pair – Burton favouring Arab robes and Speke wearing English hunting flannel under a broad-brimmed felt hat. They carried tents and bedding, chairs, tables, navigational aids, brandy and food, cloth and wire, assorted medicines, and an arsenal of daggers, swords, rifles and pistols. Progress averaged less than six miles a day, beginning after an early breakfast, halting in midday for a respite from the heat, then continuing again to late afternoon. As the sun set and the porters danced or told stories around the fire, Burton would record observations in his journal. Latitude and longitude were noted. Elevation was determined by using a thermometer to check the temperature at which water boiled. Burton was taken with the adventure, but found the continent much more brutish and forbidding than he'd imagined it could be.

Among their caravan was a hard-working young African named Sidi Mubarak Bombay, whom Burton referred to as 'the gem of the group'. Bombay was a member of the Yao tribe who had been captured by Arab slave traders at the age of twelve, then sold in the Zanzibar slave market to an Arab merchant. When the Arab moved to the city of Bombay shortly after, his young slave came along. When the Arab died, the slave was given his freedom and the adopted name of Bombay. Upon returning to Africa sometime in his early thirties, Sidi Mubarak Bombay joined the Sultan of Zanzibar's army as a soldier, and was posted to a garrison in Chokwe. That outpost seven miles from the Indian Ocean coastline was where Burton and Speke met up with the industrious, grinning former slave. By arrangement with the garrison commander, Bombay and five other soldiers were hired to accompany the British caravan. Bombay's work ethic and linguistic skills soon made him invaluable to Burton and Speke. Unbeknown to Bombay, his soldiering career was at an end, replaced by a new line of work that would lead him into the history books.

Bombay spoke fluent Hindustani, as did Speke, so Bombay served as Speke's gunbearer and translator. 'He works on principle and works like a horse,' Burton wrote of the short ugly man with filed-down teeth and an aversion to bathing, 'candidly declaring that not love of us but duty to his belly makes him work. With a sprained ankle and a load quite disproportionate to his puny body, he insists on carrying two guns. He attends us everywhere, manages our purchases, carries all our messages, and when not employed by us is at every man's beck and call.' Bombay would go on to become the talisman of African exploration, an essential roster member on any serious expedition for decades to come.

Before the expedition Burton had written that Speke was a 'companion and not a friend, with whom I was strangers'. Speke still chafed that Burton placed more emphasis on exploration than hunting, but as the journey progressed Burton and Speke became solid companions. Burton was officially the expedition leader, but he and Speke behaved more as equals. They had already fought a battle together. Now the shared agony of swamp fever, malaria and mutinous porters only brought them closer. They nursed one another through Africa's strange new illnesses and wearying tribulations. They read Shakespeare aloud to one another at night. Back home, Speke had his mother and Burton had his conquests, but neither man had a close friend. In the loneliness of Africa, however, they needed each other. Burton wrote that Speke was 'as a brother'.

The brotherhood saw great trials. The first months of the journey were a slog through claustrophobic jungle, where the thick, dank air pressed down on their shoulders and poured into their lungs. The porters deserted in ones and twos, in the dead of night, stealing precious supplies before fleeing back to the coast. A morass of palm trees, strangler figs, leopard orchids, black mambas, green mambas, cobras, monkeys, mosquitoes and tse-tse flies defined the expedition's days. The going was slow. Malaria and sleeping sickness afflicted those porters who didn't desert.

The route climbed to a plateau a little over two hundred miles inland. The scenery changed abruptly, magically, as if a new backdrop had been unfurled on a vaudeville stage. Gone was the jungle. In its place was a vast dun-coloured grassland. Acacia trees, with their stratified branches looking like low wispy clouds, hovered randomly. Clusters of shrubs seemed like islands on the sea of grass. Otherwise the land was wide-open space as far as the eye could see. Herds of elephants, zebras, giraffe, hyenas and wildebeest became commonplace. Lions and hyenas were a nightly threat, prowling outside the camp in the darkness, waiting for the campfire to burn too low, sniffing for stragglers and scraps. Water was scarce. Shade was a luxury. Burton and Speke were sick frequently but they pushed on. By November, after travelling six hundred miles, they arrived in the village of Tabora. It was a snake-infested, dusty oasis of mud homes surrounded by low rolling hills, but the Arab traders had made it the premier stopover on their way inland. Canned goods, goats and bulls for milk and slaughter, and reminders of home such as tea were available. Burton and Speke regained their strength. There were women, too. Burton was sated.

After five weeks they pushed on. Speke was in favour of travelling north, to where a large lake was reputed to exist, but Burton insisted they go west. The path changed from savannah to swampy sycamore forests. Both men were almost killed by malaria and had to be carried. But by February 1858, with Burton and Speke blinded by illness, Bombay first spied the shining waters of Lake Tanganyika. The caravan soon stood on the banks of the enormous lake. As Burton and Speke's eyesight returned they saw before them a lake like none they'd ever seen, wider than the English Channel and stretching far over the northern and southern horizons. Surely, they agreed, this was the Source. Speke, enraptured by the peaks surrounding the lake, wrote confidently in his journal: '. . . this mountain range I consider the true Mountains of the Moon.'

Burton and Speke stayed three months, searching for that elusive river leading north out of the lake into the Nile. They never found it. Regardless, the journey home began on 26 May 1858. The porters who had deserted had stolen most of the cloth and beads necessary to barter for food. It was urgent that Burton and Speke race for the coast or risk starving to death.

However, malaria again crippled Burton. The impoverished caravan was forced to halt in Tabora so he could recuperate. Speke, who found the Arabs repulsive and disliked Burton's fondness for their clothing and customs, wanted to investigate those rumours of another great lake to the north. Taking Bombay and a handful of porters, Speke began the journey in July 1858. The Burton and Speke expedition had been travelling through Africa for thirteen mostly agreeable months. All of that, however, was about to end.

Six weeks after leaving, an excited Speke strode back into Tabora. He had not only found the rumoured lake, naming the hill from where he'd seen it after Somerset and the lake itself after Queen Victoria, but he had immediately set aside his previous convictions about Lake Tanganyika. Victoria Nyanza was the true source. 'I no longer felt any doubt that the lake at my feet gave birth to that interesting river, the source of what has been so much speculation, and the object of so many explorers,' he corrected in his journal. Years before, as an officer in India, Speke had harboured the secret desire to make his name by discovering the Source. On 3 August 1858, he was sure he had done so. He didn't walk around the lake to make sure the Nile flowed from it, so he never actually saw the river. But Speke interviewed the local population and drew a map of the lake based on their opinions. The map definitively showed the Nile flowing out of Victoria Nyanza. That done, Speke had raced back to Tabora.

Fearful of being rebuffed, Speke delayed telling Burton about his theory until the morning after his return. 'We had scarcely breakfasted,' Burton wrote, 'before he announced to me the startling fact that he had discovered the sources of the Nile. The fortunate discoverer's conviction was strong, but his reasoning was weak.'

Their relationship would never be the same. 'Jack changed his manners to me from this date,' Burton later wrote of 26 August 1858 in a profound understatement. And while Burton had tolerated the non-intellectual aspects of Speke's personality before, he began treating the younger man like a fool.

Burton demanded that they walk north to double-check Speke's claim. Speke, however, reminded Burton that they lacked the cloth and beads vital for purchasing food. They had no choice but to head straight for the coast. The hotheaded Burton reluctantly agreed.

The feud escalated during the four-month walk back to Bagamoyo. Speke endured an African illness that made him delusional and racked with pain, and both men almost died of malnutrition, but their argument raged. When they finally reached the coast, the two men split up, returning to London on different ships. Their goodbyes in Aden were the last words they would utter to one another.

Speke's HMS *Furious* arrived in England first. He raced to the Royal Geographical Society and pronounced himself the discoverer of the Source. His claim was audacious and unproven, but the world was ready to believe that the Source had been found. By the time Burton made it home just weeks later, Speke was the toast of London. 'I reached London on May 21st,' Burton wrote. 'My companion now stood forth in his true colours, an angry rival.'

For five long years the debate raged – in the most elite circles of society and in commoners' pubs as well. There were other world events to draw England's attention during that time (across the Atlantic, America was now embroiled in a civil war that the British, for the sake of trade and naval supremacy, were keen for the South to win) but nothing had eclipsed it. England had endured a decade of wars in the 1850s, and the escapism of Burton and Speke's adventures proved much more intriguing in London than worries about another nation's internal strife.

The two men traded slings and arrows in public speeches, published articles and competing books. Burton accused Speke of being an incompetent geographer. Speke accused Burton of 'incompetence, malice, cowardice and jealousy'. Burton married. Speke returned to Africa with another man to prove his claim. 'The Nile,' Speke pronounced upon locating the river's effluence from Victorian Nyanza, then following the river three thousand miles north to the Mediterranean, 'is settled.'

But it wasn't. Not definitely. Speke had failed to circumnavigate Victoria, meaning a river could have fed into it without his knowing, which would prove Burton's argument. And at one point he had taken a cross-country shortcut rather than follow the river's snaking course. Short of the two men returning to Africa together, the only way to settle the matter was through a scientific presentation of facts.

In this way, 16 September 1864 was chosen as the date for the Nile Duel. Under the auspices of the Royal Geographical Society and the British Association, against the backdrop of Bath's fading Georgian splendour, in the East Wing of the Mineral Waters Hospital, mankind's last geographical mystery would be settled. The hospital contained the only auditorium in town large enough to hold the debate's crowd. When first constructed in 1737, its creation represented a newfound scientific belief in water's restorative properties. That a divisive debate over water would be held within its walls was the sort of grand irony the occasion demanded. *The Times* – known as The Thunderer for its *gravitas* – would be on hand to report the action, as would the more accessible papers like the *Daily Telegraph* and Manchester *Guardian*. The Bath *Chronicle* imported forty extra typesetters from London to churn out a new edition immediately after the verdict.

On 15 September, the day before the Duel, Burton and Speke had settled into their chairs for RGS president Sir Roderick Murchison's opening remarks, seeing one another for the first time since Africa. Speke was overcome. 'He looked at Richard and at me, and we at him,' Isabel Burton wrote of that afternoon. 'I shall never forget his face. It was full of sorrow, or yearning, and perplexity. Then he seemed to turn to stone. After a while he began to fidget a great deal, and exclaimed half aloud, "Oh, I can't stand this any longer." He got up to go out. A man nearest him said, "Shall you want your chair again, sir? May I have it? Shall you come back?" and he answered "I hope not" and left the hall.'

Desperate to calm himself, Speke sought out a cousin who lived nearby. Speke suggested they spend the afternoon hunting partridge in Neston Park, about seven miles from Bath.

By the following morning, the debate auditorium was smelling of wet wool, stale tobacco and the myriad odours of bodies wedged cheek by jowl. There were as many women as men. Stomachs rumbled in anticipation of lunch. Eleven o'clock came and passed. Burton waited for Speke. With every tick of the clock, the crowd's murmurs about tardiness turned to angry rumbles about impertinence and cowardice.

At 11.25, the doors finally opened. All eyes turned quickly, but saw neither Speke nor Livingstone. Instead, the wiry, bald Murchison solemnly entered with a handful of men comprising the Society's inner council. They took their seats on the speaker's platform. Murchison waited for the crowd to hush, then began to speak in his usual convoluted delivery. 'I have to apologize but when I explain to you the cause of my being a little late in coming to take the chair you will pardon me.' The next sentence, however, was as direct as a punch to the solar plexus.

'Captain Speke has lost his life.'

Speke had lodged his Lancaster breech-loading rifle, which had no safety catch, into a low stone wall before attempting to climb over. Something had jarred the rifle, making it fire. The coroner would avoid the word 'suicide', but his report would show that Speke pressed the barrel directly into his heart as he climbed over the wall. The bullet, the coroner wrote, 'led upwards towards the spine, and passing through the lungs, dividing all the large vessels of the heart'. Even though the shot passed through his heart, Speke's suicide was slow. He bled for ten minutes before dying at the base of the wall.

'Sensation', as the *Chronicle* reported the moment, swept the audience when Murchison broke the news. 'Richard sank into a chair, and I saw by the workings of his face the terrible emotion he was controlling and the shock he had received,' wrote Isabel. 'When called upon to speak, in a voice that trembled, he spoke of other things, and as briefly as he could. When we got home he wept long and bitterly, and I was for many a day trying to comfort him.'

Murchison proposed a resolution regretting Speke's death, with condolences to be passed along to his family. After a unanimous show of hands, it was passed.

As for Livingstone, people were wondering about his absence. When Murchison was asked where the missing explorer might be, he merely shrugged. 'I expect him at any hour, but I cannot account for his absence.'

'In fact,' Murchison concluded, knowing full well that Livingstone had been in seclusion, writing the speech he would deliver a few days later in Bath, 'he might be in Africa for all I know.'

Two months later, Murchison finally got what he wanted. The Nile Duel was still alive and well, Speke's theories were being closely scrutinized, and Burton couldn't be trusted to seek the Source for obvious reasons of non-objectivity. James Augustus Grant, Speke's companion on the second journey, would be equally subjective; he had thrown himself on the coffin and keened like a grieving widow at Speke's funeral. Sir Samuel White Baker, the barrel-chested engineer who discovered Lake Albert, was still somewhere in Africa, position unknown. Even John Kirk, the botanist from the Zambezi expedition, was out of the question. He had fallen in love and was about to be married. The timid young minister's son, who harboured a deep and secret hatred for Livingstone, wanted to settle down and get a good job, not take off for two years in Africa.

Murchison finally approached Livingstone. Livingstone adored Murchison. He owed his fame to the regal geologist. And while Livingstone was aching to return to Africa, having said so during his triumphant speech in Bath on 19 September and then again during an RGS meeting in London on 14 November, his financial concerns were too great to ignore. He wanted to ensure that his retirement would be comfortable, and that his children – Bob (when he returned, which was looking more likely as the American Civil War drew to an end), seventeen-year-old Agnes, six-year-old Anna Mary, fifteen-year-old Tom and thirteen-year-old Oswell, who was his father's spitting image – would have an inheritance. He couldn't, in good conscience, return to Africa without solving his money problems first.

Livingstone was living with his children at Newstead Abbey, Lord Byron's former estate north of London, now owned by his good friend James Young. He was writing his Zambezi memoirs. Livingstone despised the tedium of being indoors for long hours as he distilled his journals into publishable form, but considered it a necessary task. If the Zambezi book sold as well as his first book, *Missionary Travels*, Livingstone would achieve a measure of financial serenity.

'Why cannot you go?' Murchison implored upon arriving at Newstead. 'Come, let me persuade you. I am so sure that you will not refuse an old friend.'

Livingstone's defences were wavering. Despite their deep friendship, it was an extraordinary breach of Victorian social protocol for a man of Murchison's wealth to make such a vulnerable appeal to a man of lesser social standing. With Murchison and Livingstone both getting on in years, finding the Source would likely be the last expedition on which they would cooperate – and their greatest triumph if it succeeded. 'Never mind about the pecuniary matters. It shall be my task to look after that,' Murchison reassured him. 'You may rest assured your interest will not be forgotten.'

Livingstone, the man who walked through Africa without fear, cared so deeply for Murchison that he felt powerless to say no.

'You,' Murchison enthusiastically reminded his friend, 'will be the real discoverer of the Source of the Nile.'

Four months later, on 16 April 1865, Livingstone made a public statement of his intentions. 'I have no wish,' he wrote, with sentiments that would change as the Source became a fixation, 'to unsettle what with so much toil and danger was accomplished by Speke and Grant, but rather to confirm their illustrious discoveries.'

On 14 August 1865, *Narrative of an Expedition to the Zambezi and Its Tributaries* safely delivered to the publisher, Livingstone sailed for Africa.

TWO

INTO AFRICA

19 JUNE 1866
Along the Rovuma River, Africa

'WE PASSED A WOMAN TIED BY THE NECK TO A TREE AND DEAD,' Livingstone wrote in his journal exactly three months since leaving Zanzibar. 'The people of the country explained that she had been unable to keep up with the other slaves in a gang, and her master had determined that she should not become the property of anyone else if she recovered after resting for a time. I may mention here that we saw others tied up in a similar manner and one lying in the path was shot or stabbed, for she was in a pool of blood.'

It had been two and a half months since Livingstone's journey inland had begun. He was marching along the Rovuma River delta, through a towering, omnipresent wall of bamboo forest, creeping vines and mangrove trees. The air was heavy and humid, and smelled of genesis and rot. His physical health was robust, but the combination of insubordinate porters, gruesome daily evidence of the slave trade and painfully sluggish pace had him battling bouts of depression. He had averaged just three miles of travel per day since leaving the coast. It certainly wasn't the quickest way to verify Speke and Burton's theories about the Source, but marching inland via the Rovuma was the only possible way for Livingstone to ascertain facts about his own, wildly improbable, Source theories. He believed the Nile and Zambezi were connected by a chain of lakes – from south to north: Nyassa, Tanganyika, Victoria. The Source, in Livingstone's estimation, lay much further south than Speke or Burton theorized.

The obvious, and quickest, way to Lakes Victoria and Tanganyika was by travelling from the Indian Ocean to Lake Tanganyika via the Arab caravan route followed by Burton and Speke. Livingstone, however, was taking the long way. His march had begun three hundred miles south of Burton and Speke's point of departure. He planned to march due west along the banks of the Rovuma River until reaching Lake Nyassa, which he had first explored during the Zambezi trip. From there he would travel north towards Lake Tanganyika and the likely location of the Source. He was undaunted that a German geologist, Dr Albert Roscher, had been butchered by hostile tribes six years earlier while following the same path, or by reports that a rogue Zulu splinter group known as the Mazitu were marauding and killing near Lake Nyassa. When trouble came, Livingstone would sidestep it and move forward. Always forward.

He was glad to be back in Africa, but the rest of his caravan lacked Livingstone's enthusiasm. There was no trail along the Rovuma, so paths had to be hacked through the brush. His pack animals were dying from sleeping sickness, and after the first hundred miles of travel the terrain had angled upward as they left the coastal plain behind. The temperature was dropping as the elevation rose, and cold south winds began to blow. Livingstone had hired a band of porters to supplement his original contingent, back at the mouth of the Rovuma, but they chafed at the hard work and turned back on 11 June. That left Livingstone with his original band of twenty-six porters and soldiers, who had grown tired and surly in the extreme conditions.

Part of the blame rested on Livingstone. Not only had he chosen his companions poorly, but his habit of wandering ahead to scout the trail left the group unsupervised. The result was chaos: the Johanna porters stole Livingstone's precious cloth and beads, dawdled, and conveniently lost his non-essential supplies when they grew tired of carrying them; the sepoys, those Indian Marines hand-picked by their country's governor to protect Livingstone from hostile tribes, were useless. Livingstone complained 'they would not get up in the mornings to march, lay in the paths, and gave their pouches and muskets to the natives to carry'. The sepoys grew so desperate to go home they tried to sabotage the expedition by poking the pack animals with their bayonets, and encouraging the porters to run off with them. Only a small handful of men, led by Chuma and Susi, were committed to staying by Livingstone's side for as long as it took to complete his work.

Livingstone endured the personnel issues, treating them as a necessary distraction. He focused his attention on exploration. With a chronometer and sextant he pinpointed the latitude and longitude of villages and rivers. A thermometer helped him divine altitude. His interests veered far from the merely scientific, however, and Livingstone wrote down anything else of interest that struck his fancy. He wrote about the holes dug in the ground so tribes could slow-cook the heads of zebra, the feet of elephants and the humps of rhinoceros. He noted that fire was so important for safety from wild animals and mosquitoes at night that villagers carried their kindling with them wherever they went. He wrote about how pottery was made, and casually noted that pottery shards were everywhere. But for every anthropological notation, a remark about slavery was sure to follow: the little girl orphaned because she was too weak to walk alongside her parents as they were taken away; the tribes who sold other tribes into slavery and wore the expensive white calico that was their reward; the well-dressed woman with the slave-collar around her neck, demanding that someone free her but receiving no reply from bystanders. Livingstone wrote of those in-justices with growing rage, furious with the Arabs and Portuguese for their behaviour, and with the Africans who assisted them. 'At Chenjewala's,' he wrote of a village visited on 27 June, 'the people are usually much startled when I explain that the number of slaves we see dead on the road have been killed partly by those who sold them; for I tell them that if they sell their fellows, they are like the man who holds the victim while the Arab performs the murder.'

The journal entries often stretched to several pages per day, jotted with a small fountain pen with a steel nib. Livingstone kept his journals in a watertight tin box he'd purchased just for that purpose. The box would protect his words from the elements, and with luck even float if swept down a river. For the words were his gold, his future. They would be moulded into a book about his search for the Source, and provide raw scientific and anthropological data to the Royal Geographical Society. But the journals, on a much deeper level, were also Livingstone's connection to his roots. He had been a prolific reader as a boy. Through the simple act of absorbing the printed word, the first seeds of exploration were planted in the unlikely explorer over four decades earlier.

Livingstone was born in poverty, in a three-storey tenement outside Glasgow in 1813. He was the second of seven children. His forefathers had been highland rogues before moving to the city, but the adventure gene was recessive in Livingstone's impoverished father. While Neil Livingstone's brothers became soldiers of fortune, he sold tea and ran a small market. He was such a zealous member of the Independent Congregational Church that he impulsively dropped the 'e' from the family name, imagining a connection between a 'living stone' and witchcraft.

The explorer spent his childhood working fourteen-hour days inside the din and chaos of the Blantyre Works cotton mill. The introspection, stoicism and need for wide open spaces that later became Livingstone's trademarks could be traced to the claustrophobia of the mill, where the noise was so great that all communication was conducted at a yell. As a man, walking through Africa, he rarely spoke at all.

Evenings in Blantyre were for school. Sunday, the only day off for the adolescent Livingstone, was for church. Afterwards, Livingstone was fond of escaping into the countryside for solitary hikes and rock hunts. The rare leisure time was passed reading. Books were readily available at the mill library. Travel books were the most popular genre in the Livingstone household, telling of a marvellous world far beyond in-dustrial Glasgow. Among others, he read books by Australia explorer Matthew Flinders, South America explorer Francis Head and Arctic explorer John Franklin. Scottish explorers such as Mungo Park, who'd explored Northern Africa's Niger River, and James Bruce, who emerged from his explorations of the tributary known as the Blue Nile unscathed only to die falling down a flight of stairs in the safety of his own home, were Livingstone's early heroes.

The two most powerful books in Livingstone's life, however, combined adventure with Christianity. The first book was Thomas Dick's *Philosophy of a Future State*, which reconciled the disparities between science and creationism. For a teenager contemplating medical school and newly passionate about Christianity, Dick's book was a powerful affirmation that his chosen path wasn't heretical.

The second book, Karl von Gutzlaff's *Journal of Three Voyages along the Coast of China*, sealed Livingstone's fate. Gutzlaff's tale of mission-ary life enchanted the twenty-one-year-old cotton spinner. Livingstone had long dreamed of a life beyond the mill and even beyond Scotland. Gutzlaff's book showed how it could be done. After putting himself through medical school, Livingstone travelled south and entered the London Missionary Society's seminary in suburban London. He wanted, Livingstone told his new employers, to go to China.

But by the time he finished seminary, Britain and China had gone to war over opium. The year was 1840. Instead of China, Livingstone was given a choice between saving souls in the West Indies or in Southern Africa. He chose Africa. The dashing twenty-seven-year-old idealist, virgin, teetotaller, medical doctor and ordained minister travelled from London's hustle-bustle to the somnolent mission station of Kuruman, six hundred miles due north of Africa's southernmost cape. He was still suffering from his first broken heart, having being spurned by a young woman named Catherine Ridley before leaving London. Africa seemed like the ideal location in which to focus all his energies on sharing the good news about Jesus Christ, and to leave the real world's disappointments behind. It would become a recurring theme in Livingstone's life.

Missionary work hadn't yet taken on the imperialist reputation it later earned – and to which Livingstone's explorations contributed. There was nothing sinister about Livingstone's intentions as he sailed for Africa on 8 December 1840, no great political conspiracy to steal the independence of Africa's tribes. He was simply a devout young man heeding Christ's admonition that his followers 'go and make disciples of all nations'. He would wander the hinterlands like the Apostle Paul, enduring great personal risk to touch those far-flung souls who might otherwise never know Christ.

If Livingstone hadn't grown restless, his whole life might have been spent in that simple, unremarkable bubble of mission life, leading Bible studies and prayer services. But the boredom set in just weeks after arriving at Kuruman's dreary, parched scrubland location. Not only his own boredom, but the natives'. 'Our attendance at public worship would vary from ten to fifty,' he wrote, 'and these very often manifesting the greatest indecorum. Some would be smoking, others laughing, some working, some would be employed in removing their ornaments.'

Desiring a more effective way to do his job, Livingstone requested, and received, permission to 'go forward into the dark interior' to survey new mission sites. The prospect filled Livingstone with 'inexpressible delight'.

There was a simplicity to exploring Africa during those early days, a purity. Livingstone was an ambitious young man whose energy was boundless. Life's burdens slipped away as he left the vestiges of civilization behind. He wasn't famous yet, didn't carry England's expectations on his slumped shoulders. But now, twenty-five years later, both those things had happened, conspiring just as surely as the Nile Duel to lead him back to Africa one last time.

Livingstone knew that if he failed to find the Source (and, curiously, even if he succeeded) the expedition would be his last. He was not only old chronologically, but Africa had whittled at his constitution for years. The sense that the British Government and the Royal Geographical Society were always looking over his shoulder, even in the middle of Africa, added an additional undercurrent of daily stress. And then to wrangle with balking, thieving porters and surly soldiers whose language he barely understood – well, sometimes it all became too overwhelming for Livingstone. 'The sepoys had now made themselves such an utter nuisance that I felt I must take the upper hand with them,' he had written on 18 June, upon learning that the sepoys had left a sick porter named Abraham to die along the trail. 'So I called them up this morning and asked them if they knew the punishment they had incurred for disobeying orders, and attempting to tamper with the Nassick boys to turn them back . . . Their limbs are becoming contracted from sheer idleness. While all the other men are well and getting stronger, they alone are disreputably slovenly and useless looking. Their filthy habits are to be reformed, and if found at their habit or sitting down or sleeping for hours on the march, or without their muskets and pouches, they are to be flogged.'

Ten days later Livingstone gave up all hope that the sepoys would change, and dismissed them outright. He sent them back to the coast on 28 June. Livingstone and his caravan were on a highland plain at the time, surrounded by stands of pine trees and sparse grassland. Soon after, his path descended in elevation once again, as he approached the dense greenery surrounding Lake Nyassa. On 8 August 1866, he reached the lake. Its shape was long and slender, just like its northern cousin, Lake Tanganyika. Nyassa was three hundred miles long and sixty miles wide – almost identical in size to Tanganyika, as well.

Livingstone had a proprietary connection to Nyassa, having discovered and partially charted it during his Zambezi expedition. After now slogging four months up the Rovuma delta's morass to get there, the understated explorer was understandably relieved to stand on its rocky shores. The wind sweeping the lake produced small waves. He walked into Nyassa and let the cool waters drench him. 'It felt like coming to an old home to see Nyassa again and dash in the rollers of its delicious waters – I was quite exhilarated by the roar of the inland sea.'

Reaching Nyassa was also a vital first step in narrowing the Source search. Livingstone believed Victoria and Tanganyika were two links in the chain that led to the Nile. He hoped that Nyassa was another link – he just needed to find the connection. Years later, when the geographical feature known as the Great Rift Valley, stretching from the Mediterranean to Southern Africa, became understood, parts of Livingstone's theory would be proven true.

Thus, exploring Lake Nyassa for signs of the Source was a vital aspect of Livingstone's search. His plan was to cross the lake or travel around it to the north in an anti-clockwise motion. However, hearing reports of a hostile tribe around the lake's northern shores, and frustrated in his attempt to hire a boat to ferry him and his men across, Livingstone angled due south. He would travel round the lake clockwise. Random observations continued to fill his journals: 'A lion killed a woman early yesterday morning, and ate most of her undisturbed'; 'The agricultural class does not seem to be a servile one: all cultivate and the work is esteemed'; 'A man had been taken off by a crocodile last night. He had been drinking beer and went down to the water to cool himself, where he lay down and the brute seized him.'

As always, his symbiotic relations with the Arabs and the slave trade drew the most pointed commentary. 'The fear which the English have inspired in the Arab slave traders is rather inconvenient. All flee from me as if I had the plague, and I cannot in consequence transmit letters to the coast.'

After 150 miles along that southerly course, Livingstone reached the southernmost tip of Lake Nyassa. He crossed the crocodile-infested Shire River as it flowed south from Nyassa into the Zambezi. He began travelling north again, up Nyassa's western shores. The terrain was wooded, sometimes covered with clear brooks and limestone hills, and sometimes swampy from a dense black loam.

Life had been uneventful since the sepoys left – or as uneventful as any journey of African exploration could be – but trouble came Livingstone's way on 26 September. He encountered an Arab man flee-ing towards him, alone. Arabs generally travelled in large groups, for the lone Arab traveller was likely to be killed by Africans as revenge for the slave trade. The lone traveller was a strange sight.

Without being asked, the terrified Arab warned Livingstone's caravan that the country he'd just come from was thick with the Mazitu. They'd killed the other forty-four members of his party. He was the only survivor.

Livingstone was knowledgeable about the Mazitu. They were fond of surprise attacks on any tribe that lay in their path. Male victims were hacked to pieces. Women and children were kept alive for use as slaves and concubines. The very name Mazitu, meaning 'those who come from nowhere' in Bantu, gave the marauders a sinister, terrifying countenance.

Livingstone's men were understandably terrified. The most vocal about the danger was Livingstone's most abrasive porter, a native of the Comoros Islands. Musa, as he was known, was singularly surly and lazy, fond of stealing and stirring up trouble. He had worked as a sailor for Livingstone during the Zambezi expedition, earning a reputation for lying and sloth. Livingstone, however, had a forgiving, if slightly oblivious nature. He not only chose to forget his poor experience with Musa when he rehired him in Zanzibar, but he also hired eight other companions of Musa's from the Johannas. Musa and the Johanna men repaid Livingstone's largesse during the six months of travelling up the Rovuma and along Lake Nyassa by stealing from his stores whenever they thought he wasn't looking. So Livingstone had ample reason to want them gone. And with Musa equally eager to leave, the time seemed right for them to sever their relationship. 'Musa and all the Johanna men now declared that they would go no further,' Livingstone wrote. 'Musa said, "No good country that. I want to go back to Johanna to see my father and mother and son."'

But Livingstone needed Musa and the Johanna men. The hard truth about exploration in Africa was the reliance on porters. No explorer could extend his journey beyond the reach of his supplies, so porters served as a human supply line for an expedition. Everything a European explorer needed to sustain his expedition could be found on the backs of the African men he hired: the beads and cloth that would be traded for food in local villages, gunpowder, medicine, even dinner plates and silverware. Livingstone was painfully aware of his dependence upon the porters. Despite his daily battle to disregard personnel issues, the fact was that he couldn't go it alone.

Livingstone took Musa along as he approached a local tribal leader to confirm the rumours. The chief explained that the disturbance was not caused by the Mazitu, but by a tribe known as the Manganja, who were tired of the Arabs bringing guns and ammunition into their lands and stealing their people. 'There are no Mazitu near where you are going,' the chief assured Livingstone and Musa. Musa's look of terror was so great that his eyes seemed to leap from his skull. 'I no can believe that man,' he yelped, refusing to calm down.

Though Livingstone himself could not have known whether the chief's information was accurate, he continued to assure Musa that the path was safe. There would be no change of course. Then, acting as if the issue were settled, although for Musa it was not, Livingstone ordered the entire caravan – Musa and the Johannas included – to pick up their loads and push forward. He was eager to travel north towards Lake Tanganyika.

In the coming months, all of Britain would mourn Livingstone's decision.

THREE

SCARED STRAIGHT

26 SEPTEMBER 1866
Karahisar, Turkey
3,500 miles from Livingstone

AS THE DOOR TO THE TURKISH DUNGEON SWUNG CLOSED BEHIND HENRY Morton Stanley, it was clear that the journey begun on the South Platte River five months earlier had veered out of the swashbuckling realm of adventure, and into a horrific display of stupidity, miscalculation and imminent personal danger. The overcrowded cell reeked of stale urine and unwashed bodies. As Stanley's eyes adjusted to the darkness, he was swarmed by other prisoners. He was powerless to stop the Turks as they stuck their hands in his pants and fondled him roughly, and did the same to William Harlow Cook and young Lewis Noe, a former Union Navy shipmate of Stanley's who had accompanied them since New York. 'You can imagine our feelings when surrounded by these people, who were too ready to induct us into their sodomitical practices,' Stanley wrote. 'I really pitied the poor boy Lewis, as he was mentally marked by these ruffians as their night's victim.'

The problem began nine days earlier, as the three were travelling on horseback through a remote region of the Pontic Mountains. They were attempting to cross the Anatolian Plateau, into the Caucasus, but were down to their last few dollars and their horses were breaking down from exhaustion. Stanley, who never let his morals get in the way of his ambitions, attempted to waylay a Turkish traveller in order to steal his two horses. To lure the middle-aged man, named Achmet, off the main road, Stanley used sign language and broken Turkish to intimate that the boyish Noe was available for sexual favours. When Achmet dismounted and reached over to fondle Noe's genitals, Stanley deftly plucked Achmet's sabre from its scabbard and hit the Turk over the head with the handle. Achmet was saved by his fez, which deadened the blow. Though dazed, he quickly drew his knife and squared off against Stanley. The American was no match for the Turk, and within seconds Achmet had Stanley on his back. Stanley's hands had been deeply cut and were dripping blood as he desperately tried to push the blade of Achmet's knife away from his heart.

Fortunately for Stanley, Noe had the presence of mind to club the Turk over the head with the butt of a rifle. The man toppled off Stanley, staggered to his feet, then fled on foot. Just then Cook, who had been lagging behind Stanley and Noe, caught up and learned what was happening. The three quickly tried to flee the scene, with Stanley and Noe riding their new mounts. But after less than an hour of travel, they glimpsed a vengeful Achmet coming after them on horseback – this time accompanied by a group of friends. After a gruelling four-hour chase through thick forest and steep mountain trails, the three Americans were caught on a plateau. They were beaten, tied up and led to a small village, where they were tied by the neck to posts in a courtyard.

Over the next nine days, Stanley and his companions were beaten with fists and with the handle of a sword, pelted with mud and rocks by women and children, and had bullets fired just over their heads from point blank range. Worst of all, three Turks untied the seventeen-year-old Noe one night, and took turns sodomizing him. They held a knife to his throat, promising he would be killed the instant he cried for help. Stanley and William Harlow Cook were just a few feet away, but could do nothing for their young friend. Stanley wrote later that the Turks 'had no pity or remorse, but one by one they committed their diabolical crime which is, I think, or I hope, unknown to civilized nations, especially Christian America'.

Eventually, Achmet and his friends brought their captives into the nearby city of Rashakeni to be arraigned before a magistrate. There, the Americans were clapped in irons and banished to the Karahisar prison. It was in the foetid dungeon of Karahisar that Stanley and his companions were crudely molested on 27 September, and where Stanley suspected the inmates were making plans to rape Noe later that night.

Just when things seemed their worst, the three were saved by an unlikely summons to the prison commandant's office. He had heard there were Americans in his prison, and he wanted to size up their character in person. Filthy and bruised, their clothes torn and their bodies racked with fatigue and fear, they were marched from the dungeon and paraded before the commandant. Sensing that keeping the three contrite Americans in his prison any longer might be politically sensitive, the commandant bound them over to the region's governor, who released them on their own recognizance. The US minister in Turkey, fifty-one-year-old Edward Jay Morris, was alerted. 'We are all in excellent spirits,' Stanley wrote on 30 September, 'Lewis especially.'

With Morris's assistance, the Americans were cleared of all charges. On 14 November, they left Turkey by ship. By 14 January 1867, after one stop-off in Wales, Stanley arrived in New York aboard the *Denmark*. He had split amicably with Cook back in Turkey, and parted ways on a less friendly note with the traumatized Noe in New York. And though Noe blamed Stanley for his rape – and would continue to do so for the rest of his life – he saw a charismatic combination of strengths and weaknesses in Stanley's personality. 'Stanley is a daring adventurer,' Noe said after returning home, 'bold and unscrupulous, but intelligent and specious. His manners were those of a quiet man.'

The adventure to Turkey hadn't continued on to China, as Stanley had once planned. And it hadn't yielded any freelance writing assignments. In fact, Stanley had done no journalistic work whatsoever. But the trip – perhaps the most ludicrous and avoidable of Stanley's list of failures – provided the forward momentum his career in journalism needed. He was chastened by his time in prison and abuse by the Turks, and had begun to examine the folly of his loose morals. Stanley had also developed two specific career goals. The first was to write for the New York *Herald*, America's greatest newspaper. The second, inspired in part by David Livingstone, was to write adventurous stories about travels through Africa. 'Stanley spoke to me of Dr Livingstone's exploration in Africa,' noted Noe. 'He expressed a desire to go to Africa himself, and said he should aim to do so as a correspondent of the *Herald*, and thereby make a story and a sensation, and gain both fame and money.'

Stanley, however, didn't have the journalistic credentials to get hired by the *Herald* – yet. So he took the train from New York to St Louis and secured a full-time position with the Missouri *Democrat*. His salary was fifteen dollars a week, and his first assignment was covering the Missouri State Legislature in Jefferson City.

Covering an august political body was a sharp contrast to the dungeon of Karahisar, and not normally the type of adventurous subject the burly, uncouth Stanley preferred to write about, but his work was so impressive that within just two months he was reassigned to the biggest story of his career thus far. It was March of 1867. The *Democrat* ordered Stanley to return to the West to cover the American Indian Wars. The great cavalry of the United States Army was galloping across the Kansas prairie, 1,400 men and horses and cannon strong, hell bent on evicting the Cheyenne nation once and for all from the Great Plains. Everything about the operation was epic, from the force's mass to the plain's endless sweep to the undeniable truth that history was about to be written.

Stanley, much to his glee, would be the one writing it.

Meanwhile, from England, came the shocking news that Livingstone was dead.

FOUR

THE PERFECT ADVENTURE

7 MARCH 1867
Portsmouth

FIVE MONTHS AFTER LIVINGSTONE TRIED TO CALM A TERRIFIED MUSA ABOUT the Mazitu, a Royal Navy gunner named E. D. Young read the 7 March 1867 *Times* with shock and revulsion. It was a raw Thursday morning in Portsmouth as a numbing east north-east blow strafed the wooden decks of Queen Victoria's new royal yacht *Osborne*. Young read that his beloved Livingstone was dead.

It was there in black and white: Livingstone was missing and presumed murdered. The story was heart-wrenching. An emotional cover letter from Sir Roderick Murchison referring to his 'lamented friend' in the past tense was accompanied by a missive from Zanzibar confirming that Livingstone's entire expedition had been butchered by the Mazitu.

'On the fifth of December nine Johanna men of the party which accompanied Dr Livingstone came to Zanzibar,' read the letter from Vice-Consul John Kirk, 'reporting that on the west of Nyassa, sometime between the end of July and September, they were suddenly attacked by a band of Mazitu, and that Dr Livingstone, with half his party, were murdered. Those who returned escaped, as they say, through being behind and unseen, and they all depose to having helped bury the body of their dead leader the same evening. Although in details and other things the accounts of the various men differ, they all agree that they saw the body, and that it had one wound – that of an axe – on the back of the neck. One man saw the fatal blow given.

'The attack was sudden, and Dr Livingstone had time to overpower those who faced him, and was struggling to reload when cut down from behind. I fear the story is true, and that we shall never know more of its details.'

There were several aspects of the tragedy that Kirk's letter failed to mention. For instance, the poignant reaction to Livingstone's demise from the hardened citizens of Zanzibar: a period of mourning began immediately. All international vessels in port, the various foreign consulates and even the Sultan of Zanzibar lowered their flags to half-mast.

Less poignant was Musa's behaviour. After expressing his deep sadness about Livingstone's death, Musa began badgering Kirk and Consul George Seward to pay the Johanna men for their time in Livingstone's employ. They had worked six hard months for the quirky employer, he argued, breaking trail along the Rovuma River and putting themselves in harm's way when Livingstone insisted on travelling through the Mazitu's territory. Since Livingstone was a British consul to the tribes of Africa and had sometimes flown his consular Union Jack, Musa insisted the British Government pay them what was rightfully theirs.

Kirk, the same man who had travelled as expedition botanist on Livingstone's Zambezi journey, and Seward proceeded cautiously. It seemed strange to them that the only survivors were Johannas. Before sending the news back to London, they conducted a thorough investigation into the murder. For three long weeks Seward and Kirk cross-examined the Johannas, listening for inconsistent stories, trying to trip them on their own words.

Not a single story matched. Some Johannas said Livingstone was hunting elephants with some local villagers at dawn, others said he was simply exploring, and the death occurred at noon. Some Johannas swore they hid in the bushes during the attack, while others stated they'd been told to return to the village for supplies. Some said Livingstone shot one man, others said two. However, the stories weren't that different from one another, either. And specific details fitted with known facts: the order and manner of a Livingstone caravan on the march (a detail Kirk knew first-hand), and that Livingstone's route took him around Lake Nyassa's northern shore, a path he'd announced to Seward before leaving Zanzibar.

It finally came down to motive. Why would the Johannas risk criminal penalties for desertion and insubordination in Zanzibar unless they were telling the truth? No salary was worth that risk. As Christmas 1866 drew near, Ali Musa and the Johannas were shipped home without payment. But even as the Sultan of Johanna stepped forth to demand that his subjects receive the monies due them for their invaluable service to Great Britain, Seward and Kirk came to the conclusion Livingstone was dead.

Seward, a physician from Edinburgh who had become Livingstone's good friend during the explorer's stay in Zanzibar, wrote to the Foreign Office with the news. He ordered Kirk to pass on the news to the Royal Geographical Society. It was the day after Christmas, 1866. Kirk wanted the news to arrive as soon as possible so he wrote two letters. One was sent via Atlantic mail ship. The other travelled by way of the Red Sea – Mauritius to Aden, up the Red Sea then across the Suez peninsula by train. Both reached the RGS two months later. 'If this cruel intelligence should be substantiated,' Murchison wrote to *The Times* in the letter that aroused E. D. Young's fury on 7 March 1867, 'the civilized world will mourn the loss of as noble and lion-hearted an explorer as ever lived.'

The people of Britain were mortified by the loss of Livingstone, and also the manner in which he died. The savagery of the Zulus was well known. An infamous, true tale still haunted British society – that of a group of South African colonists who were killed by thick wooden stakes driven into their hearts via their rectums. Of course, in Livingstone's case, without a body it was impossible to verify the specifics of his death, but there was little argument he was gone. Seward and Kirk's investigation made it clear that Livingstone's luck, after decades of wandering through Africa unscathed, had run out in spectacular fashion.

More germane to the rage E. D. Young felt as he read the news aboard *Osborne* was his personal knowledge of Musa's character. Young, a thirty-five-year-old who held the rank of warrant officer, had served with Livingstone's Zambezi expedition between January 1862 and March 1864. He piloted *Pioneer*, the second of three steel steamboats Livingstone used to navigate the Zambezi delta. In Young's opinion Ali Musa and the Johannas were nothing but thieves, layabouts and liars. It was his belief that the Johannas abandoned Livingstone because the exploration had become too rugged, then concocted the story about Livingstone's death to collect their pay.

Young was a thin, impulsive man. As a boy he had voluntarily joined the Royal Navy, a career infamous for its brutality, sodomy and squalid living conditions. Most men didn't volunteer for such a life. Rather, they were coerced into service by groups of sailors roaming seaside towns, plying young men with drink, hitting them over the head or just clapping them in irons, then carrying them onto a ship. Young, however, enjoyed navy life. During his twenty years of service he worked his way up through the ranks to become a gunner and warrant officer. It was while serving as gunner on *Gorgon*, a supply ship plying the Mozambique Channel, that he first met Livingstone in 1860. Young admired the explorer so greatly he resigned his hard-won commission in 1862 to serve on board *Pioneer*. Initially, Livingstone had doubts about the sailor's character, suspicious that Young's overzealous work ethic was an attempt to coerce him into paying extra wages. But over time Young earned Livingstone's trust and became a mainstay of the Zambezi expedition. 'The *Pioneer*,' Livingstone wrote in his journal on 16 June 1863, as he struck out for an overland segment of his exploration, 'was left in charge of our active and most trustworthy gunner, Mr Edward Young, RN.'

The time with Livingstone was a boon to Young's naval career, which he resumed upon returning to England. The plush billet as *Osborne*'s gunner was tangible evidence – the position was almost honorary, for armament on *Osborne* was negligible. He'd been there two years. His Africa tan had been replaced by the ruddy pallor synonymous with life in windblown Portsmouth. Her Majesty's yacht was a far cry from life aboard *Pioneer*, where uniforms were washed in muddy water, food was whatever could be fished from the river or purchased from water-front tribes, and 'the reed fringe of the river, weariness and the monotonous hum of the mosquito' passed for ambience.

Though the temperature in Portsmouth reached no more than thirty-four degrees Fahrenheit the day Young read of Livingstone's alleged murder, every other facet of serving aboard *Osborne* was quite com-fortable. The ship docked silently, with all commands unspoken. The decks were always polished. Young was immaculately dressed every day, tucking his uniform jumper smartly into his starched trousers. He ate hot food at regular hours and quaffed a daily rum ration. Busy, blustery, nautical Portsmouth, the home of the Royal Navy, with its sailors' pubs and 'gunny bunny' gunners' groupies, was just a train ride from a good social weekend in London. There was even an offbeat charm to life aboard *Osborne*, one found nowhere else in the Royal Navy: it was no secret that *Osborne* had a preponderance of homosexual sailors – nicknamed the 'screaming queens' by other members of the Royal Navy. A regular highlight of shipboard life was the 'Sods Opera', cabarets performed by the queens in full drag. Their performances were lively and polished, and a sight seen nowhere else on the high seas.

Young, however, was willing to give up the luxury, prestige and high jinks for the sake of an outlandish scheme gathering momentum in the back of his mind: the gunner wanted to go to Africa and lead a search and rescue expedition to find Livingstone. Young's plan focused on following aquatic paths to the interior. A small group of dedicated searchers and a sturdy boat was all he would need. 'To take a large force of men into the country, even a boat's crew from a man o' war, much less a gunboat, was out of the question,' he later noted.

Young planned to follow the Zambezi inland from the coast, having learned that massive river well in his years piloting for Livingstone. He was familiar with its eddies and sandbars, side channels, cataracts, gusting easterly winds and the inevitable late afternoon downpours. The Zambezi was far wider and more easily navigable than the swampy, crocodile-infested Rovuma Livingstone had followed inland to start his Source expedition, with more villages along the shore where Young could trade for food. From the Zambezi he would make a right turn into the narrower Shire, which he would follow upriver until entering Lake Nyassa, through its southern egress. Upon reaching Lake Nyassa Young planned to travel from village to village around the shoreline, questioning tribes about a white man who might have passed through. He would learn for certain whether the explorer was dead or alive. Young needed to know the truth. He could not stomach the maudlin limbo of doubt.

One major obstacle, among others, stood in Young's way: the very notion of a search for a lost explorer was outrageous. When they went missing, they stayed missing. With one notable exception, British exploration had been this way for centuries. In the earliest days of exploration, when travelling over a hill from one valley into another was an act of daring, finding a lost explorer wasn't difficult. But once explorers began trekking thousands of miles from home, or sailing hundreds of miles over the horizon just to find the earth's limit, rescue was not an option. Searching for overdue explorers would represent a physical hardship akin to exploration itself; the sheer breadth of the globe and slow pace of communications would render the task like finding a needle in a haystack.

The notable exception was Sir John Franklin. The year was 1845. Franklin was sixty, a robust white-haired veteran Arctic explorer, leading an expedition through the ice-floes north of Canada in search of the Northwest Passage. In July of that year, normally a hospitable month for Arctic exploration, Franklin disappeared.

Under normal circumstances, the progression of public status for a lost expedition went from 'overdue' to 'missing' to 'presumed dead'. Memorial services were held, and statues might be erected to honour the fallen heroes. Franklin, however, was rich, with an adoring wife and Sir Roderick Murchison for a friend. Murchison leveraged his personal and political connections to continue the search after all was thought lost. 'He never ceased to stimulate public interest in the matter by the most urgent and moving appeals,' marvelled Indian explorer Sir Henry Rawlinson. Thanks to Murchison's zeal and Lady Jane Franklin's hopes, thirty-two ships took part in various searches before Franklin's death was confirmed in 1859.

Ironically, Livingstone and Lady Jane Franklin met in late 1865, when he stopped in Bombay en route to Africa for the Source expedition. He was emblematic of exploration, she of the indefatigable search for lost explorers. A year later, Livingstone was in the process of assuming both mantles.

Young, unlike Lady Franklin, couldn't finance a search. Based on the rigid social delineations of Victorian England, Young was considered lower class, a broad stratum including all except the wealthy. Typically, a member of the lower class would never mingle with members of the upper class. But Livingstone – also lower class – was an inspiration in that regard. He represented a newly developing middle class in England, living proof that a man could bridge the void between upper and lower class through achievement and bravado. As Young's ruminations about Livingstone's alleged murder grew more intense, and as his certainty that Musa was lying became set in stone, he knew such a societal leap was the only way to prove Livingstone was alive.

On 13 March 1867, a week after *The Times* announced the murder, Young boldly composed a letter to Murchison on a small sheet of stationery.

'Sir,' the note began. Young's script was taut, nervous. 'Having seen this sad intelligence of the murder of Dr Livingstone, I beg you will pardon the liberty I take in writing to you on this subject. First, I must inform you that I served upwards of two years in the Zambezi

Expedition under Dr Livingstone, being in charge of the *Pioneer* steamer under his orders, during which time I had a very good experience of Johanna men, having had twelve of them in the crew of the *Pioneer*. And Sir, I can confidently assert that, at all times, and under all circumstances, there was not the slightest dependence to be placed on them, more especially as far as the truth was concerned, added to which they were great thieves.

'I have, therefore, great reason to hope that their story respecting the murder of the Doctor will prove a mere fabrication, more especially if they brought nothing belonging to him, for they well know the value of books or papers, etc., which the Mazitu do not.

'I have the honour to be, Sir, your very obedient servant.'

Young signed his name and mailed the letter. The 'E' in his signature looked like a 'G' and his name would appear in *The Times* incorrectly. Regardless, the angry note launched the humble, eager gunner on the improbable odyssey that would define his life.

In writing to Murchison, Young found an unlikely ally. Not only had Murchison led efforts to find Franklin, he had sent relief money to Speke and Grant when they were overdue during their Nile journey. And like Young, Murchison doubted Livingstone's death, even as the old Africa hands Kirk and Sir Samuel White Baker were pronouncing the explorer dead and buried.

Murchison passed Young's letter along to *The Times*, then summoned the sailor to London. When Young boldly put forth his offer to lead a search party, Murchison was delighted. 'Doubt,' Murchison agreed with Young, 'was not to be endured.'

Preparations began in earnest. Even as the papers continued to run proof that Livingstone was dead – including a 6 April piece telling of a follow-up investigation by Consul Seward – Murchison's connections and verve shot the search expedition quickly from concept to reality. By May, Young was named Commander of the Livingstone Search Expedition and received permission from the Admiralty to take leave from *Osborne*. Thanks to Murchison's intercession and Livingstone's fame, the government offered Young ten times the necessary funding for his farfetched quest, and encouraged him to 'use every available means to secure success'.

Young wasn't lavish with the money, but he didn't hesitate to spend it on the one vital aspect of his plan: a steel river boat. *Search* wasn't much to look at, just an open boat thirty feet long and eight feet wide. But she was modelled after a craft named *Lady Nyassa*, designed by Livingstone, and was ideal for the Zambezi and Shire. There was a mast to hoist a sail and oar locks for paddling when the wind was dead. She drew just eighteen inches of water. And while the thirty-eight pieces of elastic steel *Search* was constructed from would be blazing hot to the touch under the African sun, she could also be completely disassembled. Porters could carry her up and around the journey's pivotal portage past a thirty-five-mile-long series of waterfalls and rapids on the Shire. Those cataracts, which Livingstone had named Murchison Falls, were the major obstacle between the Zambezi and Lake Nyassa.

As commander, Young also had carte blanche for personnel selection. He invited three trusted friends to join his grand quest. It was a brilliant idea, ensuring that camaraderie wouldn't be forced and Young's authority wouldn't be threatened by a power-hungry outsider. There was John Reid, who'd been ship's carpenter on *Pioneer*; Henry Faulkner, a former army officer with the 17th Lancers; and Patrick Buckley, a shipmate from *Gorgon*. Their expedition would be an adventure in the finest sense, just a few friends sallying into the wilds, attempting a goal beyond the ken of ordinary men.

As the departure date drew near, the expedition became a symbol of hope to England. Four brave men setting out to find Livingstone didn't guarantee anything, but it implied he just might be alive. This was important. When the nation was demoralized by the slaughter of her young men in the Crimean War between 1854 and 1856, it was Livingstone's walk across Africa that made her stand tall again. And when England was devastated by the news that Indian nationals had slaughtered innocent British men, women and children in the Punjab in 1857, it was Livingstone's triumphs that provided a diversion. And again, when social division and widespread unemployment during the 1850s sparked unrest and sapped British morale, it was Livingstone who stepped forth as their lion. He was more than just an explorer, he was a symbol of the potential greatness lying within each man, but tapped only by those willing to push beyond the limits of comfort and fear. In a smaller manner, Young had become such a source of hope.

There was, however, a double edge to the hope. A considerable sum of money had been spent to outfit the expedition. Expectations were getting so high that people were losing sight of the hard fact that locating Livingstone would be a miracle (as Murchison noted, 'the scheme would be stigmatized as the Livingstone Utopian Search'). He was a lone man in the middle of a vast continent. It had been a year since he'd even been seen alive, and stories of his demise seemed disturbingly plausible. If the rumour was false, a year would have also offered ample opportunity for Livingstone to put a few thousand miles between himself and civilization. So if Young was sincere about finding Livingstone, that might mean abandoning *Search* and beginning an overland expedition – a task for which he wasn't prepared.

On 10 June 1867, Young and his expedition sailed from Portsmouth aboard the mail ship *Celt*. By July, just four short months since his letter to Murchison, Young's expedition had travelled to Africa, launched *Search* and prepared to sail up the Zambezi delta. If all went well, he and the men had arranged to be picked up at the delta's mouth by a British warship on 2 December for the cruise home.

The journey up the Zambezi was like a homecoming for Young. The fourth largest river in Africa, the Zambezi also ranks as one of the largest in the world. The delta at its mouth is fifty miles wide, and the river itself is almost two miles across where it empties into the Indian Ocean. Livingstone had travelled almost every inch of the mighty river. The low-lying areas along its lush green banks were a breeding ground for malarial mosquitoes, tse-tse flies, spiders, scorpions and smallpox. Mary, Livingstone's wife, was buried along those banks, in the village of Shupange, after she died in April 1862. Young was at the funeral, and would stop to tend her grave on his quest to find her husband.

For Young and his mates, the romance of their journey was soon replaced by the realities of life on a dangerous body of water. There were mosquitoes to infuriate them all day and night. The foetid banks stank of rot and vegetation. The current was sometimes languid, sometimes swirling. When Young made the lazy right turn from the Zambezi into the narrower, serpentine Shire, the complexion of their journey changed, too. The Shire was a river of contrasts – miles of impassable rapids and miles of equally daunting marsh, choked with tall grasses. So many elephants wallowed in the shallows of the marsh that Livingstone had once, because firewood was scarce in the great Shire marsh, ordered the men to pluck elephant bones from the river and burn them as fuel in his ship's boiler. More ominously, the Shire was so thick with crocodiles that Livingstone's men during the Zambezi expedition called it 'a river of death'.

Young and his companions pushed up the Shire, reaching Murchison Falls on 19 August. There, they spent five days taking *Search* apart.

Those were nervous times for Young. Not only would the loss or damage of a single piece of *Search* render the boat useless, but also reports from local villagers confirmed that the Mazitu lurked somewhere nearby. Time hadn't made them any more docile. Young quickly hired 240 men from the Makololo tribe to carry the pieces of *Search* up the falls. The journey took four and a half days and there were no signs that the Mazitu had followed.

Clues about Livingstone's fate began to emerge as the expedition neared Lake Nyassa. Twelve months before, a white man stopped at the village of Maponda for a few days' rest. Members of the Makololo tribe hadn't heard about a white man being ambushed, and laughed out loud at the notion that such a thing could happen without word getting around, for the bush telegraph was too effective.

On Lake Nyassa, more telling clues. In one small village, Young purchased English-made tokens a white man had traded with the people – a knife, a razor, a spoon, a length of frayed calico, a book of English Common Prayer. All appeared to be Livingstone's, but there was no sign of him and no one knew which way he'd gone.

On 14 September *Search* was caught in a gale and sought refuge in a small village on the shore. As the men stepped from the boat, they were reminded again that the Mazitu were close. The huts were all empty, there was no wood smoke from cooking fires, and there were no shouts of children playing. 'Skeletons,' Young wrote, 'now met our eyes in great numbers.' The few villagers still alive knew of a white man, but said he was long dead. Young and the men rested until the wind died, then fled the ghost town to continue their detective work elsewhere.

Five days later *Search* steered towards the large village whose chief's name was Marenga. As the boat prepared to dock, Young and the men were originally mistaken for Portuguese slavers. Warriors lined the beach with guns aimed at *Search*, hoping to drive the boat away. But when Young cried out that they were Englishmen, the guns were lowered and the expedition was welcomed warmly. Chief Marenga rushed forward to greet the boat. Shaking Young's hand profusely, he asked, 'Where have you come from and where is your brother that was here last year?'

When Young eagerly told Marenga of his search for the missing explorer, he was regaled with stories of Livingstone's visit. 'He said he had come there from Maponda,' Young wrote, 'had stopped there two days. He was very kind.'

Search sailed on, combing the southernmost shores of Nyassa for clues. What became clear to Young was that Livingstone had travelled along these same shores to elude the Mazitu. He had not travelled north around the lake as originally planned – and as Musa had sworn. Clearly, Livingstone didn't die like Musa said, because he'd never travelled anywhere near the scene of his alleged death. Weighing that logic, Young was sure Livingstone lived.

Now Young was faced with a dilemma. Clause Nine of his orders from the Royal Geographical Society gave him the option of pressing forward to make contact with Livingstone or turning around once he had verified the explorer was alive.

Young turned around. He had Livingstone's personal effects to show the RGS and first-person testimony from locals that Livingstone was living. Moreover, Young was a creature of his training – after a lifetime spent on the water, the career sailor was incapable of tracking Livingstone over land. The mission, as far as Young was concerned, was accomplished. The journey home began.

By 2 October Young was disassembling *Search* for the portage back down the cataracts. By 2 December he and his men rendezvoused with HMS *Raccoon* at the mouth of the Zambezi. By 17 December they were in Cape Town. On 19 December they boarded *Celt* once again for the cruise to London. And on 27 January 1868, just ten months after the fit of pique prompting the impossible adventure, E. D. Young's official expedition report was read at a meeting of the Royal Geographical Society. 'I have the honour to be, Sir, your very obedient servant,' it concluded.

'How thoroughly and sincerely the whole British nation rejoiced at the good news of our great explorer's safety,' botanist H. G. Adams exulted.

Young hadn't explored anything, and he hadn't laid eyes on Livingstone. But if ever there was a perfect expedition, Young's was it. There were no casualties. Livingstone was shown to be alive. Based on Young's findings the Sultan of Johanna sentenced Musa to be thrown in chains for a period of eight months. And Young and his compatriots were lionized as heroes. Given voice by his success, Young was empowered to speak out about Livingstone's place in history. 'His extensive travels,' Young concluded, 'place him at the head of modern explorers, for no one has dared penetrate where he had been. No one has, through a lengthy series of years, devoted so much of his life to seeking out tribes hitherto unknown. I believe his equal will rarely, if ever, be found in one particular and essential characteristic of the true explorer.'

Gunner E. D. Young's audacious adventure came to a close. In the amazing year of 1867, when America purchased Alaska from Russia, Alfred Nobel invented dynamite and Karl Marx published *Das Kapital*, the accomplishments of an ambitious gunner from Portsmouth grabbed a healthy share of the headlines. Young's journey was important because it showed Britain that she didn't need to worry about Livingstone. He would bash on, regardless, to return one day.

CHAPTER FIVE

THE HERALD

DECEMBER 1867
New York

NEW YORK WAS COLD, DAMP. CHRISTMAS WAS JUST FIVE DAYS AWAY. Henry Morton Stanley, fresh off the train from the Great Plains, prowled the cobbled streets of Lower Manhattan, craving the newspaper job that would at last place him in the highest echelon of American journalism. New York reeked of promise, political corruption and arrogance; old money, new money, gangs and immigrants. It was an upstart city, longing to find its place on the international stage. A great Central Park, designed to compare with the monumental urban parks of Europe, had been carved from the swamps along what was then known as Bloomingdale Street – later Broadway – less than ten years before.

The city's newspapers were its collective voice. An astounding eleven dailies battled for readers. Editors were more powerful than politicians and more famous than actors, and a sharply worded editorial had the power to make careers and ruin lives. And while established titans like the *Sun*'s Charles A. Dana, Abraham Lincoln's Assistant Secretary of War, and the *Tribune*'s Horace Greeley of 'Go west, young man' fame, dominated the landscape, the most popular newspaper in all New York, selling sixty thousand copies each day, was the New York *Herald*. Readers didn't mind that the *Herald* was more expensive than its competitors – its nickel price a penny more than the *Times* and three pennies more than the *Sun*. The *Herald*'s combination of hard journalism, sensationalism and bizarre human-interest stories was worth the extra cent. The personal ads placed by the city's prostitutes didn't hurt any, either.

The *Herald* was Stanley's destination as he walked through Lower Manhattan, under skies threatening snow. Its headquarters was at the corner of Broadway and Ann, in a bright white building that looked very much like a French chateau. He was emboldened by the knowledge that his coverage of the American Indian Wars for the *Missouri Democrat* during the spring and summer had been so powerful dozens of other American newspapers – the *Herald* among them – had picked it up. The minor renown of being the journalistic voice of the Indian Wars had allowed Stanley to rub elbows with men of accomplishment, men like General Ulysses S. Grant, General William Tecumseh Sherman, General George Armstrong Custer, Buffalo Bill Cody and 'Wild Bill' Hickok, who threw a saloon patron over a pool table after the man insulted Stanley. It was a minor, temporary elevation in social status, but a great motivator. Stanley had become impatient to leave the isolation and anonymity of the prairie once and for all, and so he impulsively quit the *Democrat* in the autumn of 1867. He took the train to New York, ready and willing to pit his journalistic skills against the best reporters in the business.

Stanley didn't have an appointment with James Gordon Bennett, Jr, the *Herald*'s infamous young editor, as he approached the corner of Broadway and Ann. Nor did Stanley hold a letter of recommendation that might help him win a job. All Stanley had – all he had *ever* had, through good times and bad – was determination, bluster and the almost masochistic ability to endure rejection. Each quality, in its own way, made Stanley fearless.

He would need those qualities in abundance, for Bennett was equal parts genius and ass. Tall and without muscle, an icy-gazed whippet with a thick brown moustache hiding his upper lip, the twenty-six-year-old Bennett raced horses until they collapsed beneath him and fired reporters for something as simple as a bad haircut. He was so rich he once threw a bulky wad of cash into a fireplace because it interfered with the cut of his suit. Bennett was a lightweight who drank to excess, a loner who terrorized his Manhattan neighbours by driving his coach and four naked at midnight, and a brawler who fought with a passion beyond his ability. He was an adventurer, too. Once, Bennett raced his yacht across the Atlantic in the dead of winter on a drunken bet. It was the first ever trans-Atlantic sailboat race. He won.

Bennett was, without a doubt, the *enfant terrible* of the New York publishing world. Ironically, the same combination of arrogance, fondness for risk and embrace of change that made Bennett socially notorious also made him a phenomenal newspaperman. He was willing to do whatever it took to win New York's daily circulation wars. 'I want you fellows to remember,' Bennett once lectured his staff, 'that I am the only one to be pleased. If I want the *Herald* to be turned upside down, it must be turned upside down.'

Bennett ordered layouts and fonts altered in order to help the reader's eye track down the page easier. He increased the paper's heft by expanding international coverage. The bylines of Mark Twain, Walt Whitman and Stephen Crane graced the *Herald*'s columns.

Most important, Bennett revolutionized the concept of newsgathering by creating 'exclusives' – a one-of-a-kind story no other newspaper was bold enough to cover. 'A great editor,' Bennett believed, 'is one who knows where hell is going to break loose next and how to get a reporter first on the scene.' To that end, he would invest thousands of dollars in a piece, knowing the payoff might not come for years, or at all.

But much of the time it did. The result was a monstrous $750,000 annual profit, even after Bennett's million-dollar salary. Bennett ploughed it all back into the newspaper. He sent reporters to Asia and Europe in search of stories that would generate a groundswell of public opinion and create a news cycle. When the trans-Atlantic cable was perfected in 1866, he gladly paid for the quicker news it provided. Once, when a reporter cabled back the entire contents of a speech given by the King of Prussia, it cost Bennett seven thousand dollars.

'No rival journalists dared to go to bed before seeing a copy of the early edition of the *Herald*,' Oswald Garrison Villard of the *Evening Post* wrote, 'which they picked up in fear and trembling lest they find in it one of those record-breaking stories which made its name as famous as that of The Thunderer in every corner of the globe.'

It was small wonder, then, that Stanley would want to write for the *Herald*. When he arrived at their offices Stanley wandered the hallways until he located Bennett's office. Then, as if Bennett were the editor of a small newspaper of no consequence, Stanley talked his way past Bennett's secretary and found himself face to face with the publisher of America's most popular newspaper.

Stanley quickly introduced himself. He wrote later that he was surprised when Bennett admitted to having read – and enjoyed – his dispatches from the Indian Wars. But Stanley was rebuffed when he asked for work. 'I wish I could offer you something permanent,' Bennett lamented, preparing to brush Stanley off, 'for we want active men like you.'

Stanley, however, had planned for such a dismissal. Instead of marching back out the door into the cold December air, Stanley – in words that he later wrote down verbatim – parried, 'You are very kind to say so, and I am emboldened to ask you if I could not offer myself for this Abyssinian campaign.'

'I do not think this Abyssinian expedition is of sufficient interest to Americans,' said Bennett, before slyly inquiring, 'On what terms would you go?'

That was the opening Stanley had been waiting for. He quickly laid out a plan to travel to Abyssinia, a land of desert and mountains situated on the horn of Africa, and cover an escalating hostage crisis. Theodore, Emperor of Abyssinia, a man with a history of mental illness, had imprisoned 67 British diplomats and their 187 dependents in Magdala, his mountain stronghold. The British Army would soon march inland to rescue them. Stanley would accompany the British on their march then write about the heroic rescue. Covering the British Army in Africa wouldn't be too different from covering the American Army in Kansas. The scenario, Stanley argued, seemed perfect for a segue from the national to international stage.

Stanley offered to work without a contract, covering his own expenses. He would stand or fall based on his professional merits. If Bennett liked the stories and the *Herald* printed them, he would be paid by the letter for the exclusive. Otherwise, Stanley would absorb the loss. Bennett was being offered a no-lose situation.

The editor agreed. If only on a trial basis, Stanley was officially a reporter for the New York *Herald*. On 22 December 1867, Stanley boarded the steamer *Hecla*, bound for Europe. By New Year's Day he was in Paris. A month later, Stanley found himself in Annesley Bay on the Red Sea, where he linked up with the British expeditionary force about to march inland to Magdala.

What followed was a journalistic tour de force.

Not only were Stanley's missives brilliant, but through foresight and sheer luck, he scooped the British journalists who were also covering the campaign. After the British military force under General Sir Robert Napier not only rescued the hostages, but also killed Theodore in the process, Stanley raced back to Suez to send his stories to the world via telegraph.

Luckily, before the initial march to Magdala had begun, Stanley had had the forethought to bribe the lone telegraph operator in Suez. Thus Stanley ensured that his dispatches would be sent across the wire before any other journalist's. By a stroke of luck, not only did the telegraph operator send Stanley's work before any of the British writers', but the underwater telegraph cable mysteriously broke before any other stories could be sent.

New Yorkers, much to the embarrassment of papers such as *The Times* of London, received word of the British Army's triumph before Londoners. Angry British editorials called Stanley a liar, saying he had made up the stories, finding it impossible an American could outdo their best war correspondents. But when writers from the *Telegraph*, *Times* and *Standard* finally got their stories to London a week later, Stanley was exonerated. 'Here is *The Times*, which for half a century has beaten every journal in Europe in energy and enterprise, actually publishing the latest news of a British expedition through the favour of a London correspondent of the New York *Herald*,' London's *Spectator* marvelled, framing Stanley's achievement.

Stanley's writing style was purple and intimate, as if penning a letter to a dear friend he was trying to impress. The sentences were meandering, sparsely punctuated, sometimes lazily crafted – yet always evocative. Stanley's true brilliance lay in getting the story first, getting it right, and getting it no matter what the cost. 'Our readers will not fail to perceive the vast superiority in style of writing, minuteness of detail and graphic portrayal of events which the *Herald* correspondence possesses over the same matter printed in the London journals,' a *Herald* editorial boasted of Stanley's Abyssinia piece.

Abyssinia made Stanley's reputation. More than impressed by the upstart journalist's ingenuity and pluck, Bennett hired Henry Morton Stanley as the *Herald*'s new roving correspondent, to be based out of the London bureau. His assignment: to go anywhere he was ordered.

SIX

TWO YEARS

MARCH 1868
Cazembe, Africa

'A VERY BEAUTIFUL YOUNG WOMAN CAME TO LOOK AT US, PERFECT IN EVERY way, and nearly naked but unconscious of indecency – a very Venus in black,' Livingstone wrote on 18 March 1868.

A day later, his very next journal entry read, 'Grant, Lord, grace to love Thee more, and serve Thee better.' Together, in words notable for their honesty and simplicity, the entries dovetailed Livingstone's barely suppressed sexuality and unashamed spirituality within the span of just two sentences. The date was 19 March. It was his fifty-fifth birthday, and the second anniversary of the start of his search for the Source.

In the year and a half since Musa and the Johanna men had abandoned him, Livingstone's caravan had experienced extreme hardships – but not, as those in England had believed, death. Yet his prediction to friends back home that he would return in two years was not to be. Livingstone was now deep in Africa, on the banks of the Lualaba – a mighty river similar in appearance to his beloved Zambezi. And though Livingstone was growing weary, he felt the Source was almost his. He felt confident there was a connection between the Lualaba and the Nile – a connection that would prove his theory about a chain of lakes and rivers coursing north from the southern reaches of Africa all the way into the Mediterranean.

*

The juxtaposition between sensual and spiritual in his journal entries mirrored the unconventional manner in which Livingstone had explored in the time since Musa's desertion. After the initial shock of losing valuable men, and being forced to shed the supplies they would have carried, Livingstone had been relieved. The Johanna men's churlish behaviour was a drain on the caravan's spirits. Pressing forward with, by now, just a few porters, a small herd of goats he'd purchased for milk, and two faithful attendants, Chuma and Susi, Livingstone had continued his march north. He had veered away from Lake Nyassa to the north-west. He had crossed over the four-thousand-foot mountains Livingstone had named for Kirk and reached the Loanga River on 16 December 1866. The rainy season was upon them and food had grown scarce. The group subsisted on goat milk and handfuls of dried corn.

'We have had precious hard times,' Livingstone wrote on New Year's Day, 1867. 'I would not complain if it had not been for a gnawing hunger for many a day, and our bones sticking through as if they would burst our skin.' He prayed for grace and truth and God's mercy. The goats died during the first two weeks of 1867. Game was nowhere to be found, and Livingstone took his 'belt up three holes' from starvation. 'I feel always hungry, and am constantly dreaming of better food when I should be sleeping,' he wrote.

The rains of January overflowed the rivers and raised the levels of swamps, bringing misery and sickness. The land seemed like one giant marsh. The only foods to forage were mushrooms and leaves, and Africa's myriad assortment of dangers was everywhere. 'Sitting down this morning near a tree my head was just one yard from a good sized cobra, coiled up in the sprouts of its roots,' Livingstone wrote. 'A very little puff adder lay in the path.'

The twentieth of January 1867, however, brought the blow that sent Livingstone reeling. In a carefully planned escape, two more porters deserted, stealing as much of the expedition's supplies as they could carry. The theft was devastating. 'They left us in a forest and heavy rain came on, which obliterated every vestige of their footsteps. To make the loss the more galling they took what we could least spare – the medicine box, which they would only throw away when they came to examine their booty,' Livingstone wrote. 'The forest was so dense and high there was no chance of getting a glimpse of the fugitives, who took all the dishes, a large box of powder, the flour we had purchased dearly to help us as far as the Chambeze, the tools, two guns, and a cartridge pouch. But the medicine chest was the sorest loss of all. I felt as if I had now received the death sentence.'

Livingstone struggled to find God's presence in the loss. Instead of diminishing his faith, or leading him away from Christianity towards African beliefs in ancestor worship and witchcraft, the explorer's years in Africa had deepened and transformed his Christian faith. It was his habit each Sunday to read the Church of England service aloud, but otherwise he set aside organized religion in favour of a more personal relationship with God. In the manner of King David probing God's nature through the Psalms, so Livingstone undertook a series of one-to-one conversations with God in his prayers and journal. He sought God's presence in all things, in good times and bad, speaking and writing words that came from the heart. Even in the furthest reaches of Africa he prayed on his knees at night and read his Bible daily. So when the precious medicines that protected him from malaria were stolen, Livingstone began a rambling discussion with God, wondering how he was going to survive without those vital supplies. 'Everything of this kind happens by the permission of One who watches over us with most tender care, and this may turn out for the best,' he wrote. 'It is difficult to say "Thy will be done," but I shall try.'

He concluded his prayer, though, with an admission that worry was threatening to supersede his faith. 'This loss of the medicine box,' he wrote, 'gnaws at my heart terribly.'

Despite his fears, Livingstone placed his trust in God. Instead of turning back to race for the safety of the coast, he resumed his search for the Source. He pushed on as the trail entered thick woods and chin-deep swamps. He looked for God's hand in the loss of his medicines, and prayed for the strength to prevail. Livingstone was in a land of empty silence, gloom and thick air. Blood-sucking leeches crawled down his clothing, into his shoes, attached themselves to his genitals. Their s-shaped, black-and-blue bruise marred his body for days after he'd picked them off 'with a smart slap of the palm'. For food, Livingstone ate rats. Travelling in heavy daily rain, through a land of 'dripping forests and oozing bogs', he found himself almost destitute. It was a testimony to their loyalty that Chuma, Susi and the small handful of porters remained at Livingstone's side.

Then, just when things looked their worst, Livingstone's life was saved by the people he despised most. On 1 February 1867, he encountered a band of Arab slave traders. They took pity on the destitute, failing traveller, and gave Livingstone food to restore his strength. He accepted it, in spite of the compromise he was making. Before the Arabs could leave, Livingstone wrote to the British Consulate in Zanzibar, begging that a second packet of relief supplies be sent to Ujiji, where he would meet them. Livingstone's supply list read like a starving man's fantasy: coffee, French meats, cheeses, a bottle of port. With his original supplies so depleted, this additional shipment would be vital. The Arabs accepted his letters and promised to deliver them.

Livingstone's compromise seemed relatively minor – accepting food for himself and his starving men, entrusting his mail to their care – but showed how greatly the search consumed him. Few men of his era spoke out as passionately against slavery as Livingstone. To eat food that was paid for with money earned from slavery was against everything for which he stood.

In his journal, there was no attempt at rationalization, just a matter-of-fact admittance that he'd come across a caravan led by a slaver named Magaru Mafupi. The slaver was a 'black Arab', born of an Arab father and an African mother.

The lineage might have confused the outside world, but Livingstone knew well the symbiotic relationship between Africans and Arabs. Although Europeans perceived the African continent to be an uncharted land populated by indigenous cultures, the truth was that Arabs had lived alongside Africans for over a thousand years. It was the seventh century AD when Arabian ships began trading beads for ivory with Bantu tribes along the East African coast. A mingling of their cultures began: the Arabs brought Islam; Swahili, meaning 'coastal', was formed by merging Arabic and Bantu; the financiers of India and Persia set up shop in Zanzibar to outfit caravans; African men found work hauling ivory, giving birth to the occupation of pagazi – porter. Little boys of the Nyamwezi tribe even carried small tusks around their village, training for the great day when they would join the mighty caravans.

That relationship between Arab and African had been corrupted, though, as slavery became lucrative in the sixteenth century. Losers in war were routinely enslaved, and children were often kidnapped as their parents worked the fields. But more than any other segment of the African populace, tribes residing below the equator suffered. As early as the seventh century, men, women and children from sub-equatorial Africa were being captured by other African tribes and spirited north across the Sahara's hot sands. Two-thirds of those surviving the epic walk were women and children about to become concubines or servants in North Africa or Turkey. The males comprising the remaining third were often pressed into military service.

That slave trade route – known as the Trans-Saharan – was augmented by the opening of the East African slave trade a century later. Instead of Africans, it was the Arabs driving this new market, focused mainly along the easily accessible coastal villages. They found that slaves were a more lucrative business than gold and ivory, and began capturing clusters of men and women for work as servants and concubines in India, Persia and Arabia. Even with the second slave route open, however, slavery was not a defining aspect of African life, but a gruesome daily footnote.

When the Portuguese came to East Africa in 1498, however, and as other European colonial powers settled the Americas during the following century, that changed. Slavery became the continent's pivotal force. By the end of the sixteenth century, England, Denmark, Holland, Sweden and France had followed Portugal's initial example, and pursued slavery as a source of cheap labour and greater national wealth. A third slave trade route – the Trans-Atlantic – opened on Africa's west coast. Slaves bound for America, the Caribbean, South America, Mexico and Europe were marched to the west coast ports of Luanda, Lagos, Goree, Bonny and Saint Louis, then loaded on ships for the journey.

Great Britain's economy was once so dependent upon slavery that some maps of Western Africa were divided by commodities: Ivory Coast, Gold Coast, Slave Coast. But as Britain began to see itself as a nation built on God and morality, and as it became savvy for politicians to align themselves with the growing Christian evangelical movement, slavery was abolished in all British colonies and protectorates in 1834. During his first trip to Africa in 1841, Livingstone was terribly unaccustomed to the sight of men, women and children being bought and sold. As he insinuated himself into the fabric of African life over the years that followed – speaking with the natives in their tongue wherever he went, sleeping in the villages, making friends as he shared meals and nights around the campfire – the barbarism of the practice incensed him even more. He grew determined to stop it.

Even as other nations slowly abandoned the practice on humanitarian grounds, Portugal continued to dominate the slave trade. Slavery was, in fact, the cornerstone of its economy. The tiny nation exported African men and women by the hundreds of thousands, from ports on both the east and west coasts of Africa. Livingstone's focus was on the east, where Portugal had supplanted the Arabs as the coastal region's reigning power. African tribes were raiding other tribes then selling captives to the Arabs in exchange for firearms. The Arabs, in turn, marched the captives back to the east coast, where they were either sold to the Portuguese or auctioned in Zanzibar. The slaves were then shipped to Arabia, Persia, India and even China.

As Livingstone was pushing into Central Africa from the south in the 1840s and 1850s, still a missionary but on the verge of becoming a bona fide explorer, the Portuguese were entering the same region from the east. At first, they didn't pay much attention to Livingstone. He was just a missionary in their eyes – a fearless missionary, and one who travelled to places few other men considered going, but a missionary nonetheless. As his journeys mounted over time – three trips across the Kalahari Desert, and an east-to-west walk across Africa – all that changed. Livingstone's fame began to grow. Back in England, which he hadn't seen since leaving in 1840, Livingstone became a national hero. He was an adventurous cipher, a man few knew personally, but who was single-handedly charting the African interior in the name of God and country. That he was nearly shipwrecked off Malta, just like the Apostle Paul, on his way back to England after the walk across Africa, was the sort of fine coincidence heightening Livingstone's veneration in the British public's eyes. Heroes like Livingstone didn't come along every day.

When Livingstone finally returned to England in 1856, after fifteen consecutive years in Africa, he used his new-found fame to denounce the slave trade. The Portuguese Government began scrutinizing Livingstone and his achievements. They were concerned his journeys would lead to a greater British presence in Central Africa and a reduction in their lucrative slave trade. At Whitehall, Sir Roderick Murchison, president of the Royal Geographical Society, found himself apologizing to the Foreign Office on behalf of his intrepid protégé. Livingstone's anti-slavery speeches, it seemed, were offending Prince Albert, Queen Victoria's husband. Albert's cousin Pedro also happened to be King of Portugal.

By then, it was too late to divert Livingstone from his outspoken anti-slavery course. He was being hailed as the world's greatest explorer. His fame was phenomenal. By coincidence, the recent repeal of a stamp tax made newspapers affordable to the masses for the first time. Britain's population of four million was one of the world's most literate, and was becoming zealous for news. Livingstone's exploits made great press, and his fame continued to grow. Crowds mobbed him on the streets and even in church. He was given the keys to cities, and received great endowments to continue his explorations.

There was something miraculous in the son of a poor tea merchant making nations tremble. Livingstone revelled in the power, even as his life became more and more complex. The cloak of quiet Christian missionary had been cast off once and for all, and he spoke with the zeal of a man demanding to be heard. Livingstone resigned from the London Missionary Society to focus his work exclusively on ending the slave trade through his 'three C's' – Christianity, commerce and cotton (later amended to 'colonialism'). He felt that an influx of legitimate trade to the interior would empower the natives. His new employer was the British Foreign Office, which officially designated him Consul to the Tribes of Eastern Africa. Even his father felt something special in the air. In 1857 Neil Livingstone impulsively reattached the 'e' to the family name.

In his speeches, Livingstone didn't gloat about his discoveries à la Burton and Speke. Instead, he spoke out against the slave trade in the most graphic terms. 'This was no idle boaster, no self-sufficient egotist,' noted naturalist H. G. Adams, 'proclaiming his doings upon the house-tops and calling all men to speak and applaud. He was compelled to speak and describe what he had seen and heard, for only by so doing could he advance the great cause to which he had devoted himself.'

Livingstone's anti-slavery speeches were scathing and volatile, one of the few forums in which the quiet man expressed public rage. He was not anti-slavery because it was convenient or politically correct, but because Africa had become his home. It was the destruction of a people. Population size, population distribution, class structure, marriage patterns, ratios of men to women – all were altered by the forced diaspora of mostly peaceful, mostly agricultural tribes to other lands.

By 1867, as Livingstone travelled once again in Africa, his ideals had been forced to change. Still passionate in his anti-slavery stance, Livingstone now had a new concern – finding the Source. Nearly starving and with nowhere else to turn, he decided to accept the aid of slave traders rather than return home. The Source bid had officially become Livingstone's obsession.

*

Almost as soon as the Arabs who had given him aid left on 3 February 1867, Livingstone became sick with rheumatic fever. He recovered, but was buffeted by a series of fevers and delusions in the months that followed. 'I had a fit of insensibility that shows the power of fever without medicine,' he wrote on 1 April 1867. 'I found myself floundering outside my hut and unable to get in. I tried to lift myself from my back by laying hold of two posts at the entrance, but when I got nearly upright I let them go and fell back heavily on my head on a box. The boys had seen the wretched state I was in, and hung a blanket at the entrance to the hut, that no stranger might see my helplessness. Some hours elapsed before I could recognize where I was.'

Clearly, Livingstone would not be able to find the Source without further assistance. On 20 May 1867, in a village whose chief's name was Chitimba, he crossed paths with another Arab caravan led by a man named Hamees, and quietly joined their ranks. Whereas the British were fond of travelling into Africa in ones and twos, the Arab caravans numbered in the hundreds, making it possible to carry huge amounts of food and creature comforts. Because their objective was not a cursory exploration, but a lasting trade presence, the Arabs made frequent use of outposts like Ujiji and Tabora as resupply points, making it possible for some traders to remain in the interior – and maintain a relatively comfortable lifestyle – indefinitely.

Livingstone was not party to the Arab slave raids, nor did he assist in their ivory gathering, but he subordinated the moral imperative of battling slavery to the greater goal of finding the Source. Rationalizing his actions by inflating his Arab rescuers' importance, he wrote of the Arabs in his journal, 'They are connected with one of the most influential native mercantile houses in Zanzibar. Hamees has been particularly kind to me in presenting food, beads, cloth, and information.'

Hamees, however, was also at war with a powerful African chief named Nsama, whose village blocked travel to the west. The trader had no intention of moving his caravan until the bloodshed was ended. When Livingstone argued that he would travel on alone rather than spend months waiting out the impasse, the Arabs insisted he would be mistaken for one of them and murdered. Thus, Livingstone did no exploration whatsoever for over three months. From 20 May until 30 August he lingered impatiently in Chitimba's village, cared for by Hamees and the Arabs, waiting for the trail west to open. Then, after travelling just one hundred miles at a dawdling pace, Hamees brought his caravan to a halt for three more weeks. It was the Koran, Hamees insisted, that told him he must stop.

Livingstone was growing furious with the frequent stops, but he had become too accustomed to the luxury of Arab travel to strike off alone. He continued the journey to the west with Hamees when the caravan began moving again. And though Livingstone enjoyed debating with the Arabs about their beliefs, contrasting the wonders of Christianity with his disdain for Islam, he was becoming more and more like them every day. Not even the sight of slavery repulsed him any longer. It had become just another aspect of the African scenery. 'These valleys along which we travel are beautiful. Green is the prevailing colour,' he wrote on 1 November, as the caravan marched towards a village named Casembe, home to yet another powerful regional chief. 'But the clumps of trees assume a great variety of forms, and often remind one of English park scenery. The long line of slaves and carriers, brought up by their Arab employers, adds life to the scene: they are in three bodies and number four hundred and fifty in all.'

On 21 November 1867, Livingstone arrived in Casembe with Hamees and his caravan. The path into the village was lined with red anthills towering twenty feet high. The chief, also named Casembe, was a cruel man. He was fond of cutting off the hands and ears of his subjects. His chief advisor was a pompous dwarf with a broken back named Zofu, measuring three feet, nine inches tall.

In Casembe, Livingstone was introduced to another powerful Arab trader, named Mohamad bin Saleh. The new acquaintance was about to become Livingstone's third Arab benefactor. He was an older man, heavy and black, with a thick white beard and a broad smile. 'Mohamad bin Saleh proposes to go to Ujiji next month. He waited when he heard we were coming in order that we might go together,' Livingstone wrote in his journal on 27 November. Bin Saleh promised Livingstone the caravan's march from Casembe to Ujiji would take just one month.

As Livingstone waited three weeks for the day of departure from Casembe, battling a fever and observing the chief and Zofu with bemusement, his will to find the Source inexplicably wavered. Thoughts of Ujiji were prompting emotional images of home. The village was a natural stepping-stone from the interior back to British civilization. 'I am so tired of exploration, without a word from home or anywhere else for two years, that I must go to Ujiji for letters before doing anything else,' he wrote.

But as Livingstone marched out of Casembe with Bin Saleh on 22 December, the desperation ebbed. The act of moving forward once again, and through a region that was not only new to him but delightfully beautiful, boosted his morale. The wide open country was populated by many villages. Wildlife seemed to be everywhere, and Livingstone wrote of zebras, lions, hippos, buffalo and leopards glimpsed along the way. He waxed eloquently about the beauty of the countryside. 'The number of new notes I hear,' he wrote after a day walking through a bird-filled forest, 'astonishes me.'

During those hours of each day the caravan was on the march, Livingstone and his attendants quickly fell behind. His pace was a slow, deliberate plod. But he rarely paused for very long, and so rejoined the Arabs at the end of every day. Livingstone didn't like that the Arabs often lingered for two or three weeks at a time in one spot, for he longed to reach Ujiji and lay his hands on his supplies. But he stayed with the Arabs anyway, lacking the strength or resources to press on alone.

Despite Bin Saleh's promises to reach Ujiji in one month, the caravan was still hundreds of miles south and west of Lake Tanganyika – and Ujiji, across the lake on the eastern shore – after three long months on the trail. By March of 1868, they were still on the banks of the Lualaba River, still well south of Tanganyika. The rainy season had begun, swelling the rivers to waist deep and turning the swamps to interminable seas of black mud. At the broad, overflowing Lualaba, Bin Saleh called a halt. The rainy season was making the paths worse and worse. The land through which they marched was often what Livingstone called a 'sponge' – ground so waterlogged that a man could slip down into what looked like solid earth, as if he were falling into water. Bin Saleh ordered that travel would cease until the rains stopped – yet another halt which could take several months. Livingstone pleaded with him to continue, even though his remaining faithful followers were reminding him that they were too tired to continue. 'They were tired of tramping,' Livingstone noted in his journal, 'and so am I.'

The need to find the Source had become an obsession once again, however, and Livingstone could not stand the monotony of waiting for the rains to end. If he couldn't move forward to Ujiji, he rationalized it was better to backtrack and look for the Source. He had heard rumours of a lake named Bangweolo eighty miles off, which was connected by a river to a lake named Mweru he knew of. Livingstone wanted to explore the possibility that these were somehow part of the chain of lakes that became the Nile. Bin Saleh was adamant that Livingstone should not go. Almost all of Livingstone's porters, emboldened by Bin Saleh's opposition, and reluctant to leave the good life as a caravan member, deserted Livingstone to remain with the Arabs. On 13 April 1868 he marched deliberately away from Bin Saleh's caravan. Livingstone began his journey with just six attendants, chief among them Chuma and Susi. Two days later, an attendant named Amoda turned around and fled back to the luxury of Bin Saleh's caravan. Livingstone was down to just five men.

His march south was through the same swamps of black mud and parasites and leeches from which he had just come. His attendants often carried Livingstone through the rivers, and lifted him up when he sank into one of the great underwater depressions left by elephant footprints.

Starvation became a constant once again. Willing to eat anything, Livingstone often gnawed unripened ears of corn down to the husk. His teeth moved over the cobs with such intensity that his two front teeth loosened in their sockets and fell out. Trying to make light of his new look, Livingstone joked in his journal that he looked like a hippopotamus, but his physical decline was serious. His dysentery was becoming chronic. His hair was turned from brown to grey-streaked. It had always been his habit to shave daily, but he'd given that up and now wore a bushy white beard. Livingstone truly looked like a feeble old man.

On 26 June 1868, honestly appraising his decline, he pondered where he would like to be buried when he died. 'We came to a grave in the forest,' he wrote. 'It was a little rounded mound, as if the occupant sat in it in the usual native way. It was strewed over with flour, and a number of large blue beads put on it. A little path showed that it had visitors. This is the sort of grave I should prefer. To lie in the still, still forest, and no hand ever disturb my bones. The graves at home always seem so miserable, especially in the cold, damp clay, and without elbow room.'

Livingstone threw himself into his work. There seemed no rhyme or reason to it: north one day, south another. Investigate one river, then another. He was not lost, just performing a marvellously thorough, detailed exploration. His location was south-west of Lake Tanganyika, almost a thousand miles from Zanzibar, walking in broad circles about the countryside. The commitment to a two-year journey was long forgotten. 'I hope I am not premature in saying, that the Sources of the Nile rise from ten to twelve degrees south – in fact, where Ptolemy placed them,' he wrote to his friend William Cotton Oswell, hoping to mail the letter when he finally made his way to Ujiji. The missive was a detailed explanation of the course of various rivers – and, through that explanation, an argument for his Source theory. 'The Chambeze is like the Chobe, forty to fifty yards broad. But the country is not like that at all. It is full of fast-flowing perennial burns – we cross several each day, and crossed the Chambeze in ten degrees, thirty-four minutes south. It runs west into Bangweolo. Leaving that lake it changes its name to the Luapula, then into Lake Moero. On leaving it, the name Lualaba is assumed.'

Then Livingstone's tone changed abruptly. 'I hope you are playing with your children instead of being bothered by idiots. In looking back,' he wrote, 'I have but one regret and that is that I did not feel it my duty to play with my children as much as to teach the Bakwains. I worked very hard at that and was tired out at night. Now I have none to play with.' Livingstone was showing himself to be far more than merely a one-dimensional heroic Victorian archetype. He possessed, in fact, a very human mixture of hope, dreams, longing, depression, spirituality, sexuality and regret.

As July of 1868 came to an end, even a three-year journey became less and less likely. Livingstone's search for the Source, with all the redemption, financial peace and everlasting glory it promised, held him tightly in its grip. He would not return to civilization until he found it. However, unable to continue his search without supplies, he finally turned around on 30 July and marched north to rejoin Bin Saleh's caravan. He planned to travel with them to Ujiji. There, Livingstone would resupply, then resume the search. He was becoming sure that the Lualaba River was the Source. He just needed to prove it by finding the Fountains of Herodotus, then following the Lualaba to where it linked with the Nile.

It took ten weeks to journey north and rejoin Bin Saleh's caravan, a task made easier because the Arabs still hadn't made progress. Several other Arab traders had joined with Bin Saleh since Livingstone left, including Mohammed Bogharib, a flamboyant man whom Livingstone met at Casembe's village. The traders hoped to use their strength in numbers to travel safely through the region's hostile tribes – including the Mazitu, who had migrated from Lake Nyassa.

On 8 November 1868, waiting for the new caravan to begin marching for Ujiji, Livingstone summed up his thoughts on the great search. 'The discovery of the sources of the Nile is somewhat akin in importance to the discovery of the North-west Passage, which called forth, though in a minor degree, the energy, the perseverance, and the pluck of Englishmen. And anything that does that is beneficial to the nation and its posterity. The discovery of the sources of the Nile possesses, moreover, an element of interest which the North-west Passage never had. The great men of antiquity have recorded their ardent desires to know the fountains of what Homer called "Egypt's heaven-descending spring". That which these men failed to find, and that which many great minds in ancient times longed to know, has in this late stage been brought to light by the patient toil and laborious perseverance of Englishmen.'

Another four weeks later, on 11 December, the march for Ujiji finally began.

SEVEN

A SHARP LOOKOUT

NOVEMBER 1868 TO FEBRUARY 1869
Aden
1,600 miles from Livingstone

THE FIRST LIVINGSTONE 'DISAPPEARANCE' STORY IN A UNITED STATES newspaper ran in the New York *Herald* on 9 April 1868. The *Herald* ran another two weeks later. So when rumours out of Bombay predicted that Livingstone would emerge from Africa some time close to New Year's Day, 1869, the *Herald* dispatched Henry Morton Stanley on a top secret mission to the continent. Banking on the hope Livingstone would emerge in either Cairo or Zanzibar, Stanley based himself in Aden. The ancient port lay roughly halfway between the two cities. He arrived on 21 November 1868, took a small room in a local guesthouse then sent out feelers in both directions. Stanley was prepared to launch north by train to Cairo or south by ship to Zanzibar at a moment's notice.

Stanley, charging through life with a massive chip on his shoulder, was eager to prove Abyssinia wasn't a fluke. The years of drifting and failure weren't that far in the past. His grasp on success was still tentative. 'I must keep a sharp lookout that my second coup shall be as much a success as my first,' he wrote in his journal.

There was no doubt that Livingstone was alive – in addition to Young's evidence, Arab caravans had returned to Zanzibar bearing year-old letters from the explorer, written after the date of his supposed slaying. Still, three years was a long time to dodge western civilization. Livingstone's previous expeditions were frequently punctuated by visits to villages, trading centres, missionary outposts and ports on the Indian Ocean. During the Zambezi expedition, Livingstone had even left the African mainland entirely, travelling several hundred miles by boat down the Mozambique Channel to pick up fresh supplies. Clearly, something out of the ordinary was taking place. It was as if Livingstone had secretly cast himself into exile.

As the mystery deepened, public fascination over Livingstone's whereabouts had grown. The world joined Britain's wondering. Newspapers in Europe, India and South Africa were running stories. In the absence of facts, rumours sprouted like weeds, tawdry and epic alike. London wags were gossiping that Livingstone had fallen for an African woman and begun a new family. Sir Roderick Murchison, on the other hand, was publicly predicting Livingstone might be walking across Africa again, this time following the mighty Congo River's route through the uncharted rainforests west of Lake Tanganyika.

Of all the places Stanley could have chosen to wait for Livingstone – Cairo, Zanzibar, Suez – Aden was the most horrid. It was volcanic, notorious for flies and wind and heat. The only reason it had been carved from the desert thousands of years before was because it over-looked the mouth of the Red Sea. That strategic location made Aden irresistible to empires. The Egyptians came first, in the third century BC. Then the Romans, the Persians, Ethiopians, Yemenis and Turks. It was the British, however, taking residence by force in 1839, who were about to benefit more from their conquest than any previous tenant. By con-trolling the narrow slot dividing the Red Sea from the Indian Ocean, Britain would control trade through a new French-built waterway at the other end of the Red Sea, the Suez Canal. The shortcut from Europe to the Orient via the waters Moses once parted was due to open in November 1869. 'A strange place this,' Stanley noted in a rare wry moment during his otherwise bleak two and a half months stuck in Aden. 'Fit only for a coal depot.'

That quiet nature was on display in Aden. With the conclusion of his dream so near, Stanley should have been ecstatic as he waited for Livingstone – but he was miserable. The locale's claustrophobia was punctuated by British disdain for the American in their midst. Other than a short trip across the Red Sea to officially set foot in Africa and have his picture taken on a camel, Stanley passed the days alone in his room. He smoked cigars, wrote in his journal and read. No book was too obscure to pass the time, with Stanley absorbing authors from Milton to Homer to Virgil to Dickens. Aden became his university, a place to resume the education that ended at fifteen. By Christmas 1868, however, one month into his stay, the intellectual depth of the reading commingled with boredom, rejection, the solitary holiday season and Stanley's massive insecurity. Depression swallowed him whole. He pondered death.

Low moods were nothing new to Stanley. They seemed to strike whenever he had too much time to think. Action – physical exertion, travel, accomplishment – was his typical stepladder whenever the depths consumed him, but with nothing to do in Aden Stanley was forced to look inward. Between Christmas and New Year he plumbed his heart for vice. He binged on self-improvement goals. Gone were the cigars and sexual immorality. The Stanley who had used Lewis Noe as sexual bait to steal horses in Turkey was no more. The journalist's New Year's resolutions were to quit smoking, to rid his mind of 'vile thoughts that stained' and to be 'better, nobler, purer'.

Stanley craved a corner of the globe where he would be the ultimate authority, beyond ridicule. Only then would he know peace during his lifetime. 'I know not what I lack to make me happy,' he admitted to his journal in an exceptionally intimate revelation. 'If I could find an island in mid-ocean, remote from the presence or reach of man, with a few necessaries sufficient to sustain life, I might be happy yet; for then I could forget what reminds me of unhappiness and, when death came, I should accept it as a long sleep and rest.'

Stanley found no rest in the first days of 1869. He was tense and withdrawn, craving a smoke. In lieu of cigars Stanley busied his hands with scissors and glue, clipping inspirational phrases from books and pasting them into his journal. The theme, expressed through Johnson, Shakespeare and Addison, was warriors – brave men battling long odds. Stanley against nicotine. Stanley against himself. Stanley against the world.

Stanley lasted exactly one week without tobacco. But the quest towards long-term change continued. His goal was to fit in. He wanted to say the right things, do the right things. Stanley was well aware he tended to grate on people. Once, through the inexpensive walls of a railway station hotel room, Stanley overheard two travellers he'd just shared a train compartment with compare him to a leper. In Abyssinia, a British general found Stanley so annoying he called him a 'howling cad'. And on his way from Alexandria to Aden, Stanley had endured a Scotsman sneering about the 'active little Yankee'. Stanley was disgusted with rejection. Just six months shy of his twenty-sixth birthday, having failed to develop a single lasting relationship with either man or woman, American or British, he wanted to be liked.

His journal entries turned philosophical. Stanley reminded himself to 'count the raindrops falling during a storm or snow flakes as they drift through space'. He analysed his personality and wrote that 'curiosity undefined may turn itself into a deleterious agent' and 'man has two voices: the silent and the articulable'.

And through all the introspection, Stanley waited for Livingstone. His source of information was the American Consul in Zanzibar, a former ship's captain from Salem, Massachusetts named Francis Rope Webb. The thirty-six-year-old Webb was a diplomat in title only. The bulk of his time was spent directing a merchant shipping business. His consular title was a convenient tool for waging trade wars against the British on behalf of himself and other US expatriates in Zanzibar. For though the United States once dominated the flow of goods into East Africa, re-allocation of American naval assets to wage the Civil War had seen Britain take over the market. In the nearly four years since war's end, Webb had been unable to reverse that trend. If anything, Britain's influence grew more each day. A frustrated Webb was developing a profound dislike for all things British – particularly his nemesis and peer, Vice-Consul John Kirk. Webb had never met Stanley. But when the journalist wrote inquiring about help locating Livingstone, Webb was thrilled – anything to thwart the British. Because there was no telegraph service from Zanzibar to Aden, the plan was for Webb to send word to Stanley by ship when Livingstone appeared.

In effect, Stanley and Webb were positioning themselves against the British Empire. They were not paranoid for sensing anti-American sentiment, and it was not of their making. Rather, it was part of a genuine, enduring tension between Britain and the United States. Part of the problem was perception – almost a century after the War of Independence and fifty years after its 1812 coda, many Britons still considered the United States their prodigal child. British politician Charles Dilke's book *Greater Britain*, which trumpeted this belief in 1866, was widely popular in England. To Britain's annoyance, though, not only did the United States reject the claim, it sought to expand its sphere of influence at Britain's expense.

That America was ascendant in the late 1860s defied logic. The Civil War should have decimated the nation. Lincoln's assassination had been staggering, a bare-knuckled punch to the windpipe. Post-war reconstruction, with its carpetbaggers and Ku Klux Klan, was a reminder that racial hatred didn't disappear with the end of slavery. The nation was still very much divided. But America was unbowed. Like an adolescent staring into a mirror, examining the heft and might of newly adult muscles, the nation gazed at its potential in awe. 'The United States,' American customs inspector Herman Melville noted in a post-Civil War essay, 'wore empire on its brow.'

Britain did too, and in a much more proprietary fashion. Inevitably, the two nations quarrelled. Britain and the United States came to loggerheads over the sovereignty of Oregon, British claims of global naval supremacy, reparations for US shipping sunk by British-built vessels sailed by the Confederacy during the Civil War, Newfoundland fishing rights, the Canadian frontier and control of the Pacific Ocean. Most appalling to the British were America's designs on Canada. 'Nature designs this whole continent, not merely these thirty-six states, shall be sooner or later, within the magic circle of the American Union,' promised Secretary of State William Seward after purchasing Alaska from Russia in 1867. With an auspicious chunk of Canada dividing America from her new Alaskan territory, it seemed only a matter of time before Canada became part of the United States. Britain's Hudson Bay Company, though, had blazed the first trails through that wilderness, setting up trading posts and towns. The British, historically far more in love with commerce than colonies, didn't plan on letting Canada go.

Stanley's *Herald* bosses had forbidden him to use Aden's British-run telegraph services, for fear the London papers would get wind of his top secret mission. But when a letter arrived from Webb in mid-January saying Livingstone wouldn't be coming anywhere near Zanzibar, Stanley quickly telegraphed the news to the *Herald*'s London bureau. By the end of the month Stanley received a response: the search for Livingstone was over. Stanley was being reassigned to Spain to cover their Civil War. Stanley sailed from Aden on 2 February. 'I am relieved at last,' he rejoiced in his journal.

Stanley's commitment to self-improvement, though, continued long after boarding the *Magdala* and leaving Aden in his wake. He continued clipping and pasting exhortations in his journal for several months after leaving Aden, as if preparing for some great endeavour not yet revealed to him. Occasionally, he transcribed Biblical passages from Proverbs or Jonah by hand. 'Heavens,' he wrote in his journal on 16 February 1869. 'What a punishment it would be to have no object or aim in life.'

Even as Stanley buoyed his mood with positive thinking and self-assurances, frustration set in. He was annoyed to learn that his employers considered the journey to Aden a failure. The notion filled him with impotent rage. 'I am hardly to blame because Livingstone has not shown himself to the world,' he wrote. 'It is unjust that I am in disgrace when I cannot alter events or change destiny.'

Unjust or not, Stanley had a penchant for turning even the slightest snub into a chance to prove his worth. The *Herald*'s disappointment raised his personal stake in finding Livingstone.

EIGHT

TROUBLE

MARCH 1869
Lake Tanganyika

UJIJI REPRESENTED LIFE ITSELF TO LIVINGSTONE, AND BY THE TIME HE BEGAN his rugged overland journey to the inland trading Mecca, almost two long years had passed since that horrible rainy night when his medicines were stolen. Despite the Arabs' great kindness in that time, Ujiji also represented a return to independence. Fully resupplied with the cloth, gunpowder, brandy, cheeses and vital medicines awaiting him there, Livingstone would once again be able to sally forth into the wilderness at his own pace – and without compromise.

The journey to Ujiji, however, which should have seemed like a triumphal march, was almost the death of Livingstone. He celebrated New Year's Day, 1869 fording rivers in a driving rainstorm, wishing he could stop for a rest but fearing the Lofuko River might flood in the meantime, then block his path to Ujiji. Two days later, on 3 January, he collapsed. Pneumonia had set in. His attendants were forced to carry him in a litter. He was too feeble even to sit, and the only food he could keep down was a spoonful of gruel. 'Can not walk,' he wrote on 7 January. 'Pneumonia of right lung, and I cough all day and all night: sputa rust of iron and bloody, distressing weakness. Ideas flow through the mind with great rapidity and vividness, in groups of twos and threes. If I look at any piece of wood, the bark seems covered with the figures and faces of men, and they remain, though I look away and turn to the same spot again. I saw myself lying dead in the way to Ujiji.'

In his thoughts of death, Livingstone also pondered home, and the desire that his loved ones felt comfort in his pending demise. 'When I think of my children and friends, the lines ring through my head perpetually:

> I shall look into your faces,
> And listen to what you say,
> And be very often near you,
> When you think I'm far away.

'Mohammed Bogharib offered to carry me. I am so weak I can barely speak,' Livingstone wrote on 9 January. 'I am carried four hours each day on a kitanda, or frame, like a cot. Then sleep in a deep ravine . . . Mohammed Bogharib is very kind to me in my extreme weakness, but carriage is painful. Head down and feet up alternates with feet down and head up. Jolted up and down and sideways – changing shoulders involves a toss from one side to the other of the kitanda. The sun is vertical, blistering any part of the skin exposed, and I try to shelter my face and head as well as I can with a bunch of leaves, but it is dreadfully fatiguing in my weakness.'

He was too sick to write another word for five weeks. Livingstone finally reached the western shore of Lake Tanganyika on 14 February 1869. Ujiji and his medicines lay just sixty miles across on the other side. However, there was a shortage of canoes for ferrying men and material, and the lake's waves were too high for easy paddling. Livingstone was forced to wait. He extracted 'twenty funyes, an insect like a maggot' from large pimples on his arms and legs on 25 February. These subcutaneous maggots were feeding on his flesh. In addition, Livingstone was suffering from an anaerobic streptococcus bacterial infection on his feet, causing bone-eating tropical ulcers.

On 26 February canoes finally became available. The agonized Livingstone and his men, along with Bogharib's caravan, began paddling for Ujiji. They stayed close to Lake Tanganyika's shores, preferring the safety of the longer path along its coast to the large swells of the tempestuous direct route across the middle. As Chuma and Susi paddled, Livingstone lay in the bottom of the broad dugout canoe. Finally, on 14 March, a shattered and emaciated Livingstone arrived in the village of Ujiji for the first time. He rose and walked into the Arab trading post, brimming with satisfaction and happy anticipation of receiving his new supplies.

To Livingstone's horror, almost nothing remained. His supplies had reached Ujiji, but his stores had subsequently been plundered. The medicines, food and mail were gone. Of the eighty pieces of cloth – so vital for bartering with native tribes for food – just eighteen were still there.

Livingstone was devastated and destitute, and in his anguish once again threw himself on the mercy of the slavers. They found him a small lean-to in which he could sleep. A salve of butter, beeswax, copper sulphate and coconut oil was procured to heal his sores. Rest and hygienic improvements banished the maggots. The Arabs taught Livingstone the revolutionary concept of boiling his drinking water as protection against parasites and bacteria, decreasing the risk of dysentery. However, fearful he would reveal insider's truths about the slave trade, they rarely carried his letters back to Zanzibar.

By 1 June, Livingstone's strength was returning. He became fluent in the Masai language. He ate. He moved into a small home the Arabs rented for him. He planned the continuation of his journey. He studied algae growth along the shoreline and determined that the current flowed north out of Lake Tanganyika, meaning his theories about the Nile were likely correct. And slowly, very slowly, he regained the ability to wander.

Livingstone's health was still frail as he made plans to bid Ujiji farewell, but an Arab caravan led by Mohammed Bogharib was assembling on Lake Tanganyika's north-west shore. Lacking supplies of his own, Livingstone had no choice but to join the slavers once again. Their path was due west into Africa's heavily forested Manyuema region, an area that would later be named the Congo. Bogharib had little to gain by assisting Livingstone – indeed, taking the explorer into one of the slaving industry's most bountiful and relatively untapped new territories could endanger Bogharib's future ability to harvest slaves there – but the Muslim was a compassionate man. Despite their profound religious differences, he liked the ailing Scot. The slave traders who made Ujiji their home were an aggressive, arrogant group – 'the vilest of the vile' in Livingstone's words – who would surely allow Livingstone to die if left behind. And though there was also a good chance Livingstone would fall ill on the trail into Manyuema, at least Bogharib would be able to assist him.

Livingstone paddled out of Ujiji on 12 July 1869, carrying just a Bible, his journal and a pair of chronometers. After a three-day paddle, Livingstone and his men crossed the lake, making landfall at the base of the Mugila Mountains. On 1 August Livingstone and his small group of attendants successfully linked up with Mohammed Bogharib's caravan.

The trail went further into the centre of Africa than Livingstone had ever before travelled. It was a region of mountains, rainforest and head-hunters. However, it was vital to Livingstone that he risk the difficult journey. The Lualaba River flowed through there somewhere and he meant to trace its course. Based on his explorations thus far, the north-ward-flowing Lualaba's path was identical to the upper reaches of the Nile as drawn by Ptolemy on his map of AD 140. Livingstone intended to travel there to prove that the two rivers were one and the same.

NINE

THE HOME FIRES

MAY TO SEPTEMBER 1869
London

SPRINGTIME IN LONDON WAS MARKED BY THE DELICATE EXPLOSION OF primrose flowers, swans returning to the Thames, school groups excited to be outdoors again and, for the rich, the frivolous bustle of the social season. From May to July England's most powerful families moved from their country estates into their London townhouses. Grosvenor Square, Park Lane, Piccadilly and Belgrave Square pulsed with aristocratic men in top hats and waistcoats, wives and daughters in bustles and bonnets, family dogs, Siamese cats, black-and-white-clad household staff, the clip-clop of horse-drawn carriages on cobblestones and early morning delivery wagons bearing meat, milk and produce. Three intoxicating months were spent on debutante balls, social calls, croquet, horse racing, symphonies, shopping and intellectual events such as the Royal Academy of Art's annual exhibition of influential painters. From the riding trails in Regent's Park wafted the unforgettable aroma of horseflesh and money. Parliament was in session, adding the daily routine of governmental work for the peerage. Evenings were long and warm, perfect for strolling along Park Lane or drinking a tall gin on the terrace.

The majority of the Royal Geographical Society's membership belonged to this elite, and Sir Roderick Murchison appropriately chose this time of year to deliver his annual RGS president's address. Year in and year out, it was a centrepiece of the social season. The clubby Whitehall Place headquarters would be abandoned for the night, in favour of a Burlington Gardens lecture theatre. Gentry and aristocracy came by the hundreds. In an age when there was no cinema, for one night only they would live vicariously in the world of adventure.

Murchison would speak of the RGS and its ongoing explorations. Jungles and savannahs and untouchable Himalayan peaks came to London, punctuated by inspiring field reports from the men Murchison had tasked to conquer them. The geologist was an aristocrat, a Scot, a baron and a knight, but most of all Murchison was a showman. He never used one word when it was possible to use three, and his addresses often stretched long into the evening, after London's famous pastel twilight was replaced by the mute sparkle of gas streetlights. The RGS was so in vogue, though, and the tales of adventure so breathtaking, that the length was forgiven. Murchison would stand before a map of the world, speaking with such passion that he held the crowd in the palm of his hand. Everyone in the room became a lion. And that was important. For a month or a year later, when Murchison sought exploration funding, many in the audience would hold the purse strings. Murchison's every word was a reminder that he worked night and day to make Britain the most far-reaching nation on earth.

The 1869 address, however, was different. Murchison was still centrestage – in addition to the regular president's address, he also formally accepted re-election to his seventh two-year term. But the evening's focus lay elsewhere – on Dr David Livingstone. There was no escaping talk of the explorer. Murchison didn't mind, confiding to the audience his 'ardent hope that my dear friend Livingstone might soon return to us, so that I might have the joy of presiding at the national festival which would then unquestionably take place in his honour'.

In fact, while Murchison was still passionate about each and every one of the RGS's ongoing expeditions in Australia, Canada, the Middle East, South America and Central Asia, his friend's whereabouts were his reason to live. He admitted as much to the audience. Speaking in the lucid tones of a man glimpsing impending death, Murchison placed Livingstone's return in the context of his own demise. 'If I live to witness this completion of my heartiest aspiration,' he stated, 'I will then take leave of you in the fullness of my heart.'

For a change, Murchison wasn't being melodramatic. At seventy-seven, the RGS president was no longer the athletic young geologist who trekked up and down the Swiss Alps. He had grown frail and bald, with jowls sagging noticeably and caterpillar-like salt-and-pepper eyebrows shooting hairs in all directions. His mansion at 16 Belgrave Square was still one of London's leading intellectual salons, a place where debates and parties ensured Murchison's social stature and brought his adventures before polite society. But his wife Charlotte, to whom he had been married for fifty-four years, had died in February after a long illness. He had been the unlikely architect of the British Empire, cobbling it together outpost by outpost; she had been his champion, advocate and inspiration. They had no children, so in the days leading up to her death, Charlotte's failing health was a daily reminder their salon would soon close for ever.

So when Murchison spoke of death it was not as a distant, abstract idea, but as an interloper whose presence grew stronger every day. The Livingstone uproar, though it pained him, was the ideal summation for a life dedicated to advancing public interest in geography. It was almost a homage to Murchison. He was the Richelieu, the Boswell – the man turning everyday adventurers into exploration's superstars.

History had never known a man like Roderick Impey Murchison. At first glance the aristocratic Scot was just another visionary patron synonymous with exploration: Queen Isabella standing behind Christopher Columbus, Lord Sandwich bestowing funding and political intercession for Cook, Thomas Jefferson (whose vision for exploring the American West was inspired by Cook's journals) giving marching orders to Lewis and Clark. But Murchison was much more than that. Not just the driving force behind a single expedition, he fathered an entire generation of global unveiling. Some members of the Royal Geographical Society – Charles Darwin, notably – felt Murchison's showmanship detracted from its scientific aims. But Murchison's legacy was nothing less than the growth of the British Empire and expansion of the known world. His explorers thanked him by naming twenty-three topographical features on six continents in his honour – waterfalls, rivers, mountains, promontories, glaciers and even an island. In Australia, the Murchison River's tributaries were the Roderick and Impey. 'To relate the doings of the Royal Geographical Society under Murchison's supremacy,' the official RGS record formally admitted, at the expense of those powerful men borrowing the presidency when Murchison took a few years' rest, 'would be almost to write a history of geographical discovery in the most crowded years of its modern development.'

Empire building was a calling Murchison came to by accident. He was born in 1792, into a family of Scottish highlanders disenfranchised by their pro-Jacobite leanings. His father, Kenneth, was a surgeon, philanderer and duellist. He recouped the family wealth by taking work in India, where he was paid a substantial reward for curing the sick child of a prince. Kenneth fathered five children. Three of them, however, were illegitimate. As his father's oldest legitimate heir, it was four-year-old Roderick who inherited Tarradale, the family estate, when his father died of natural causes in 1796. Roderick went on to become an army officer, fought in the Napoleonic Wars, then resigned his commission. In 1815 he married Charlotte, the intellectual, dynamic only child of a wealthy general. They lived in Switzerland, France and Italy from 1816 to 1818. The time was notable for long Alpine walks and Murchison's first concerns about the United States' growing international presence.

Murchison sold Tarradale after returning to England. Lacking a career, he spent the next several years living aimlessly, a sporting squire who devoted himself so thoroughly to the outdoors that he was considered 'one of the greatest fox hunters in the north of England'. By the time Roderick was thirty-three, however, the Murchisons were in the advanced stages of squandering his inheritance. Idle living and bad investments had taken their toll. Roderick and Charlotte moved to London to start over. He took her advice and settled down to the life of a gentleman scientist. 'She had studied science, especially geology, and it was chiefly owing to her example that her husband turned his mind to those pursuits in which he afterwards obtained such distinction,' said her friend, physicist Mary Somerville.

Science was considered a glamorous way for a man of means to pass his days. Geology allowed him to indulge his passion for the outdoors at the same time. He attacked it with the obsessive ferocity that was becoming his calling card. Beginning with explorations of the Thames Valley, Murchison began roving into Scotland and Russia to examine new rock formations. He was credited with defining the Silurian, Devonian and Sedgwick geological periods. His understanding of the earth's structure grew so profound that though he never set foot in Australia, he predicted that a massive vein of gold would be discovered there. It was.

Science changed Murchison. He was still capable of great arrogance, but his focus shifted from glorifying himself to serving his country. At some point in his education Murchison developed a prescient vision of what was right for Great Britain. On 24 May 1830 he became a charter member of something called the Geographical Society of London. Soon after, the name was changed. The Royal Geographical Society's charter was to further scientific exploration worldwide and accumulate a geographical library of books and charts. It was a body whose time had come. Exploration needed a firm hand to guide it through a time of transition.

Prior to the turn of the nineteenth century, exploration was primarily a naval endeavour. Expeditions were government financed. Commissioned officers were in command. The focus was oceanic, the goal conquest. The great geographical questions revolved around finding undiscovered landmasses in the southern hemisphere and vetting them for potential settlement. With rare exceptions, only the ships and officers of the Royal Navy were capable of the complex global circumnavigation necessary to do the job properly.

By the time Captain James Cook was murdered by Hawaiian natives in 1779, each and every continent had been sketched, and most of the Pacific islands had been plotted. Two years later, the British Government ceased funding all voyages of exploration. France, the world's other great exploration power, became embroiled in revolution and war soon after. The French set aside exploration, as well.

But the pursuit of exploration did not stop. The call to adventure is genetic in a handful of men and women, not quieted by something as mundane as lack of bureaucratic interest. These private citizens began mapping the unknown world on their own. The focus switched from sea to land. The Amazon, the Indian Subcontinent and the Australian Outback called to men with courage and initiative. But the area with the greatest allure, perhaps because it was the most terrifying and closest to Europe, was Africa. The animals were carnivorous and prehistoric. It was a land in which human beings could easily become prey. Mysterious diseases, theoretically caused by bad air – 'mal'aria' to Italians, hence malaria – brought on fever, chills, madness and death. The inhabitants were considered cannibals or emasculants.

Playboy botanist Joseph Banks had formed the African Association in 1788 to foster exploration of what was popularly known as 'the Dark Continent'. While the term later took on racial overtones, it came about because cartographers coloured the unknown regions of Africa black – which, at the time, meant almost everything south of Cairo and north of Cape Town. The African Association commissioned American adventurer John Ledyard to lead their first expedition, a journey up the Nile. Ledyard died in Cairo before the journey began. The mysterious nature of his illness only added to Africa's cachet.

Banks had sailed with Cook and been a fishing companion of Sandwich's. When the Royal Geographical Society (then the London Geographical Society) absorbed the African Association shortly after their founding, the botanist became the bridge from one generation of explorers to another. Murchison quickly took up where Banks left off. His showmanship meant he once arrived for a public rock-gathering trek dressed in white breeches, white shooting jacket and white top hat. And because he was a bastion of London society, Murchison could be shameless in using his high-level political connections to obtain expedition funding. That faculty was much-needed: global exploration was an expensive undertaking and the RGS was continually short of funds.

'Industry and energy, a clear head, a strong will and great tenacity of purpose' defined Murchison's character, marvelled friend Henry Rawlinson. As did 'kindness of manner, his entire absence of jealousy, his geniality, fine temper, tact and firmness'.

In time Murchison and the RGS became synonymous, just as RGS explorations became synonymous with Britain's global expansion into an empire. The RGS gold medal for achievement became one of the world's most prized decorations. Generals, statesmen and scientists from both Britain and Europe clamoured to join so they could affix 'FRGS' – Fellow, Royal Geographical Society – to their signature and dine at the exclusive Geographical Club on Whitehall Place. In all, RGS memberships rose from the founding five to a select 2,300 in Murchison's lifetime.

In the early 1850s Murchison set geology aside to focus on imperial expansion. The introduction of disciplines such as organic chemistry was making science too complex for him to keep pace. Even geology began requiring physics, chemistry and mathematical skills, so he became the 'gentleman geologist' in name only. Enhancing the link between exploration and global power became his speciality.

By a twist of fate, it was during this period that Livingstone entered Murchison's life. An evangelical revival had swept through England. Groups like the London Missionary Society, mindful that Britain had been a pagan nation until missionaries arrived on her shores in the sixth century, were returning the favour by sending men and women around the world to proselytize. They were not explorers in the traditional sense, but the missionaries caught Murchison's eye because they were venturing far into the wilderness to spread their faith. They set up schools and churches on the frontier, and lived among the natives of Polynesia, Asia, South America and Africa. They learned the local languages. The missionaries ate the local food. Sometimes, as in the case of one New Zealand tribe whose favourite recipe called for Anglicans, the locals ate the missionaries. On all levels, the missionary connection with the local peoples and cultures was deeper than anything a passing explorer might experience.

To Murchison, Livingstone was the perfect hybrid of explorer, missionary and scientist. Livingstone's Christianity was muscular, which was appealing to an empire claiming the faith as its official religion. His travels, though he was far from perfect and certainly not a saint, had a righteous heft. When word of the young Scot's early, relatively tentative, explorations trickled back to London in the late 1840s, Murchison took note. They finally met in 1856, when Livingstone returned to London after sixteen years away. Their friendship blossomed. When Livingstone was mobbed in the streets and even churches of London because of his bold walk across Africa, it was due to Murchison organizing a massive public relations campaign. When Livingstone received the Society's gold medal for excellence in exploration, it was Murchison who presented it. And when a middle-aged Livingstone needed funding for his Zambezi expedition, it was Murchison who handled negotiations with the Foreign Secretary. Murchison not only wangled the money, he convinced the government to fund a river steamer, as well.

Owing in great part to Livingstone's unrelenting travels, Murchison 'adopted and made his own the great field of African discovery', in Rawlinson's words. His focus became finding the Source of the Nile. Thus Murchison gave his greatest encouragement to those travellers wishing to investigate Africa. In time Murchison's African explorers developed into his core group of 'lions', as Burton called them. The pride was Livingstone, Burton, Speke, Grant, Baker, the French-American gorilla expert Paul du Chaillu, and the British authority on Ethiopia, Charles Beke. But it was Livingstone, of Scottish Highland origin, who received Murchison's greatest attention. For even though Murchison lived in London for over fifty years, he always carried a powerful sense of Scottish clan loyalty.

Admiration between the two men flowed both ways. It also seemed as though Livingstone worshipped Murchison. He 'was the best friend I ever had – true, warm and abiding', the searcher wrote. He once lugged a portmanteau full of Central African rocks home as a gift for his geographer friend. But while Livingstone did the hard work of exploration, there was no doubt the elder Murchison held the upper hand in their partnership. Their relationship was not a son to a father, but of 'a highlander to his chief'. The two shared many a private hour walking the countryside, hunting rocks and talking Africa. Each man benefited from the other's prominence: Murchison revelled in the worldwide interest in himself and the RGS that came with Livingstone's discoveries, while the explorer received government assistance, public subscriptions to fund further expeditions and the fame he quietly coveted.

It was Murchison who sheltered Livingstone from the fallout of the failed Zambezi trip, instructing the explorer to avoid all media and public appearances for two months after arriving home, knowing any negative editorials would be forgotten over time. It was Murchison who, knowing that his friend's finances were dwindling, introduced Livingstone's speech at the British Association's conference in Bath on the night of Monday, 19 September, just three short days after Speke's suicide, publicly alluding to the explorer's financial situation in the hopes that Her Majesty's Government would step forward and offer a pension. 'Dr Livingstone has had honours in abundance showered upon him, but he cannot live nor provide for his family on honours merely. I think he is entitled to public and national recompense,' Murchison said. Murchison was such a stirring speaker that he was interrupted for applause three times during the introduction alone. By the time Livingstone took the stage the audience was at fever pitch. The pairing of Murchison's display of affection and Livingstone's earnest, adventurous remarks rendered Livingstone's Bath speech the highlight of the 1864 British Association meetings.

As the summer of 1869 arrived, however, and with his annual president's address behind him, Murchison was coming to the end of methods to help his friend. He became obsessive in pondering the vagaries of African travel and how they might be slowing Livingstone's return. For instance, he noted that if Livingstone was following the Nile from Lake Victoria north to the Mediterranean, he would have to catch the boat from Gondokoro to Khartoum that left each April. From there it was twenty-five days to Alexandria. That would place Livingstone home by the end of June – but only if he made the Gondokoro boat. Otherwise he might have to wait a year for another.

In April it had been reported that Livingstone was in Zanzibar en route to Europe. A July article in the *Medical Times and Gazette* said Livingstone was somewhere in the region of Lake Victoria. Livingstone rumours ran in *The Times* on average once a week. Murchison immediately wrote rebuttals to any mentioning his friend's death. He cautioned the public against despondency.

The social season ended quietly in late July without sign of Livingstone. The landed gentry returned to their estates. August passed, and still no word. The question of his whereabouts lurked beneath the veneer of daily English life. The mystery threatened to go unsolved and taunt the curious for ever. No one, however, took action. Like the boy who cried wolf, Livingstone had been reported overdue and dead, only to reappear, one too many times in his career. Based on what E. D. Young had seen and written, the British Government had begun an unspoken policy of not funding Livingstone search expeditions. Not even Murchison was stepping forth to suggest differently.

Then, on 28 August, a tragic occurrence cast a shadow over all African exploration. In their 'Deaths' section, *The Times* reported that Alexandrine Tinne, the Belgian heiress and veteran African explorer, was attempting to become the first woman ever to cross the Sahara when she was murdered by robbers in Northern Africa. They had ridden into her camp and slaughtered her companions. Then, as the men charged their horses at Tinne, she held up her hand as if to halt them. One of the intruders quickly pulled his sword and cut the hand off as he galloped past. Another Arab then shot her in the heart. Alexandrine Tinne was thirty-three.

Miss Tinne's explorations and bravery were well known to Britons. She had explored the upper Nile at the same time as Speke and Grant, and was respected as a very capable explorer, regardless of her gender. The manner of her death was unsettling, as was its timing.

In the outpouring of public sorrow that followed, Isabel Burton wrote to *The Times* and publicly suggested what many were already thinking: it was time to find Livingstone. And not just evidence of his existence, as Young had found two years before, but the man himself. Isabel, whose penchant for independent thinking was so notable among women in Victorian England that the *Edinburgh Review* was inspired to comment on her character – 'a clever capable woman, self-reliant in difficulties, with a pretty sense of humour' – wrote the letter without any prompting from her husband. Richard Burton was on his way to Beirut to serve as Consul to Damascus. He didn't worry about his fellow lion. Burton felt Livingstone had to be alive, for when he finally died the bush telegraph would wire the news back to Zanzibar within days. Isabel's letter, then, was notable for its independence and compassion.

It also forced Murchison into a tight spot. To seek funding for a rescue mission would be publicly admitting that his steadfast belief in Livingstone's safety was a sham. Yet if he didn't, his friend might perish. 'Sir Roderick,' Rawlinson once noted, 'never deserted a friend in need.'

On 29 September help arrived in the form of a letter from Sir Samuel White Baker. Barrel-chested, with light bags under his blue eyes, a pronounced nose, greying brown hair parted on the right and a frizzy beard draping down to his sternum, the fifty-seven-year-old Baker was the most animated and emotionally stable of Murchison's lions. He was at the Nile's mouth in Alexandria, he wrote to Murchison, about to journey upriver with his new spouse and long-time travel companion, the former Florence von Sass. She was blonde, Hungarian, a second wife fifteen years his junior.

Baker's letter explained his itinerary and goals, offered Mrs Baker's warmest wishes, then added a compelling postscript: 'I see a letter in the papers from Mrs Burton, proposing an expedition in search of Livingstone. Although well meant, it will be a useless undertaking, as I shall arrive south of the Albert before any expedition from Zanzibar could reach Tanganyika. There I shall be certain to hear of him.'

So it was settled. Baker would not aggressively search for Livingstone, but he would travel up the Nile to Gondokoro. His intention was to build a settlement and open up the interior to commerce. The settlement would serve as a listening post. Baker, who thought Livingstone's Nile theories were absurd, would race to his fellow lion's assistance if Livingstone's location became known.

Murchison affixed a cover letter and forwarded Baker's missive to *The Times*, confident there could be no better caretaker of Livingstone's safety. Baker was intelligent, thorough, bold and fluent in the local language. If any explorer could divine word of a fellow white man, it was he. The RGS would not launch a search expedition. There was no need.

Isabel Burton's letter, however, was a call to arms. Adventurous men throughout England disregarded Baker's assurances. Inspired by

E. D. Young's new bestseller *The Search for Livingstone*, they sent applications to the RGS, hoping to join the search party. All were turned away. 'No such expedition had, however, been intended,' the RGS finally stated publicly. 'Dr Livingstone had been more than three years and a half in the heart of Africa without a single European attendant.' Murchison 'was not sure that the sight of an unacclimatized young gentleman sent out from England would not produce a very bad effect upon the Doctor. Because, in addition to his other labours, he would have to take care of the new arrival.'

Almost loving in his staunch defence of Livingstone's ability to prosper, Murchison never broached the subject of a search party again. Livingstone would return on his own or not at all.

It never occurred to Murchison that search and rescue could be attempted without RGS participation; that Livingstone's disappearance didn't just belong to Britain and the RGS any more. The man and the story belonged to the world. And even as Isabel Burton's letter ran in *The Times*, followed by Samuel White Baker's, events were unfolding in New York that would directly affect Livingstone.

It was October 1869. Winter was coming to London. War was brewing in Europe. And James Gordon Bennett, Jr, in that time of upheaval, was about to decide it was time to go looking for Livingstone in earnest.

TEN

LUALABA

OCTOBER 1869
Bambarre

THERE WERE TWO MAIN VILLAGES OF THE MANYUEMA REGION WEST OF Lake Tanganyika through which Livingstone was travelling. The first was Bambarre, located in a valley beneath high granite mountains that reminded Livingstone of glaciers. Those mountains were also named Bambarre. Further inland, and at a much lower elevation along the banks of the Lualaba, was the lush oasis of Nyangwe, which was Livingstone's ultimate goal. The terrain was intensely rugged in the miles between Lake Tanganyika and Nyangwe, however, and the going was very slow. Livingstone was only halfway to Nyangwe when he finally reached the village of Bambarre on 21 September 1869. He had travelled just two hundred miles in the two months since leaving Ujiji.

Those two hundred miles, however, were some of the most arduous in all of Africa. The mountains of Bambarre were like towering castle walls protecting Africa's innermost kingdoms from easy incursion. The heavily forested slopes were so steep that hiking upward often meant scrambling on all fours, clutching trees and creeping vines to avoid tumbling back down. The ground near the summit was moist and cool, protected from the sun by the stifling density of the primeval forest. The air was dank and oppressive from lack of light and circulating breezes. Moss and ferns sprouted on the trees. The creepers twined up and around the great tree trunks so tightly that even dead trees remained upright, supported by the same parasitical vines that had killed them.

As Livingstone descended into the valley on the other side, the ground was riven with deep gullies and ravines. The forest was even more awesome, with trees growing to three hundred feet tall, canopies intertwined. But slowly, as the base of the mountains came closer, the clear blue sky and rays of sunshine began filtering through. The forest thinned, and the trees became smaller. When the mountains had finally tapered out, and Livingstone was in a land of green fields, sparkling streams and scattered clusters of mighty trees, he had done much more than merely cross a mountain range. He had, in fact, entered a place like none he had seen before in Africa.

The village of Bambarre was arranged like a European city, with long boulevards and bright-red square houses made of clay. Palm trees grew in the village centre. Communal granaries protected food supplies from birds and animals. 'The houses are all well filled with firewood on shelves, and each has a bed on a raised platform in an inner room,' he wrote. 'Very many people come running to see the strangers. Gigantic trees all about the villages.'

Bambarre was the sort of place a man could call home – and Livingstone did. He was so weary from travelling, and so enjoyed the abundance of peoples and food in Bambarre, that he immediately postponed his march to the Lualaba River. On 22 September, having decided to take a sabbatical from exploration, he had his men build a house for him in the village. Mohammed Bogharib and the other Arabs left Livingstone behind and moved quickly to find slaves. Livingstone had just enough cloth and copper wire to pay his way, and the people took to him. It was a little jungle village just a few degrees south of the equator, where the chief was polite, and the people were interested in the location of England and the words of the Bible. The men dressed in aprons made of deerskin, and carried a single spear and a cutting knife. Using clay, they moulded their hair into elaborate animal shapes – horns, gills, scales – and decorated the design with rings of iron and copper. The fact that they sometimes practised cannibalism didn't scare Livingstone in the slightest.

Meanwhile, back in Zanzibar a cholera epic was sweeping through the island. Vice-Consul Kirk's five-year-old daughter Marion was among those suffering the intestinal spasms and vomiting. She was lucky to survive. Kirk and his wife never got sick, thanks to the new technique of separating the ill from the well known as quarantine, developed by Florence Nightingale during the Crimean War. Almost seventy thousand slaves, however, did not survive. The island's plantations depended upon their labour, and owners frantically sought replacements. The result was a mad dash towards the interior by slavers eager to quench the market's demand.

The impact on Livingstone was great. More than ever, the traders feared his letters would incite anti-slavery passion once they reached London, thus shutting down their line of work at a most lucrative time. So though Livingstone would write letters and pass them to caravans marching east, most of the letters disappeared as if they had never been written at all. Livingstone was cut off in Africa.

As a result, the relative safety of Bambarre was misleading. Livingstone was not only trapped, but his health also continued to fail. Almost all his back and bottom teeth had fallen out. Eating was a chore. He was too weak to travel great distances. The ulcers on his feet had returned. So instead of wandering and seeing the world from a broad perspective, his explorations turned to minute details. He wrote about white ants, for instance, while resting in Bambarre, and how easy it was to catch them for frying after they had done battle with the larger and more deadly driver ants. Most of all, he pondered his Nile theories, and came to the conclusion that the Lualaba was definitely the Source. 'I have to go down and see where the headwaters join, then finish up by going round outside or south of all the sources. I don't like to leave my work so that another may cut me out and say he has found sources south of mine. I am dreaming of finding the lost city of Meroe, but reality reveals that I have lost nearly all my teeth. That is what the sources have done for me,' Livingstone wrote.

Once able to wander hundreds of miles a month, Livingstone was now barely making a few hundred a year. Taking assistance was one thing. Being carried, however, was averse to Livingstone's identity as one of history's great wanderers. The stroll, the saunter, the march, the gambol – all held a place in his repertoire. Like a leaf swept through the sky by a gentle breeze, Livingstone wafted through life, landing where the wind decided, then lifting again with a fresh gust. 'No one,' he once wrote, 'can truly appreciate the charm of repose unless he has undergone severe exertion.' Now, his health and fortitude were flagging. Livingstone's days of extreme exertion seemed to be over.

*

In 1841, when Livingstone first came to Africa, the natives laughed when he offered to accompany them on walks in the bush. They pointed to his baggy pants and untanned skin and said he would never last. Every word of their ridicule was spoken in their native Setswana, not knowing Livingstone was fluent in it. He wandered with them, however, earning their respect as he kept the pace with ease. Not only was he undeterred by Africa's extreme temperatures, Livingstone embraced them. 'A merry heat doeth like a good medicine,' he wrote. His travels taught him about the topography and climate and soil quality and dangers of Africa – the aspects that interested Europe – and also about its great, underappreciated history.

It was his wondrous ability to wander that led the Royal Geographical Society, that fulcrum of British exploration, to embrace Livingstone as one of their own. They awarded him a gold chronometer in absentia for his Kalahari crossing in 1850, followed by their prestigious gold founder's medal for the four-year journey across Africa. On that expedition Livingstone named a geographical landmark after a member of royalty, the only time he did so in his career. The story of Livingstone measuring Victoria Falls soon made its way around London, and added to his growing legend. The feat happened in November 1855. Livingstone was following the Zambezi's course from its source in the Central African highlands. He was puzzled that the Zambezi lost almost no elevation for hundreds of miles from its origin. It sprawled a mile wide across the landscape, languorous and imposing. The shores were lined with rat holes and vegetation. Hippos, otters and tiger fish were predominant in the river.

Livingstone knew it had to narrow and begin descending towards the sea at some point, but the miles passed without a drop in elevation. He was exhausted, suffering from insect bites, infectious running sores and debilitating bouts of dysentery. His journey began to take on a Sisyphian quality. After following the river for five hundred miles, Livingstone seemed no nearer the secret than when he started.

Finally, he heard the sound of distant thunder. As he gazed down the river to the sound the entire massive body of water disappeared into a fissure in the earth. Approaching the edge carefully, he was shocked to see the Zambezi spilling 360 feet off a cliff into the merest sliver of a gorge. Compressed into the narrow space, it became a frothing, roiling juggernaut, racing to the sea.

Livingstone had been taking careful notes throughout his journey. He was determined to measure the falls' depth exactly. Slipping into a borrowed canoe, he paddled alone to an island in the centre of the river. The island jutted out over the edge of the falls. On hands and knees, Livingstone crept to the lip. Dropping flat on his chest he peered into the chasm and carefully lowered a weighted rope into the thundering abyss. Great plumes of mist rose into the air, making it hard to judge where the falls ended and the river began. The roar reverberating off the gorge's wall deafened him and made the ground tremble. Livingstone carefully recoiled his rope and backed away from the edge. He was normally calm about his discoveries, but the enormous waterfall awed him. It was, he later wrote, 'the most wonderful sight I have seen in Africa'.

When David Livingstone returned to London in December 1856 he was at the zenith of his fame and popularity. He was forty-three. He had money and prestige for the first time in his life. In between his explorations he'd managed to marry and father four children. Africa hadn't yet ravaged him physically, and the tragedies that would mar his final years had not yet begun.

Livingstone's fame was so great that when Murchison threw a 'Farewell Livingstone Festival' on 13 February 1858, just before the explorer's departure for a second Zambezi expedition, 350 of England's most prominent citizens filled the Freemason's Tavern. Notably absent was Lord Clarendon, head of the Foreign Office. Having a commoner gain so much attention irritated him. British explorers were supposed to be gentlemen of money and pedigree. 'For some time past,' Clarendon told Murchison by way of excuse, 'I thought Dr L. was being too much honoured for his own good, and that the public was being led to expect more from his future labours than will probably be realized.'

Clarendon's prescience proved tragically accurate. Livingstone's aim for the grand new expedition was to explore the entire Zambezi basin, a massive undertaking that involved journeys on water and foot to the source of several major rivers. If anyone but Livingstone had announced such a plan he would have been mocked. But Livingstone had already done the impossible by walking across Africa. The public expected phenomenal things from the second Zambezi journey – Murchison alone foresaw the seeds of a British colony and breakthrough discoveries of coal deposits on the upper Zambezi.

The journey was a highly publicized failure. Public response was best summed up by *The Times*'s assessment on 20 January 1863. 'Livingstone,' the paper wrote, 'was unquestionably a traveller of talents, enterprise and excellent constitution, but it is plain that his zeal must outweigh his judgement.'

The Zambezi was too shallow and laden with sandbars and waterfalls for easy navigation. Slavery had decimated the region. The expedition was caught in inter-tribal war and slave raids. Dead bodies floated on the water, and children starved in the ruins of once-thriving villages. It was no place for a colony.

Within the expedition, the problem was Livingstone's travelling companions. Livingstone was a reluctant leader, expecting the men to be self-motivated, like him. He disliked travelling with white men, finding them impatient and argumentative.

'Constantly,' remembered expedition member E. D. Young, 'has he asserted his belief that for a man to succeed as a traveller in Africa he should go unaccompanied by other white men.' Parliament, however, had approved thousands of pounds in funding. The mission needed commensurate grandeur. So instead of travelling with porters alone, a contingent of British scientists and artists was assigned to accompany Livingstone. Livingstone issued strict orders that the locals were to be treated with kindness at all times. Guns were only for obtaining food and scientific specimens. 'The best security from attack consists in upright conduct,' he warned the Africa newcomers.

As Livingstone expected, the six men proved whiny and timid. With the exception of botanist John Kirk, also a Scot, they weren't fit enough to keep up when the journey switched from the river to overland. Livingstone's brother, Charles, whom he'd invited as morale officer out of misplaced loyalty, was the worst of all. Charles was a self-centred martinet whose behaviour made his older brother furious. The only times Livingstone lost his temper were to rebuke Charles. With Kirk, on the other hand, he was a warm father figure.

Most of the men mocked Livingstone behind his back. They thought he was crazy for taking too many chances – and asking the same of them. His stubbornness prevented Livingstone from backing down in favour of caution once a difficult course had been set. His motto was 'never give up', and so he pushed forward, always forward, the picture of British exploration in his blue serge pants and jacket, billed consular cap perched on his narrow head. 'If I risk nothing I gain nothing,' he groused.

The risks and resolution took their toll. The Zambezi expedition began the erosion of Livingstone's health. Despite his diligence about taking proper medication, several attacks of malaria, eczema and dysentery wore him down. It took longer and longer for the tireless energy to rebound. C. F. Mackenzie, a balding young missionary bishop travelling with the group, wrote of a typical day on the trail: 'Livingstone tramping along with a steady, heavy tread which kept one in mind that he had walked across Africa.' Tragically, Mackenzie lost a vital cache of supplies inadvertently in 1862, letting them tumble from his canoe into the Zambezi's chaotic waters. The supplies he lost were not food or plates or beads, but medicines. And in a river delta infested with mosquitoes, where anti-malarial quinine was all important, the missionary had effectively signed his death warrant. Malaria killed him soon after. Mackenzie's demise spelled the end to an endeavour known as the Universities Mission project, whose charge was to establish Christian missions deep in Africa. The idealistic venture was enthusiastically backed by the British evangelical movement. And though Livingstone could not be blamed for Mackenzie's fumbling or his unnecessary death, he would be – with still more tragic results.

As for Livingstone and Kirk, it was Charles Livingstone who drove the wedge between them. As the expedition wore on, and Kirk grew more and more homesick, Charles disparaged the sensitive botanist's skills. In a momentary lapse of judgement, David Livingstone joined in. He apologized soon after, but the damage was done. Combined with the loss of his journals to the Zambezi and his desperate need to return home, a rift was effected between Kirk and the explorer. The rift grew slowly, but it never stopped widening. 'I can come to no other conclusion,' Kirk wrote in his journal on 18 September 1862, 'than that Dr Livingstone is out of his mind.'

The most devastating aspect of the trip, however, was the death of Livingstone's wife, Mary. Theirs was an enigmatic marriage, with moments of great intimacy and adventure – at her insistence, she and the children travelled by ox cart with Livingstone during an early crossing of the Kalahari – interspersed with monumental separations. He had married the sturdy, brown-eyed woman, who wore her straight hair pulled back in a bun, in 1845. They had five children together, and suffered the loss of Elizabeth Mary in infancy. It was common in Victorian England for women to handle all child-rearing while the husbands busied themselves with making a living, so it wasn't unusual that Livingstone spent so much time away from home. But Mary, the daughter of famous missionary Robert Moffatt – Livingstone's supervisor at Kuruman, during the explorer's initial days in Africa – had begun a downward mental spiral when she returned to England with the children during Livingstone's walk across Africa. That spiral continued when Livingstone left for the Zambezi expedition. She became fond of brandy, and threw herself at other men. With her husband off for yet another long expedition, Mary could stand it no more. In 1858, Mary placed the children in the care of family friends and sailed to Africa to be with him. She briefly joined the expedition, but was forced to return to Britain in April 1858, when she found that she was pregnant. By 1861, Mary was leaving young Anna Mary with Livingstone's mother in Scotland, and returning to Africa. She met up with him at Shupanga, a small mosquito-choked port on the lower Zambezi. Within months she was dead from a devastating combination of malaria and continual vomiting, breathing her last with Livingstone at her side. But the loss shattered him. The health problems that would dog him for the rest of his life began in earnest with Mary's death on 27 April 1862. 'I cannot tell you how greatly I feel the loss,' Livingstone wrote to a friend a week later. 'It feels as if heart and strength were taken out of me – my horizon is all dark. I am distressed for the children.'

The expedition was recalled in 1863, five years after it sailed. Livingstone emerged from the interior and discharged his men. Still not ready to go home, however, he piloted his steel steamship *Lady Nyassa* 2,500 miles from Africa to India to sell it. She was forty feet long, with an awning over the stern and a steam engine. Livingstone had barely taken the helm travelling up the Zambezi, let alone piloted her on the open ocean, but somehow he managed the forty-five-day crossing. The manoeuvre was audacious. There was a swashbuckling tempo to the casual manner in which it was attempted and achieved – like an afterthought, as if the ocean was a minor obstacle after five years fending off the dangers of Africa.

Now, six years and thousands of miles of world travel later, David Livingstone was a radically changed man. As he rested in Bambarre in October 1869, he was no longer an explorer. Livingstone was a lost old man, looking for a set of fountains that might not exist, repeating the worst mistakes of his Zambezi expedition. He was down to just three companions: Chuma, Susi and a boy named Gardner.

Livingstone lacked health, resources and an ability to communicate with the outside world. As bad as things had been during the first three and a half years of this most recent expedition, Livingstone had always been capable of doing the unthinkable: giving up. He could have walked east to the African coast and found a ship to take him to Zanzibar or Cape Town, where the British Consulate would have seen to it that he received medical assistance and a cruise back to London.

But David Livingstone in the waning months of 1869 was no longer physically capable of such a feat. Unable to press onward, and equally unable to make a retreat, he was helpless. If he was going to live to see London again – see the people who loved him and cared for him, whether or not he found the Source – David Livingstone would need to be rescued.

ELEVEN

THE GREAT COMMISSION

OCTOBER 1869
Paris
4,000 miles from Livingstone

AT THE SAME MOMENT, JAMES GORDON BENNETT, JR WAS HOLED UP IN HIS Paris hotel suite trying to conjure brilliant thoughts. The twenty-eight-year-old newspaper tycoon was seeking to counteract yet another in the series of crises that had unfolded in New York over the past two months, this one having to do with a gold market scandal he'd stumbled into. With the reputation – indeed, the very future – of his New York *Herald* at stake, Bennett had fled to Paris aboard a Cunard liner. He took a suite at the luxurious Grand Hotel, the city's finest accommodation, to plot his next move. It was a situation calling for a bold gambit, a compelling distraction. He would publish an epic newspaper story or series of newspaper stories to distance the *Herald* and Bennett from the scandal. The question was: stories about what?

Bennett had spent his youth in France because New York had been unsafe for his family then. His father, a penniless Scottish immigrant who made his fortune publishing the *Herald*, was in constant physical danger because of his uncompromising editorials. The family was new-money wealthy and shunned by New York society. Bennett, Sr, was once beaten by thugs as the police stood by; on another occasion he received a bomb in the mail – both on account of his editorial perspectives. Out of fear for the children's safety, Bennett's mother relocated the brood to France while the elder Bennett stayed behind to run the *Herald*.

Almost two decades later, with the paper he'd inherited on the verge of ruin, it felt natural for Bennett to seek sanctuary in the City of Lights. Paris, too, was in upheaval. Emperor Napoleon III was pursuing war with Otto von Bismarck's Germany. More tangibly, Baron Georges Haussmann's architectural modernization was changing the city for ever. Slums were being razed, boulevards were being widened and arranged in a geometric grid, and the medieval sewage systems revamped. For many men those changes would have been a distraction, but Bennett thrived on chaos. His suite at the Grand, street level and noisy, was ideal for serious thought, business and socializing.

Bennett had no direct role in the gold market scandal that caused him to flee New York, but one of the two principal participants was his frequent drinking companion Ed Fisk, a financier who had made his fortune selling fifty-three million dollars of watered-down Erie Railway stock. Fisk's partner was the slick Jay Gould. Working in cahoots with Boss Tweed, whose Tammany Hall ring was looting New York City's Treasury, Gould and Fisk tried to boost their wealth to stratospheric levels by cornering the United States gold market in September 1869.

To prevent the Treasury from dropping the price of gold and making a shambles of their plan, Gould secretly enlisted the aid of his friend Abel R. Corbin, who was married to President Ulysses S. Grant's sister. Grant had been in office just five months and was naive about the intricacies of government finance. So when Corbin persuaded Grant to keep the price of gold high as a means of boosting the nation's economy, Grant went along with it. Fisk and Gould, with that decision, cornered the gold market – temporarily.

In late September Grant realized his error. He immediately ordered the Treasury to release the nation's reserve supplies of bullion onto the market. Gold prices plummeted. The stock market endured a horrific crash. Gould, tipped off about Grant's plans, sold his gold in time to reap an eleven-million-dollar profit. But he never warned his partner. Like gold speculators across America, Fisk, Bennett's drinking friend, lost everything.

Five days later, the devastated Fisk was prepared to tell all. He hunkered down with a *Herald* financial reporter and named names: Gould, Corbin, assistant treasurer Daniel Butterfield and, most of all, President Grant. The President was wide open to charges that his influence had been purchased. Fisk's words were bold and the story would definitely sell newspapers, but his claims about a grand conspiracy were unsubstantiated. It was just Fisk's word against the President of the United States. Running the piece left the *Herald* open to a libel suit. The public would vilify Fisk for trying to swindle the nation then ratting on his cohorts. Bennett, whose public drinking jaunts were always high profile, would become a suspect by proxy. Between a libel suit and the bad publicity, the *Herald* could be ruined. Bennett would be disgraced.

Bennett faced the greatest decision of his short career as editor. Running the story meant he could lose it all. Not running the story meant a competitor would get the scoop eventually. The *Herald*'s silence could be mistaken for a cover-up.

Bennett stalled. He ordered his writers to use every investigative means possible to prove Fisk's story. They turned up nothing. After two weeks Bennett ordered a tightly edited version of the piece to run. Grant's involvement was downplayed. Bennett's connection with Fisk wasn't mentioned at all.

Then Bennett sailed for Paris and waited for the furore to subside. Spending his days ruminating and his nights drinking champagne, the accomplished yachtsman set his course. Ideally, there would be a war somewhere for a *Herald* reporter to cover – war coverage was always popular. But the world, to Bennett's chagrin, was a relatively peaceful place. A touch of civil unrest in Japan and a minor unpleasantness in Fiji, but otherwise, peace.

On 11 October, *The Times* ran another letter about Livingstone, this one stating that Arabs returning to Zanzibar from the interior had seen a white man in Ujiji. Bennett had his story. What better way to ensure the *Herald*'s stature than tweaking the British tail one more time? Or, as Bennett liked to call it, 'twisting the lion's tail'. He cabled New York, looking for Randolph Keim, one of the *Herald*'s best reporters. Bennett wanted to give Keim the Livingstone assignment. But word came back that Keim was somewhere unreachable in America. Bennett settled for the *Herald*'s correspondent in Madrid, covering the Spanish Civil War. 'Come To Paris On Important Business,' he tersely cabled Henry Morton Stanley.

Three weeks passed. It was 27 October when a nervous Stanley rapped on his boss's door at midnight. Bennett was in bed. 'Come in,' he yelled, not getting up.

Stanley stepped inside. He was nervous, afraid he was about to be fired. The Aden failure had been followed by a few months' lazy reportage in Spain, where he'd actually spent very little time at the front. With Bennett's proclivity for firing people – most recently, Stanley's boss in the London bureau, Colonel Finlay Andersen – and with no advance word about why he'd been told to pack up his bags and race to Paris, Stanley feared the worst.

He stepped inside Bennett's room. The ceiling was vaulted and the room was large enough to be an apartment. A bed was in the corner. There was a table in a sitting area just inside the door. Stanley had met Bennett on several occasions, most recently six months before. It was Bennett who ordered the editorial praising Stanley's Abyssinia coverage. Nevertheless, Bennett was infamous for keeping his employees off balance.

'Who're you?' Bennett demanded as if they'd never met.

'My name is Stanley,' he later recounted.

'Ah, yes. Sit down. I have important business on hand for you.' Bennett got out of bed and threw on his bathrobe. He paced and spoke at the same time, the tall thin editor hovering over the short, beefy, seated reporter.

'Where do you think Livingstone is?' Bennett continued.

'I really do not know, sir.'

'Do you think he is alive?' Bennett pressed.

'He may be and he may not be.' In fact, Stanley wrote in his journal, he thought Livingstone was dead. Most everyone he knew felt the same.

'Well, I think he is alive and that he can be found, and I am going to send you to find him.'

'What? Do you really think I can find Dr Livingstone? Do you really mean me to go to Central Africa?'

'Yes. I mean that you shall go and find him wherever you may hear that he is,' Bennett answered. 'The old man may be in want. Take enough with you to help him should he require it. Of course you will act according to your own plans and do what you think best – but find Livingstone.'

Stanley was dumbfounded. He marvelled at the magnitude of what Bennett was ordering. This was a vast difference from a professional military search à la Sir John Franklin, or the humanitarian rescue impulse beating inside E. D. Young. Sending a journalist into the African interior was either an act of enormous pomposity or incredible stupidity. Africa wasn't a place for amateur sleuths.

'Have you considered seriously the great expense you are likely to incur on account of this little journey?' Stanley asked.

Bennett was unconcerned about money. What concerned him was creating the proper news cycle for the Livingstone story. It would need time to blossom. Stories would begin appearing intermittently. The *Herald*'s readers would become knowledgeable about Africa and enthusiastic about finding Livingstone. Done properly, Livingstone and Africa would insinuate itself into New York's subconscious. It would become the topic of dinner conversations. New Yorkers would find themselves worrying about Livingstone's safety. They would eagerly buy papers telling of the latest news.

To buy time – and, more important, precluding the need to spend thousands of dollars for an African expedition should the gold scandal die quietly – Bennett ordered Stanley to delay his trip to Africa. He told him to write a series of travel stories first. The first would be the 17 November opening of the Suez Canal. Bennett wanted a critical piece on the canal's viability. But just as important, he wanted Stanley to spy on the Baker expedition by following it a short way up the Nile.

Then it was off to Jerusalem to write about the Biblical archaeology in process. Then to Constantinople to check out rumours of war. 'Then – let me see – you might as well visit the Crimea and those old battle-grounds. Then go across the Caucasus to the Caspian Sea. I hear there is a Russian expedition bound for Khiva. From thence you may get through Persia to India – you could write an interesting letter from Persepolis,' Bennett continued.

On and on, until finally, a year in the future, Stanley would find himself in Zanzibar. If Livingstone had been found, Stanley's orders were to sail directly from Zanzibar to China and look for trouble. Otherwise, it was straight into the interior and don't come back until Livingstone was found. 'And if you find him dead,' Bennett concluded, 'bring all possible proofs of his being dead. That is all. Goodnight, and God be with you.'

As Bennett went back to bed, Stanley stumbled back into the chill autumn night. His dazed demeanour matched Paris's chaos. The meeting had been brief, no more than half an hour. Important issues like funding and timetable had been touched on, but not clarified. The burden of initiative had switched from Bennett to Stanley. But Henry Morton Stanley's life had changed irrevocably in the course of that short meeting. So had Livingstone's. For better or worse, the fledgling reporter had just become the man who would broadcast David Livingstone's fate to the world. Not only did he still have his job, but the man who once compared being a journalist with being a gladiator was being asked to lay down his life in the name of journalism.

Most wonderful of all was this: Stanley had found his second coup.

TWELVE

LIMBO

1870
London

A YEAR PASSED IN A BLUR OF HOPE AND FAILED HOPE WITHOUT ANY SIGN OF Livingstone. He had been missing for four years and was considered, most likely, to be dead. One of his letters, dated May 1869, had arrived in Zanzibar the following November. However, his parting words had little hope for his safety. He was heading into cannibal country, he said, and would likely be eaten. Not even the Arabs reported seeing him since.

Meanwhile, Stanley was in the process of travelling the Asian sub-continent fulfilling Bennett's orders, girding for his secret impossible task. And in London, Murchison was dealing with two shattering reports about Livingstone. The first came to light on 2 February, when *The Times* published a letter from a British naval officer in West Africa swearing that Livingstone was burned by natives in the Congo. 'He passed through a native town and was three days on his journey when the king of the town died. The natives declared Dr Livingstone had bewitched him,' Captain Ernest Cochrane of HMS *Peterel* wrote. 'Then they killed him and burnt him. This news comes by a Portuguese trader travelling that way. Livingstone was in the lakes at the head of the Congo, where he was going to come out.'

There was a very good chance the news was true. As a naval officer, Cochrane was assumed to be a man of honour. And it was also true that the alleged burning took place along the same westerly path Murchison had long predicted Livingstone would follow. Murchison, however, brushed off the report as just another act of Portuguese insolence. They were jittery about losing Africa and weren't above planting lies about their unlikely rival. 'I can see no grounds for despondency,' Murchison told the RGS in his president's address.

He was, however, thoroughly disheartened by a letter Vice-Consul Kirk wrote from Zanzibar on 5 March. Murchison was fond of Kirk – the younger man's hoodwinking by Musa and the Johanna men in 1867 notwithstanding. He saw Kirk, who was both a fellow Scot and RGS member, as his conduit into Africa and Livingstone. Murchison also knew that the Arab slavers were a cornucopia of information about the African interior, fully linked to the bush telegraph. Kirk's letter, however, confessed to Murchison the sorrowful news that none of the caravans returning from the interior had a scrap of intelligence respecting Livingstone.

Murchison dealt with the news by imagining his lost friend Livingstone had concocted a brand new agenda. 'The theory which I have now formed to account for this entire want of information is that he has quitted the eastern region entirely and has been following the waters flowing from the western side of the lake,' Murchison said, publicly establishing once and for all that Livingstone was not coming out via Zanzibar. 'These will lead him necessarily across a large unknown region, to emerge, I trust, at some port on the west coast.'

Just to be safe, Murchison wanted to send a shipment of relief supplies to Ujiji. The tactic had been tried twice before, in 1868 and 1869. Arabs had looted the majority of the first shipment and a cholera epidemic had killed seven of the porters carrying the second. The survivors helped themselves to the supplies, leaving nothing for Livingstone. They were so sure Livingstone was dead they even threw away his letters from home.

Despite those failures, Murchison wanted to try one more time. He fearlessly approached Lord Clarendon, Secretary of State for Foreign Affairs and a man professing ambivalence about Livingstone's achievements, to ask a favour. Murchison requested a thousand pounds from the Government to buy relief supplies. The money would be hand-carried to Zanzibar by the British Consul, H. A. Churchill, who was in London on sick leave. Stores would be purchased and shipped by ivory caravan to Ujiji.

The request was politically risky for Murchison. While the rest of England professed great sympathy over Livingstone's disappearance, Prime Minister William Gladstone had been notably silent. Portly and balding, the esteemed legislator was a devout Christian. A favourite pastime was walking the streets of London late at night, convincing prostitutes to seek another profession. He practised self-flagellation as a means of fending off feelings of sexual temptation engendered by those encounters. That inner conflict was also on display in his feelings for Livingstone. Gladstone had been a vocal advocate of Livingstone and the ill-fated Universities Mission to Central Africa. He met personally with Livingstone before the beginning of the Zambezi expedition. They met informally again on his return, bumping into one another at a dinner party at Lord Palmerston's home. Livingstone called his conversation with Gladstone 'very affable'.

Gladstone, however, distanced himself from Livingstone after the mission's failure and the deaths of Bishop Mackenzie and his two colleagues. Politically, the Prime Minister shifted his focus from Africa and the foreign expansion favoured by his rival, Benjamin Disraeli, to focus more on domestic issues such as Irish Home Rule. By begging Gladstone for money Murchison was asking the Government to take a stand one way or another on his friend.

On 7 May 1870, during a four-hour Saturday afternoon cabinet meeting, the money was approved. Livingstone was the tenth item on a thirteen-item agenda, preceded by an Election Bill and followed by a million-pound loan guarantee to New Zealand. Gladstone knew public sentiment was firmly behind Livingstone, and would have risked unnecessary controversy by denying the request. Thanks to Gladstone's tight-fisted and widely loathed Chancellor of the Exchequer, however, the Government didn't lose face. Instead of a humanitarian gift from a grateful nation, Robert Lowe decreed that Livingstone's thousand pounds would be an advance on his next two years of consular salary.

Nonetheless, it was money. 'It will take two months or more for these supplies to reach Ujiji from Zanzibar,' a relieved Murchison explained to the RGS on 4 June. 'Therefore all anxiety must be set aside for months to come. In about seven or eight months good news might be expected, and soon after that I hope we might see our friend again in his native country.'

Livingstone's salary advance was duly transported to Zanzibar, relief supplies were purchased, a small caravan was hired, and the British

Consulate's office concluded preparations for what represented England's final official attempt to help Livingstone. Either the supplies would find him and he would come out of Africa under his own power, or he would die and be laid in an anonymous grave. By all appearances, there seemed to be nothing more Murchison could do for Livingstone.

Ironically, in October 1870, as the seven-member relief caravan finalized preparations in Zanzibar, seventy-eight-year-old Sir Roderick Murchison was paralysed by a stroke.

On 1 November, the relief caravan sailed from Zanzibar to Bagamoyo, the traditional starting point for travel inland to Ujiji. 'After a vast amount of delay,' wrote Consul Churchill, 'I have succeeded in sending off to Dr Livingstone a reinforcement of seven men, who have engaged to place themselves at the disposal of the Doctor as porters, boatmen, etc, and a quantity of beads, cloths and provisions for his use.'

In December, Churchill was stricken with a severe malaria attack and returned to England on medical leave. Until a replacement could be appointed, his post was assumed by Livingstone's old nemesis, John Kirk. Despite a recent ruling from his immediate superiors in Bombay that forbade medical officers from appointment to consular positions, and despite opposition from the old guard diplomatic corps, Kirk was determined to keep his new job in Zanzibar. It was the chance for status and power he'd always craved. 'I had been given,' Kirk later wrote of the temporary position, 'a fair chance of distinguishing myself.'

Kirk's ambitions would not be easily realized. As 1870 came to a close, Kirk was unaware that Henry Morton Stanley was, quite literally, right over the horizon. In fact, he was only days from Zanzibar. Stanley's search for a second coup, and Kirk's search for his first, could only mean a collision of egos.

Livingstone, oblivious to either man's plotting, was the prize.

II

SOMEWHERE IN THE
MIDDLE OF NOWHERE

James Gordon Bennett, Jr

THIRTEEN

ZANZIBAR

6 JANUARY 1871
903 miles from Livingstone

FOUR HUNDRED AND THIRTY-SIX DAYS AFTER MEETING BENNETT, AND nearly five years after Livingstone disappeared, Henry Morton Stanley finally went looking. He had completed Bennett's lengthy itinerary.

The air in Zanzibar was balmy and humid as Stanley stood on the creaking, weathered deck of the American whaler *Falcon*. The island had been a mesmerizing green carpet as *Falcon* followed its contour through the Zanzibar Channel. The lime-coloured countryside dazzled Stanley and the tang of tropical landfall was intoxicating. But as *Falcon* nosed into Zanzibar's busy port and the sun rose on Friday, 6 January, he became uneasy. Flat-roofed white palaces stood side by side facing the water, like a row of opulent ivory teeth. Each palace entryway featured Zanzibar's trademark, an ornately carved wooden door. The air, he wrote in his journal, smelled of raw sewage, wood smoke, stale sweat, drying animal hides and breakfast. Twenty miles on the other side of the Zanzibar Channel, cloaked in morning fog, sprawled the eminence making Stanley's morning an anxious affair: Africa.

Stanley had travelled the world since 1866. He knew the food, customs, haggling, lodging and transport of America, Europe, the Middle East and India. None of that, however, mattered in Africa. He was a novice. Everything was new. His anxieties threatened to paralyse him. Stanley was anxious to hear the latest Livingstone rumours and either to begin hunting or to turn around and take up Bennett's alternative plan – the journey to China. He was anxious about the logistics of travelling through Africa, and aware he was innocent to the morals and means of its equatorial heart. He was anxious to meet the notorious John Kirk, and pepper him with sly questions about Livingstone. He was anxious to be under way, if Livingstone was still out there, before the forty-day monsoon season began in April.

He was extremely anxious about money, because he didn't have any. The *Herald* had advanced him a thousand pounds at the start of his trip, but it was long gone. He prayed that his London bureau chief had sent a fresh supply of financing, and that the money was waiting at the American Consulate.

But most of all, Stanley was anxious about Central Africa. The 'eternal, feverish region' haunted his dreams. He'd read every book he could find since leaving Bennett – Burton, Speke, Livingstone, even E. D. Young – and as far as Stanley could imagine, the land he was about to cross was an enormous swamp of malarial mosquitoes, hippopotamus, crocodiles, lizards, snakes, tortoises and toads. The image depressed him. The journalistic code saying a correspondent stayed with a story until he got it, or until the assignment was given to someone else, went double at the *Herald*. There was no way out. Unless Bennett ordered otherwise, Stanley had to walk into Africa to find Livingstone. Only then could he return to the safety of his bureau in London.

Thanks to a phenomenal gift for suppression, Stanley turned his anxieties into action. His problem-solving began the instant he stepped from *Falcon*'s launch onto Zanzibar's stone quay. He knew just one man in Zanzibar, Francis Rope Webb, so his first stop was the American Consulate. At Stanley's side was the two-man search force he'd begun assembling en route to Zanzibar: William Farquhar, a Scottish sailor, navigator, thug and drunk he met while sailing across the Indian Ocean, and Selim, a slender teenage manservant of Arab Christian ethnicity he hired back in Jerusalem. Selim could do no wrong in Stanley's eyes, but in the two short months he'd known him, Farquhar was already the focus of Stanley's greatest journal rants. 'Farquhar is a sailor intelligent after a fashion,' Stanley described, 'but no exception. He is remarkably sulky, taciturn and unwilling to work, no matter what the job.'

Stanley, however, could not do without Farquhar. The travel plan taking shape in Stanley's head depended upon the former first mate's nautical knowledge. Instead of walking overland like Burton and Speke, Stanley planned to sail south from Zanzibar fifty miles then enter Africa via a picturesque river known as the Rufiji. 'It is this river that I intend to ascend to the Tanganyika,' he wrote in the 1871 Colonial Edition Journal he would carry into Africa. With any luck, he would find Livingstone somewhere by the lake. Then, perhaps with Livingstone at his side, Stanley would return to civilization by sailing the Nile's length. His re-emergence into civilization at Cairo would be a spectacle for the ages. The world would be astonished.

Just as important as glory, the Nile was also the fastest way to file his story. 'If Livingstone is at Ujiji my work is easy,' Stanley wrote. 'The race is now for the telegraph.' There was no telegraph in Zanzibar, which meant additional months travelling by ship to Aden or Bombay after the long walk from Ujiji. Cairo, however, had a telegraph of its own. And sailing downriver, even thousands of miles downriver, was faster than a long slow walk and a long slow sail.

The major obstacle to Stanley's plan was that technical sailing skills eluded him. He had served a short stint in the Union Navy, but as a clerk. Hence, he was reliant upon the nautically savvy Farquhar.

Stanley strode along the waterfront to the great white building flying the American flag. He hoped to meet his old friend Francis Rope Webb face to face, pick up the *Herald* expedition money and learn the latest Livingstone news.

The thirty-eight-year-old Webb showed Stanley every hospitality, offering him and his men a place to stay. But Webb also broke the withering news that there was no *Herald* money waiting. Stanley was dumbfounded. He had considered such an oversight, but for the *Herald* to make such a grievous error meant the death of the search. Money was one problem he couldn't fix through a simple attitude adjustment. He needed cash in hand to buy supplies and hire men.

The obvious solution was a quick return to Aden or even Bombay, where he could fire off a cable to Bennett. Stanley still had eighty dollars in his pocket – just enough to pay for such a trip. Either choice, however, would waste another six months at the very least. The start of Baker's journey into Africa was just as delayed as Stanley's, but Baker might still find Livingstone in that amount of time. Leaving Zanzibar was not an option.

Webb was the answer. In an act that would have been humiliating if Stanley wasn't so desperate, he begged the American Consul to sign his name to a twenty-thousand-dollar line of credit. Webb, knowing James Gordon Bennett was more than good for the money, agreed. As part of the deal Webb stipulated that all monies be spent at businesses affiliated with the United States. For all his diplomatic title, Webb's focus was strictly commercial. He doubled as the Zanzibar director for the Boston trading firm of John Bertram and Company. Thanks to the Civil War and the opening of the Suez Canal, American companies' share of Zanzibar's three-million-dollar annual market was shrinking. Britain's, thanks to John Kirk, was increasing.

The shift grated on Webb. Zanzibar was small enough that all business was personal. And, personally, American traders despised Kirk. Webb considered him an aloof 'empire builder' who spoke in haughty 'Kirkisms'. Even a member of the British clergy residing in Zanzibar once noted that Kirk was 'a great hand at contradicting you flat, and aims at being the authority on all points under debate'.

Just as infuriating was Kirk's success. He'd only been acting British Consul for a month, but already he'd made it his business to know all that was going on in Zanzibar. Having apprenticed beneath Consuls Churchill and Seward for five years, Kirk also knew the importance of sending regular dispatches to London and Bombay, reporting on all activity concerning British influence – trade, intrigue within the Sultan's palace, ship arrivals and departures, and travel into the interior.

Diplomatically, Kirk had already shown a brilliance Webb lacked by forging a watertight bond with Sultan Barghash, the new Omani ruler of Zanzibar. Barghash was portly, with a wispy beard and moustache, and constantly wore slippers because his feet were swollen by elephantiasis. He was not the sort of man with whom the buttoned-down Kirk would normally make friends, but the alliance was pivotal: Barghash controlled East African trade from Zanzibar all the way to Lake Tanganyika.

Simultaneously, the Royal Navy was assuming control over the waters off East Africa. Webb foresaw the day when American traders and ships would be muscled aside entirely. So even though Stanley's journey might change Zanzibar's dynamics little in the long term, it was a solid injection of business and international one-upmanship at a time when the American companies in Zanzibar – Bertram and Company; Arnold, Hines and Company; William Goodhue – needed it most.

Webb took Stanley around town. He introduced him to the Sultan, and to the second most powerful man in Zanzibar, customs master

Ladha Damji, in order that Stanley might gather more information about journeying up the Rufiji. Stanley lied about his intentions, telling the Hindu with the snowy beard that the *Herald* was sending him up the Rufiji to write a travel piece on the river's famous beauty. Lined by grassland and forest, densely populated with hippos, rhinos, buffaloes, giraffes, baboons and monkeys, the Rufiji was developing a reputation as one of Africa's jewels. Stanley's cover story to the customs master was novel, but believable. It was known that one traveller – Central Africa's first recorded tourist – had already come to Africa just to see Livingstone's most wondrous discovery, Victoria Falls. If anything, a newspaper reporter writing stories about the Rufiji River portended things to come.

Unfortunately, Damji knew very little about the Rufiji. It was too far south of the caravan routes to interest him. But that was exactly why Stanley planned to travel that way. There was concealment in that distance. None of the Zanzibar–Ujiji caravans would see him. No one would report his whereabouts. Word would never make it back to London, prompting a new British rescue mission or a messenger ordering Baker to make a beeline for Ujiji. It was, after all, shaping up as a race. Stanley was coming from Zanzibar. Baker was progressing up the Nile. The first man to find Livingstone would win.

It was Kirk who added a new, unexpected time element to Stanley's search. Their first meeting occurred on 9 January. Stanley and Webb had just left the customs house. The extreme heat of the sun on that day was like a passive instrument of torture. The street was narrow and squalid, 'lined with tall, solid looking houses', Stanley remembered. Kirk was a slim man of Webb's age, with round shoulders and a beard covering his jawline but not his cadaverous cheeks. 'Dr Kirk,' Webb called out, as the acting British Consul crossed their path. 'Permit me to introduce Mr Stanley of the New York *Herald*.'

The former botanist of the Zambezi expedition said nothing. He raised his eyelids until the whites of his eyes became perfectly round, as though he was lapsing into a trance. There was no movement of the mouth or nod of the head, just that look of vague disdain. 'If I were to define such a look,' an unimpressed Stanley wrote, 'I would call it a broad stare.'

The fact that Kirk was in Zanzibar at all was due to the fame earned through his time with Livingstone. But Kirk, who still considered himself an explorer of sorts, hadn't yet got over his bad memories of the

Zambezi expedition and all things Livingstone. He could still recall vividly the day in 1860 when Livingstone attempted to run the Zambezi's treacherous Cabora Bassa rapids in twenty-four-foot dugout canoes. For the rest of his life Kirk would recall the terror of rocketing uncontrollably through the walls of whitewater, then having his 'body sucked under a canoe'. Even as Kirk clawed onto the safety of a rock, he could see boats downstream snapped in half and crushed by water and jagged boulders. Just as horrifying, from a professional point of view, was the notion that somewhere inside that frothing maelstrom were eight volumes of his botanical notes – lost for ever.

Kirk spent the remaining three years of the journey nurturing his hatred for Livingstone. He especially disliked Livingstone's random exploration style, and daily willingness to risk his life – and the lives of his caravan – without a second thought. The explorer's 'reason and better judgement', Kirk wrote to a friend, 'is blinded by headstrong passion'.

That didn't prevent Kirk from pleading for Livingstone's help in securing employment after they returned to England. Livingstone, not knowing of Kirk's resentment, swallowed his pride and went to the Zambezi expedition's most vocal critic, Foreign Secretary Lord Russell, seeking a consular position for the botanist. None was available – at least, none to Kirk's liking. He turned down postings to the Comoros and Mozambique, and even rejected Zanzibar initially. What the botanist wanted was a position with prestige, easy duties, plenty of free time for hunting and collecting botanical specimens, and most of all, generous pay. Livingstone vowed to keep looking. During a stopover in Bombay en route to Zanzibar in January 1866, Livingstone pressed his friend Sir Bartle Frere, the Governor of Bombay, to give Kirk the medical officer position in Zanzibar. Frere agreed. Kirk was in Zanzibar by June 1866, missing Livingstone by two months.

When Stanley met Kirk for the first time on that stifling January morning in Zanzibar nearly five years later, he knew nothing of the animosity or of Livingstone's intercession. He just knew Kirk had been with Livingstone and was more knowledgeable than any other man in Zanzibar – perhaps in the world – about Livingstone's exploration proclivities. Like a detective ferreting evidence from an eyewitness, Stanley sought to extract information from Kirk. The challenge made him edgy with anticipation. In order to keep his secret safe, he had to extract the information without letting on about Livingstone. His tactic was to ask questions about the Rufiji. 'Met Kirk, companion of Livingstone,' Stanley wrote in his journal. 'He had never been on that river. He thought of going for some time, was pretty sure it was a large river.'

That was all. Nothing about Livingstone. And while Kirk let the moment pass without notice, Stanley began to view Kirk as an adversary. Just as Webb viewed Kirk as an impediment to American power, so Stanley began to see the former botanist as an opponent in his quest to find Livingstone.

Their next encounter was on 17 January. Kirk was holding a wine party at his home. Stanley attended as Webb's guest. Stanley was antsy in polite company, prone to distraction and eager for provocative points of view. The guests were members of the diplomatic community. All night long, Stanley watched disdainfully as they made small talk, waiting for a moment alone with Kirk. Finally, they stood together, the stocky American and the thin Scot, inspecting an elephant rifle and talking hunting. Kirk was travelling for the mainland in mid-February to hunt big game, and was fond of talking about the trip and his shooting ability. Livingstone's name, to Stanley's enormous relief, came up tangentially, without prompting.

'Ah, yes. Dr Kirk, about Livingstone,' said Stanley, who later recorded the conversation in great detail. 'Where is he, do you think, now?'

'Well really, you know that is very difficult to answer,' Kirk replied. 'He may be dead; there is nothing positive whereupon we can base sufficient reliance. Of one thing I am sure, nobody has heard anything definite from him for over two years. I should fancy, though, he must be alive. We are continually sending something up for him. There is even now a small expedition at Bagamoyo about starting shortly,' Kirk said, making mention of the convoy of relief supplies commissioned by Murchison.

'I really think the old man should go home now,' Kirk continued. 'He is growing old, you know, and if he died, the world would lose the benefit of his discoveries. He keeps neither notes nor journals. It is very seldom he takes observations. He simply makes a note or dot, or something on a map, which nobody understands but himself. Oh yes, by all means, if he is alive he should come home and let a younger man take his place.'

'What kind of man is he to get along with, doctor?'

'Well, I think he is a very difficult man to deal with generally.

Personally, I never had a quarrel with him, but I have seen him in hot water with fellows so often, and that is principally the reason, I think, he hates to have anyone with him.'

'I am told he is a very modest man. Is he?' Stanley asked.

'Oh, he knows the value of his own discoveries. He is not quite an angel,' Kirk replied.

'Well now, supposing I met him in my travels – I might possibly stumble across him if he travels anywhere in the direction I am going – how would he conduct himself towards me?'

'To tell you the truth, I don't think he would like it very well. I know if Burton, or Grant, or Baker, or any of those fellows were going after him, and he heard of their coming, Livingstone would put a hundred miles of swamp in a very short time between himself and them. I do. Upon my word, I do.'

Stanley walked back to Webb's house that night, thoroughly depressed. He considered quitting. It seemed that with every passing day, Stanley had to overcome a new hurdle to success. If it wasn't Bennett failing to send money, or the ensuing anxiousness that Bennett would fail to honour Stanley's debts, then it was Kirk coolly, calmly, surgically replacing hope with something worse than fear: doubt.

Stanley brushed aside his depression. 'I did not suppose, though I had so readily consented to search for the doctor, that the path to central Africa was strewn with roses. Had I not been commanded to find him? Well, find him I would, if he were above ground,' he wrote.

The race had taken on a new dimension. Not only was Stanley racing Baker, he was also competing against the slave caravans and the tribal telegraph. He couldn't let word of his arrival precede him. Livingstone was likely to run in the other direction. And since Stanley's great commission was to pursue Livingstone until he found him, the game of cat and mouse could go on for years.

Stanley cherished the secret more than ever as he began his first bits of shopping for supplies in the bazaars and markets, eliciting scores of questions from traders eager to know where the white man was going. The French Consul, taking note of Stanley's spending habits, thought the American 'rather eccentric in his way of doing things, refusing everyone's advice and consequently reduced to his own resources'.

Two of Stanley's first purchases were boats – the first twenty-five feet long and six feet wide, the other ten feet long and four and a half feet wide. Farquhar, Selim and a new member of the team, the British sailor John Shaw, who was stranded in Zanzibar after beating a mutiny charge, were put to work ripping the wooden sides away and replacing them with collapsible canvas. The ribs, keel, stem and stern pieces were disassembled for easier overland transport. As needed, the boats would be reassembled and floated.

When Stanley learned that the Rufiji and Lake Tanganyika did not connect and, in fact, were separated by two hundred miles of mountains and woodland, he still pretended that the Rufiji was his destination. Not even Selim, Farquhar and Shaw knew the truth. So as his three assistants spent their days in Webb's courtyard, tarring the canvas, sewing sails and tents, Stanley changed his course. He would follow the caravan routes west from Bagamoyo to Ujiji. The boats would still be used for the second half of the journey, to Cairo.

At Webb's suggestion, Stanley began relying on a powerful trader named Sheikh Hashid, for advice on necessary purchases and caravan construction. Hashid, who was also Webb's landlord, had sent dozens of caravans into the interior. He became Stanley's guidebook, and profited enormously from Stanley's naivety. From Hashid, Stanley learned the proper assortment of cloth, beads and wire needed for use as currency in the interior. They would be payment for food from villages en route, hiring new porters as needed and paying tribute to those chiefs demanding a toll for the privilege of passing through their land. Cloth, beads and wire were worth more than gold in Africa. The goods had to be functional, abundant and appealing to the eye. 'The women of Africa,' Stanley learned, 'are as fastidious in their tastes for beads as the women of New York are for jewellery.'

Then there were the basic, vital logistics. The pagazis – porters – carried a maximum weight of seventy pounds on their shoulders. They operated between Bagamoyo and the crossroads of Tabora, roughly two-thirds of the way to Ujiji. At Tabora the men would be paid off and Stanley would need to hire new men for the final push to Ujiji. If Livingstone wasn't at Ujiji, and Stanley needed to push further inland, there would be an additional charge. Payment was in doti – bolts of blue Indian calico or 'Merikani', the preferred American cotton from the mills of Salem and Nashua. Each doti was four yards long and three feet wide. Depending upon experience, a pagazi received from fifteen to twenty-five doti for his tour of duty.

Stanley purchased eight thousand yards of Merikani to pay his porters and to barter with in the interior. The cloth came folded from the mill, but would have to be unfolded and tightly rolled into seventy-pound bales for carrying. After rolling, the bale of cloth was bound with coir rope and pounded by two men until the bale was shaped like a bedroll – three feet long, one foot wide, one foot deep. The bale was placed in a mat bag known as a makanda, which the pagazi hoisted onto his shoulders for travel. Beads, on the other hand, were placed in long narrow bags weighing sixty-two pounds each. Wire was carried on poles in loads of six coils weighing sixty pounds.

But cloth, beads and wire were just the start. Under Hashid's direction Stanley purchased food, medicine, ammunition and pack mules. Anticipating the great moment he would meet Livingstone, Stanley also purchased a bottle of champagne. Stanley spent money zealously, until his little search party became the largest-ever expedition to set forth from Zanzibar – so big that Stanley was forced to divide it into five sub-caravans and stagger their departures to avoid robbery. The mules would carry those loads too heavy for porters.

As January passed, and Stanley was almost ready to sail for Bagamoyo, all of Zanzibar talked about the white man setting off into the mainland. 'This fact was repeated a thousand times in the streets, proclaimed in all the shop alcoves and at the custom house,' Stanley wrote. 'The native bazaar laid hold of it and agitated it every day until my departure. The foreigners, including the Europeans, wished to know the pros and cons of my going in and coming out.' He was getting worried. The Rufiji River facade was wearing thin. There were too many goods for such a short journey, too much money being thrown around by a simple newspaper reporter. He stuck to his story, however. The need for secrecy was still vital, no matter how obvious things were getting.

Right to the end, Stanley continued purchasing in an eager, but not impulsive fashion. A childhood of poverty had made him careful with money. Finally, 'there remained for me,' Stanley wrote months later in his first dispatch to the *Herald*, 'to raise a small company of faithful men, who should act as soldiers, guards to the caravan and servants when necessary'. The legendary Sidi Mubarak Bombay – 'the honestest of black men who served with Burton, and subsequently with Speke' – came on board as leader of Stanley's protective militia. In time, Bombay would serve as unofficial caravan leader, and as liaison between Stanley and the pagazis.

Thirteen years had passed since a young Bombay had dazzled Burton and Speke with his easy humour and insatiable work ethic. But he was still able to walk thirty miles a day at a brisk pace, had worked with more expeditions than any man, and knew the interior by heart. Bombay, however, had also passed into middle-age. He was bald, and the young pagazis didn't respect him. As the rare man in history to follow the Nile from Lake Victoria to the Mediterranean, Bombay thought himself a celebrity. He had an ego, as Stanley knew from reading the works of Burton and Speke, and could be outspoken, prone to drink and chasing women, and a procrastinator. So there were liabilities incumbent in Bombay's hiring. All in all, however, the exploration veteran was vital.

Stanley trusted Bombay so much he let the former slave hire his own soldiers. Bombay hand-picked twenty men. For defence, the force carried 'one double-barrelled smooth bore No. 12, two American Winchester rifles or "sixteen shooters", two Starr's breech-loading carbines, one Jocelyn breech-loader, one elephant rifle, carrying balls eight to the pound, two breech-loading revolvers, twenty-four flintlock muskets, six single-barrelled pistols, one battle axe, two swords, two daggers, one boar spear, two American axes, twenty-four hatchets and twenty-four long knives'.

Stanley, it seemed, was ready for anything. In less than a month he had assembled his caravan and was preparing to get under way.

On 5 February, as the sun rose over the Indian Ocean, Stanley said goodbye to Webb and his family. Four dhows bobbed in the harbour right in front of the American Consulate. As a going-away present, Webb's wife sewed Stanley an American flag. She had come to enjoy his company a great deal, though she'd thought him gruff when they first met. The flag was Mrs Webb's contribution to her husband's and Stanley's anti-British subterfuge. Stanley ran the provocation up his dhow's mast. He hadn't written any newspaper dispatches to the *Herald* from Zanzibar, for fear of giving away his intentions. That would wait until he reached somewhere deep in the interior. The homemade Old Glory, now fluttering and snapping in the wind, would add a patriotic dimension to Stanley's trip that was sure to please his readers.

Now Henry Morton Stanley was leading an expedition into the African interior, with the purpose of finding David Livingstone. It was a glorious moment indeed.

Stanley's flotilla of forty-foot-long dhows contained two other valuable presents: horses. One was a bay, the gift of an American merchant. The larger, a grey, was from Sultan Barghash. The Sultan had taken to Stanley after the reporter impressed him with travel stories of journeys through Islamic countries. The Sultan also presented Stanley with a signed paper, stating the New York *Herald* expedition could go anywhere in his domain, unhindered. The backing of such an influential friend emboldened Stanley. It was just a month since he'd arrived in Zanzibar. He had known just one person when he arrived. But through ambition, drive and even a little personal charisma, Stanley had financed the entire journey and made two very powerful friends in Webb and Barghash.

When it came time to sail that day, Shaw and Farquhar were missing. It was mid-morning when Stanley found them in a seaside bar, drinking whisky, surrounded by a dozen new acquaintances, spending their advance salary. Farquhar, in Stanley's words, 'was holding forth on the greatness of the art of African exploration'. In truth, Farquhar was scared of the unknown miles that lay ahead. He was lazy, insolent and mean. Farquhar was much too proud to admit fear aloud, but like Shaw, he was drinking to calm himself. 'Trying,' as Stanley scornfully wrote later, 'to stave off with the aid of whisky the dread presentiments that would insidiously now and then obtrude themselves into their minds, warning them that though the new lands were about to be revealed to them, with all the fantastic scenes credited to the new country, there might be something in these strange parts that might . . . well, what?'

Stanley glowered at the sailors. 'Get into the dhows at once, men,' Stanley barked. 'This is a rather bad beginning after signing contracts.'

Shaw spoke up. He was more complicated than Farquhar, more sensitive and less afraid to show his fears. Unlike Farquhar, however, who could find work on a ship that would take him away from Zanzibar and Africa if he successfully deserted from Stanley, Shaw was stuck on the island. The false charge of mutiny by the captain of the USS *Nevada* made him unemployable. Though proven innocent, no other skipper in port would hire him. Unless Shaw wanted to stay on Zanzibar for ever, earning his passage money by working for Stanley was his only option.

On the verge of departure, though, Shaw was cowed by Africa, and haunted by fears he'd signed on too hastily. 'If you please, sir, may I ask if you think I have done quite right in promising to go with you to Africa?' Shaw asked tentatively as Stanley stood over him. Farquhar remained quiet.

The question about the group's safety in Africa – unspoken for so long

– hung between the three men. Their differences in manner and background were many, and best heard in their accents: Shaw's clipped Cockney, Farquhar's working man's Scottish brogue, Stanley's curious Southern drawl. But all three had privately wondered whether going into Africa was wise. That hesitation was one of the few things they had in common. But devoid of hubris and machismo, and spoken on the verge of their journey as a plea to be released from his obligation, Shaw's question placed the issue squarely at the middle of their triangular relationship – where it would remain for the rest of their journey together.

Stanley, even as Shaw's words dangled in the air, chose to scoff. 'Have you not received your advance? Have you not signed the contract?' Stanley asked. 'Get into the boat, man, at once. We are all in it for now. Sink or swim. Live or die. None can desert his duty.'

When the *Herald* expedition's dhows finally sailed for the mainland just before noon, Shaw and Farquhar were reluctantly on board. Stanley looked back and scanned the shore. Kirk was nowhere to be seen. But Stanley spied Webb, his wife and two young children cheering him on, waving star-spangled hats, handkerchiefs and even a banner. 'Happy people, and good!' Stanley wrote of the Webbs. 'May their course and ours be prosperous, and may God's blessing rest on us all.'

Then Stanley turned his back on Zanzibar, ready to face at last the land haunting his dreams. In the final days on the island, when people asked his destination, Stanley no longer mentioned the headwaters of the Rufiji. Instead, in simple tones, he declared: 'I am going to Africa.'

Now Henry Morton Stanley had the blessing of the American Consul, and was flying the American flag. It was a moment that swelled Stanley with pride. And yet Stanley harboured one great secret – something he concealed from everyone he met and was now carrying into Africa – Stanley was not an American. He was, in fact, as British as Livingstone.

FOURTEEN

INTO AFRICA

FEBRUARY TO MARCH 1871
Bagamoyo
815 miles from Livingstone

CHARACTER IS BUILT THROUGH TRIALS AND TURMOIL. STANLEY, WHO
endured a heart-wrenching childhood, then an adolescence fraught with
hardship, sexual molestation and longing, and an international change
of residence, had seen an abundance of both in his life. Despite the
challenges and setbacks, he still indulged himself in moments of great
hope. Without that lustrous act of faith there could be no viable search
for Livingstone.

Life had taught Stanley to prepare for the worst in any new situation.
As a result he was steeled, almost resigned, to the African mainland
being a brutish place that was far more harrowing than his nightmares.
But in the days after Stanley's dhows dropped anchor on the coral reef
forming Bagamoyo's natural harbour, he was surprised to discover
Africa wasn't as bad as he thought. At least, Bagamoyo wasn't. Weary
of Zanzibar's claustrophobia and squalor, Stanley revelled in the sweet
ocean breezes and the bombast of coastal jungle greenery. 'We were able
to sleep in the open air, and rose fresh and healthy each morning, to
enjoy our matutinal bath in the sea. And by the time the sun had risen
we had engaged in multitudinous preparations for our departure for the
interior,' he wrote.

Bagamoyo would be the second, and final, stage of Stanley's launch. Zanzibar was for purchasing supplies, while Bagamoyo was for hiring the men to carry them and for indulging in last-minute organization. On the surface it was an idyllic place for a man to gather his thoughts and gain perspective. The white sand beach was a crescent curving slowly outward. Stanley could see ten miles down the coast in either direction, see the tall rows of palm and pine trees separating sand from jungle. Dhows lay stranded on their sides at low tide, making it easier to unload boats. The sounds of Swahili being spoken mingled with the thunk of shipwrights swinging short-handled axes into felled tree trunks and the clatter in the treetops of wind knocking palm fronds against one another.

Sand berms along the beach protected Bagamoyo from the sea. The town was set two hundred yards back on a single long street with a few houses made of stone and others of mud. The buildings were white-washed, like those in Zanzibar, but were mostly one storey, and without the island's signature ornate wooden doors. The population was Arab slavers, Indian merchants and slaves. The only Europeans were the French fathers of the Holy Ghost Roman Catholic mission, which resided on several acres just inland, to the north. Stanley rented a home on the western edge of Bagamoyo, with a courtyard for penning the pack animals and pitching tents. As new supply needs made themselves known, he began sending Bombay back and forth on the four-hour dhow journey to Zanzibar for last-minute items.

The paradise of Bagamoyo, however, came with a sad legacy. It was the terminus of the slave caravans, and the last African soil slaves would ever tread. Originally, the Arabs had named the town Bwagamoyo – 'throw off melancholy' – but the slaves changed it. Bagamoyo, in Swahili, means 'crush your heart'.

Life in Bagamoyo was even slower-paced than Zanzibar. With his anxieties and short attention span, Stanley grew bored. The euphoria of leaving Zanzibar was soon replaced by an impatience to leave Bagamoyo. Time was closing in. The monsoons were coming. But Stanley was stuck. The Zanzibar cholera epidemic of 1869–70 had devastated the East African coast, too, killing over one hundred thousand people. Wary of the disease, skilled porters were still avoiding Bagamoyo, which meant there weren't enough men to carry Stanley's massive load. The journalist offered double and triple the going rate, but he still couldn't find porters. There were tasks for him to oversee in the meantime, such as compressing the doti into bundles. Otherwise, all Stanley could do was wait for the manpower.

In his boredom, Stanley's fears returned. He realized again how 'impracticable' it was to search for Livingstone. And again, he went as far as to make allusions to suicide. He would kill himself, he wrote in one bizarre sentence, 'by putting my head in a barrel of sand, which I thought to be a most easy death, and one I gratuitously recommend for all would-be suicides'.

His thoughts never went beyond rumination, but they defined Stanley's mood. He was edgy, afraid of failure, trying to contain an inner foreboding. Finding Livingstone was more than just an assignment – he pictured it as the rightful conclusion to the self-help regime he'd begun two years before in Aden. He was a glory-hound, but had the prescience to realize that facing his fears by trekking across Africa would give him charge of his destiny. 'I mean, by attention to my business, by self-denial, by indefatigable energy, to become my own master and that of others,' he wrote.

He was propelled by an underdog's penchant for proving himself through extreme actions, no matter how dangerous or how much they scared him. That which did not kill Stanley definitely made him stronger. He had been a timid, needy child. But each new challenge since leaving home had hardened him and added another notch of courage. Cumulatively, they had prepared him for Africa. He knew how to camp, how to shoot, how to endure days without food and water, how to march. Instead of observing and writing about the actions of others, as the life of a journalist traditionally mandated, Stanley would write about himself. Hero or goat, he was about to take centrestage.

So he shooed the depression away and turned it into rage. The rage, in turn, was directed at one man: John Kirk. Their one-sided battle of wills and wits – a skirmish of which Kirk was almost completely unaware – wouldn't end just because Stanley had sailed to Africa.

A fresh opportunity for attacking the British Consul arose when Stanley noticed that Livingstone's caravan of relief supplies, which had left Zanzibar on 1 November, over three months earlier, was still in Bagamoyo. In that time the caravan could have almost travelled to Ujiji. Instead, the porters drew a daily salary for doing nothing, living off Livingstone's money as they made trips back to friends and family in Zanzibar. 'They lived in clover here,' Stanley fumed. 'Thoughtless of the errand they had been sent upon, and careless of the consequences.'

The problem lay with Kirk. Overwhelmed by his new duties and apathetic about helping Livingstone, he allowed the caravan to idle. He knew that in addition to the seven men hired in Zanzibar, the relief caravan required an additional thirty-five porters to carry all the loads. He had not, however, hired them. Kirk had also been an Africa hand long enough to know that heat and malaise robbed men of initiative, made them lazy, made them cowards. It wasn't enough merely to purchase supplies, trusting that the porters would deliver them. After the failure of the 1868 and 1869 resupply attempts, Kirk knew it was vital that porters be hired, and that a supervisor escort the caravan all the way to Ujiji – if only to act as a catalyst. Kirk hadn't arranged such an escort, either through his contacts in Zanzibar or by travelling to Bagamoyo and arranging it himself, so the porters showed no sign of leaving.

The more Stanley ruminated about Kirk's failure to expedite supplies to Livingstone, the more the conflict between him and Kirk escalated in his head. Stanley represented America: brash, arrogant with resources, steadfast in the belief that anything was possible. Kirk was Great Britain: sober, powerful, understated. So while Kirk was quietly sure Livingstone would carry on until the supplies inevitably reached him, Stanley was appalled Kirk could be so reckless about Livingstone's safety. 'If the British Consul puts forward a plea that he was not aware that his supplies to Livingstone were still halted at Bagamoyo, it will only prove to me that he was more culpably negligent than ever of his duty to a British subject and a brother official, who was left completely dependent on him for even the means to live,' Stanley wrote.

As if reading Stanley's mind, a rumour circulated through Bagamoyo on 10 February that 'balyuz' – the Consul – was coming to town. The relief caravan immediately packed up and slipped away in the dead of night, headed in the general direction of Ujiji. By the time Kirk stepped off the HMS *Columbine* and strolled into Bagamoyo two days later, they were long gone.

Kirk claimed he was in Bagamoyo to hunt, but really he was there to save face. Snider rifle in the crook of his arm, Kirk ventured into the bush for a day of shooting, pretending disinterest about the caravan. In actuality, he followed the caravan path several miles inland to confirm the relief caravan wasn't just loitering outside town, waiting for him to go back to Zanzibar so they could head back to the beach.

Stanley seemed to be the only man not fooled by Kirk's ruse. Stanley confronted Kirk in Bagamoyo. He scolded the Consul for being negligent with Livingstone's supplies, and Kirk responded by looking down his nose at Stanley. He sneered that the journalist knew nothing about Africa. To prove it, Kirk coldly predicted tse-tse flies would soon kill the two new horses that were the objects of Stanley's pride. Then, having had the last word, Kirk sailed back to Zanzibar on *Columbine*.

Finally, to ensure Kirk was seen as Livingstone's staunch ally, Kirk wrote to the new Foreign Secretary back in London, Earl Granville. The letter was dated 18 February. Kirk swore he had travelled with the caravan from the beaches of Bagamoyo until they were eight miles outside town. 'Had I not gone in person,' he wrote to assure Granville, 'the caravan might have loitered yet several months.'

Back in Bagamoyo, Stanley set aside his rivalry with Kirk to focus on his expedition. Porters were beginning to trickle in. Stanley hired them immediately and began sending sections of the caravan on their way to Tabora, which lay five hundred miles to the west. The first group of twenty-four pagazis left on 18 February, led by a group of three soldiers. With the monsoons due to arrive in six weeks, it was crucial that Stanley make sure the other four groups left before 1 April. After that point it was likely the rains would turn the trail into a black sludge, and travel would be impossible.

No route inland was safe from the rains. And though it was a minor detail, of the three caravan routes heading west, Stanley chose the route Arab traders considered fastest – but also the most rugged. The three routes weren't much different from one another, and even crossed each other at certain points. One had been followed by Burton and Speke. The other by Speke and Grant. Stanley's was shortest, if only by a little, but Stanley reasoned it would make a difference when the rains hit. 'My mission was one that required speed,' Stanley wrote. 'Any delay would render it useless. Forty days' rain and a two-hundred-mile swamp must not prevent the New York *Herald* correspondent from marching, now that the caravan is ready.'

Finally, on 21 March, his caravan was indeed ready. After seven interminable weeks, it was finally Stanley's turn to leave Bagamoyo. Farquhar had left on 25 February, leading the third caravan, followed by the fourth caravan on 11 March. But Shaw would travel with Stanley in the rear column. Separating the two sailors was intentional. Farquhar was a bitter whoremonger and drunkard who enjoyed baiting Shaw, a simple, witty dreamer prone to depression and rage. Separating them seemed the best hope of minimizing conflict on the trail.

Stanley had begun to compare the inactivity of Bagamoyo with doing time in a federal penitentiary. Therefore, as he rode the bay horse out of town, there was a song in his heart. Stanley's group was the largest caravan segment, including twenty-eight porters, Bombay and eleven soldiers, Selim the fourteen-year-old interpreter, Omar the dog, a tailor, a cook, John Shaw and Stanley. Mrs Webb's flag flew at the front of the column. 'We were all in the highest spirits – the soldiers sang extempore, the Kirangoze lifted his voice into a loud bellowing note, and fluttered the American flag,' Stanley wrote of that stirring morning. 'My heart, I thought, palpitated much too quickly for the sobriety of a leader. But I could not help it. The enthusiasm of youth still clung to me.'

A total of 192 people comprised the New York *Herald* expedition's five caravans. 'Altogether,' Stanley wrote, 'the expedition numbers three white men, twenty-two soldiers, four supernumeraries, with a transport train of eighty-two pagazis, twenty-seven donkeys and two horses, conveying fifty-two bales of cloth, seven man-loads of wire, sixteen man-loads of beads, twenty loads of boat fixtures, three loads of tents, four loads of clothes and personal baggage, two loads of cooking utensils and dishes, one load of medicines, three of powder, five of bullets, small shot and metallic cartridges, three of instruments and small necessaries, such as soap, sugar, tea, coffee, Liebig's extract of meat, pemmican, candles, etc, which makes a total of one hundred and sixteen loads – equal to eight and a half tons of material.'

The sheer mass of goods was a reassuring reminder Stanley would never do without. It was also his acknowledgement that his logistics were influenced too greatly by reading Burton, and from listening to Sheikh Hashid. The New York *Herald* expedition, however, could no longer afford to base itself on previous journeys. The average caravan slogged six miles per day – less than one mile per hour. Time meant little in Africa, and ten miles a day was a fair journey. But Stanley was attempting the outrageous. He needed to move faster. He needed to start thinking for himself.

In many ways, that applied to his life as well as his caravan. Africa was a big land with a big sky and empty spaces, where silence and solitude and boredom forced even a man like Stanley, at once entranced and terrified by introspection, to peer inside his soul to divine the essence of his being. It was a process, though, that he intended to suppress through activity. 'Pleasure cannot bind me, cannot lead me astray from the path I have chalked out,' he wrote, defining the facade of denial and bluster concealing his inner chaos. 'I have nothing to fall back upon but energy and much hopefulness.'

The facade, however, started to crack as soon as he began his journey into Africa, on 21 March 1871, with the glorious march from Bagamoyo. Pleasure seeped in through those cracks, and Stanley was too awash in sensation to care. 'Loveliness glowed around me as I looked at the fertile fields of manioc, the riant vegetation of the tropics, the beautiful strange trees and flowers, plants and herbs, and heard the cry of the peewit and cricket and the noisy sibilance of many insects,' Stanley wrote. 'Methought each and all whispered to me, "At last you are started."'

The pleasure was fleeting. Three days later, just as Kirk predicted, both horses died. To Stanley's smug satisfaction, when he slit them open for a field autopsy, the cause of death was parasitic worms, not tse-tse flies.

FIFTEEN

THE SOURCE

29 MARCH 1871
Nyangwe

'O FATHER,' LIVINGSTONE PRAYED IN HIS JOURNAL ON NEW YEAR'S DAY, 1871. 'Help me to finish this work to Thy honour!'

Finally, at the age of fifty-eight, through a perseverance that bordered on mania, it seemed as if Livingstone had done just that. On 29 March 1871, he reached the village of Nyangwe, on the shores of the Lualaba River. Until then, he had nearly given up finding the Source. 'It is excessively trying,' he wrote of his search a few days earlier, 'and so many difficulties have been put in my way that I doubt whether the Divine favour and will is on my side.'

But then he found it – or at least, thought he had. Before him lay the Lualaba River, which he was more convinced than ever was the Source of the Nile. Through interviews with Arabs and villagers and his own observations through five long years of withering travel, he had come to the conclusion that the Lualaba could be nothing other than the upper Nile. The Nile and Lualaba, then, were one and the same. By tracing the Lualaba south to its source, he would find the Nile's.

At one time Livingstone thought the Lualaba might be the source of the great Congo River instead, but an observation of the Lualaba's immense width and length, steady northward flow and two-thousand-foot elevation made him positive it was the Source. 'I went down to take a good look at the Lualaba,' he wrote. 'It is narrower than it is higher up, but still a mighty river – at least three thousand yards broad and always deep. It can never be waded at any point, or at any time of year. The people unhesitatingly declare that if one tried to ford it he would assuredly be lost. It has many large islands, and at these it is about two thousand yards, or one mile. The banks are steep and deep. There is clay and yellow schist in the structure. The current is about two miles away to the north.'

And north led, theoretically, to where it became the Nile. To confirm that theory, Livingstone needed to rent a canoe from the Nyangwe villagers and follow the river's flow to see where it led. Once that was accomplished, he could then backtrack down the Lualaba to its source, sure that he had also solved the mystery of the Nile's.

The villagers of Nyangwe, however, had seen Livingstone travelling with Arabs, and thought the white-skinned Livingstone to be an eminent slaver. They were convinced he wanted a canoe to cross over to the river's far side and make war. The villagers were happy to rent a canoe to Chuma and Susi, and even small groups of lesser Arabs, but the white-skinned Livingstone wasn't to be trusted. 'They were alarmed at my coming among them,' he wrote, 'and ready to flee. Many stood afar off in their suspicion.'

Nyangwe, like Bambarre, was comfortable, and Livingstone was eager to earn the people's trust, no matter how long he had to wait. The busy village was easily one of the finest places in Africa he had ever resided in. The people were enormously intelligent. Ivory was so plenti- ful that they decorated the arches of their doorways with elephant tusks. The women were stunning, with a colouring like light cocoa, fine noses, full lower lips and delicate jaw lines. They wore no clothing, save for a leather band around their waist, from which dangled thin, ornamented strands of grass cloth to cover their pubic region and the cleft in their buttocks. Their hair was woven into long, elaborate shapes that pro- truded from the front of their heads like a sun visor, then also cascaded down the back of their necks in ringlets. Many possessed a great skill for swimming and holding their breath, and would dive to the bottom of the Lualaba for freshwater oysters. Livingstone was quite taken with the women of Nyangwe.

Unfortunately, Livingstone wasn't the only outsider enchanted by the women of Nyangwe and other villages in the Manyuema region. Coincidental to his journey, the Arabs had carried their slave trade further and further into the heart of Africa due to the Zanzibar cholera epidemic. Never having seen guns before, tribes in the Manyuema region didn't understand what the Arabs fired at them in times of war. It seemed that the newcomers had found a way to trap lightning, and it was assumed that fighting back was futile. The Arabs, who were initially terrified of the cannibalistic aspect of Manyuema, were soon flooding the region, stealing ivory and people with abandon. Word had already trickled back into the interior that women of Manyuema were fetching high prices in the Zanzibar slave markets. Their beauty was considered so stunning that many of Zanzibar's Omani half-castes were purchasing the Manyuema women to be wives instead of consigning them to a harem.

Livingstone had no plans to marry these women, whom he observed daily in the village marketplace. That didn't necessarily mean, however, Livingstone was chaste. Though a man of God, he was not without weakness. The missionary who arrived in Africa as a teetotal virgin had become fond of beer and champagne, and often travelled with a small bottle of brandy when he could procure it. Livingstone was also fond of women – and sex. It was only natural in a land where the intense heat made nudity preferable to being fully clothed, where sex often took place in the outdoors because the communal family hut was too small for intimacy, where the muffled sounds of furtive lovemaking could be heard at night, and where Livingstone occasionally stumbled upon Africans in the act of intercourse. It was also not surprising that a widower enduring long absences from England would want the company of a woman.

Livingstone's thoughts of sex were actually evident in his journals long before Mary died. His entry of 8 January 1854, describing a fiery African princess named Manenko, was a commentary on the brash sexuality he encountered in his travels. Livingstone wrote that she was 'a tall strapping woman of about twenty . . . in a state of frightful nudity. This was not from want of clothing, for, being a chief, she might have been as well clad as her subjects, but from her peculiar style of elegance of dress. In the course of a quarrel with her entourage she advanced and receded in true oratorical style . . . and, as usual in more civilized feminine lectures, she leaned over the objects of her ire, and screamed forth all their faults and failings since they were born, and her despair at ever seeing them better.' Manenko referred to Livingstone as 'my little man', and he complained that she left him with 'no power'. It was common for royal women like Manenko, if they so desired, to share the bed of passing travellers. Hypothetically, if Livingstone was so ordered, he had no choice but to concede – or be killed.

Throughout his years in Africa, Livingstone's journal admissions about sex were limited to vivid appreciations of the beautiful women he saw in his travels. But in a candid personal letter to G. E. Seward, the British Consul whom Livingstone befriended during his time on Zanzibar in 1866, the explorer revealed a telling private detail. In the course of sharing insights about expedition supplies and the vagaries of life in Africa, Livingstone displayed uncharacteristic machismo by confiding in Seward that he'd had so many African women he felt like a famously prolific Biblical lover. 'I had like Solomon three hundred wives princess (but don't tell Mrs Seward),' Livingstone confessed to his fellow Scot.

Clearly, the vast continent of Africa held a deep spell over all outsiders who visited it. As 1871 marked the fifth year of the Source search, Livingstone, like Stanley, was being changed daily by its complexities.

SIXTEEN

BED OF THORNS

MARCH TO APRIL 1871
East African Coastal Plain
790 miles from Livingstone

STANLEY'S SEVEN-HUNDRED-MILE WALK FROM BAGAMOYO TO LAKE Tanganyika could be broken into rough thirds. The first third comprised the stretch from the Indian Ocean across the coastal jungle. The second portion began when the trail rose from the jungle, ascending to an elevation of fifteen hundred feet, then continuing all the way across grassy savannah and waterless desert into Tabora, where the original porters would be discharged and new men hired. The final third was the push into Ujiji, on the coast of Lake Tanganyika, which took place largely through thick, rocky forest.

The journalist knew from his research that Burton and Speke needed five months to make Tabora, so he knew better than to be too impatient over the caravan's languorous rhythm. Instead, Stanley adopted the air of a bored tourist in the first days of his journey, taking notes and gaping at the scenery. The path across the coastal plain passed through small villages and crossed rivers. Bare-breasted African women tilled their gardens, titillating Stanley even as they pointed and laughed at his safari outfit of knee-high boots, khaki pants and shirt, and the balaclava helmet that kept the sun at bay. Strangler figs, forest grass, marsh reeds, acacias, dwarf fan palms and tiger grass rioted all around them. The land and sky were alive with a stunning array of birds; pelicans, pigeons, jays, ibis sacra, golden pheasants, quails, hawks and eagles whirled. Monkeys howled, and the trail shifted with the movement of lithe and speedy black mambas, green mambas, cobras, fat puff adders, night adders and seventeen other poisonous snakes. The mauve hides of partially submerged hippopotamuses poked above the surface of the Kingani River like bulbous stepping stones.

Stanley, fancying himself a big game hunter in the manner of his rival Kirk, fired at them with his shotgun. The metal pellets only irritated the hippos. Some moved away. Most ignored him. One angry male, however, bellowed at Stanley. The journalist switched to the more powerful Winchester, and shot the hippo dead.

Despite that act of destruction, Stanley thought he was in Eden. 'The country,' he wrote during his first euphoric week of travel, 'is as much a wilderness as the desert of the Sahara, though it possesses a far more pleasing aspect. Indeed, had the first man at the time of the creation gazed at his world and perceived it of the beauty which belongs to this part of Africa, he would have no cause for complaint. In the deep thickets, set like islets amid a sea of grassy verdure, he would have found shelter from the noonday heat, and a safe retirement for himself and spouse during the awesome darkness. In the morning he could have walked forth on the sloping sward, enjoyed its freshness and performed his ablutions in one of the many small streams flowing at its foot. The noble forests, deep and cool, are round about him, and in their shade walk as many animals as one can desire. For days and days let a man walk in any direction, north, south, east and west, and he will behold the same scene.'

Stanley's caravan's day began before sunrise, with Bombay yelling, 'Set out, set out' to the camp. Tents were dropped. Breakfast was eaten quickly, and the march began by 6 a.m. Stanley always set off last to ensure nothing was left behind, then charged ahead to lead the way. Bombay kept the column in line. Shaw rode at the back, encouraging stragglers. Each late afternoon when the caravan stopped, there was a rush to collect thorn bushes for building the nightly berm, known as a boma, around camp to ward off carnivores. Tents for Stanley and Shaw would be pitched in the centre of the boma. Stanley's hammock, carpet and bearskin would be laid out in his tent by Selim, who would also unpack Stanley's travel duffel.

Meanwhile, the porters and soldiers would divide into informal groups of three to seven men. Each group would build their own fire, cook their own food and build the night's sleeping hut. The hut would begin with a single ridge pole, followed by forked uprights, rafters of small sticks and bark, then grass for the roof and sides. Grass was also spread across the ground as a mattress. When the ground was muddy the porters built raised sleeping platforms of sticks and grass.

In the evenings, after dinner, the men smoked and talked before the campfire until eight or nine. Stanley didn't fraternize with the men, preferring to retire to his tent. He donned flannel pyjamas, sat in his camp chair and described the day to his journal by lamplight. The script was neat and flowery. His notes were long and descriptive, full of personal thoughts and honest expression, admitting both fear and courage.

Livingstone was very much on his mind, but Stanley was losing his sense of haste. Africa was the first place on earth he'd ever enjoyed total control of his environment. He thought of himself as 'the vanguard, the reporter, the thinker, the leader'. He liked that the porters and soldiers called him Bwana Mkuba – Big Master.

But Stanley wasn't really in control, and he knew it. As he'd feared all along, it was Africa that held sway over his future. And almost as if poking fun at him, the continent terminated his idyll with a bit of comedy. Just a week into the journey the jungle grew thicker. The fourth caravan was stopped by illness and Stanley's group raced ahead. However, a warning came to mind from Burton's writings, something about unsupervised porters being likely to dawdle – if they travelled at all. The experience with Kirk's relief expedition in Zanzibar had proved that to be true. Afraid his fourth caravan would turn around and march back to Bagamoyo, Stanley called a halt until they caught up.

Until then, coastal breezes had made insects scarce. But with the jungle came bugs. Flies swooped about the camp in a variety of shapes and sizes that intrigued Stanley so much he ordered the soldiers to catch handfuls for his inspection. Dutifully, the men ran around camp, grabbing at air. They brought their catch to Stanley in his tent. Copying Burton, Livingstone and even Kirk, Stanley affected the air of dutiful scientist, recording his discoveries. He let the flies play on him, observing them in action. There was the large black-headed African horsefly, longer by a third than a honeybee and with a bite that drew blood. A second fly sang like a cricket but was smaller and had white stripes across its abdomen. The smallest of all was brown, with long wings that made it look just larger than the average housefly. That fly made no sound. But Stanley had previously noted that it tended to attack horses and donkeys in great swarms. The animals would cry out in pain. Blood would stream down their legs. They writhed and bit and swished their tails, but the small fly was tenacious. Once it began sucking blood, it would not let go. Only goats and antelopes, Stanley learned from his porters, were immune to this little brown pest. Even humans were targets. The porters said the little fly was known as 'chufwa'. Only later did Stanley learn it was also called 'tse-tse'.

Also unknown to Stanley, and to medical science at the time, was that the tse-tse carried a microscopic parasite known as trypanosome, which caused sleeping sickness. If a tse-tse landed and inserted its proboscis in his skin – a puncture feeling more like a sting than a bite – and began sucking his blood, it had the potential to inject the parasite which would then breach the body's immune system by altering its structure. Fevers, seizures, slurred speech, confusion and lethargy would follow within days. Death would come several weeks later. Stanley was unaware that sleeping sickness was incurable, and killed more people in Africa each year than lion, hippo and crocodile attack combined. He merely passed the evening in his flannel pyjamas, playing with the small brown fly as if it were a toy.

The next morning, still in his comfortable, unrestrictive pyjamas, wearing canvas shoes instead of boots, Stanley was in the mood to go hunting. If an Englishman had been nearby Stanley would never have dreamed of an act so gauche as hunting in pyjamas, but just a week away from Bagamoyo and Kirk, he was living by a different sense of decorum. Survival and comfort were more important than proper dress. And, having seen elephant, wildebeest and zebra tracks along the trail, Stanley was eager to bag meat for the cooking pot. Livingstone was temporarily forgotten. With the fourth caravan still nowhere in sight, Stanley was sure that 'within reasonable proximity to game, I doubted not but I could bring some to camp'.

Stanley pulled back the door of thorns marking the boma's entrance. A gunbearer accompanied him. They stepped into a field where the grass grew taller than their waists. The pace was slow, without conversation. Every culvert and rise was checked for signs of a crouching animal. Soon Stanley found the hoofprints, scat and trampled grass showing that antelope and hartebeest had recently passed through. Both were small, fast animals that travelled in herds and made good eating. Separating from the gunbearer, Stanley struck off alone down the trail. He was already a mile from camp.

The path led into a jungle and down a stream. Carrying his rifle low, his pyjamas already drenched in perspiration, Stanley tracked the animals along the water for a full hour. Footprints and trampled grass showed the way. Then, just as suddenly as it appeared, the trail vanished. Stanley instinctively turned around to retrace his steps, but in the jungle's thick undergrowth he lost his way. Not even his trusty pocket compass could point the direction back to safety. So he surveyed the horizon and guessed. 'I steered for the open plain, in the centre of which stood the camp,' he later wrote.

It was a hopeful thought, but wrong. Stanley took a bearing and made his course. But just a few steps later a thorny acacia branch snagged the right leg of his pyjamas and ripped it almost all the way off. Staggering to catch his balance, another branch reached out and grabbed his pyjamas on one shoulder, ripping the flannel again. Two steps later, an aloe plant's tendrils grabbed the left leg of his pyjamas, leaving both his legs exposed.

A less determined or more pragmatic man might have paused to calm himself, or plot another course. But Stanley, legs bare and pyjamas hanging in rags from his body, pressed on. Just one step later a low vine caught his ankle and pulled him to the ground. Instead of landing on another vine, or even plopping with indignity into the black jungle mud, Stanley prostrated himself on a bed of thorns. He cried out in pain, but the jungle canopy's thick leaves and the press of tangled undergrowth muffled his agony. His legs bled. Thorns had broken off and embedded themselves in his skin. The beautiful flannel pyjamas that gave him so much comfort at night, removing him from the hardship of Africa with their downy warmth, had been transformed into lengths of dirty cloth dangling from his body. For all intents and purposes, Henry Morton Stanley was naked.

The young journalist pried his flesh from the bed of thorns and plopped down into the mud to take stock. The saving grace was that his gun and compass hadn't been lost. Rifle in one hand, compass in another, Stanley crawled gingerly across the thorn patch in search of the elusive trail. 'It was on all fours, like a hound on a scent, that I was compelled to travel,' he wrote. Adding insult to injury, a plant whose leaves gave off a foul smell struck him in the face as he burrowed through the jungle. He experienced a sharp burning pain as though cayenne pepper juice had been squirted into his flesh and sizzled deep into his facial wounds. And through it all, he sweated as if water was being strained through his body. 'The atmosphere, pent in by the density of the jungle, was hot and stifling,' Stanley wrote later. 'The perspiration transuded through every pore, making my flannel tatters feel as if I had been through a shower.'

When he finally slunk from the jungle and stood again, Stanley looked back at the green hell. His entire body was a collage of gashes and abrasions and puncture wounds. If his torn clothing and mud-streaked body didn't mark him as an African ingenu, his uneven tan certainly did. Humiliated and exhausted, Stanley endured the stares and snickers of his caravan as he found the boma and returned to its protection once again. Stanley marched to his tent to clean himself and change clothes. He had already vowed he would never enter an African jungle again. 'When I had finally regained the plain and could breathe free,' he wrote, 'I mentally vowed that the penetralia of an African jungle should not be visited by me again, save under most urgent necessity.'

Africa would give Stanley no choice. The jungle would be an omnipresent part of his travels until the tropical coastal plain turned into the sparse, low-rainfall scrub known as *nyika* that served as a transition to the savannah's wide open spaces. Even if that weren't the case, Stanley was too enraptured by Africa to remain upset for long. Within moments of swearing off jungle travel, he was again experiencing great affection for Africa's beauty and hardships. 'Notwithstanding the ruthless rents in my clothes and my epidermal wounds,' he admitted in his journal, 'as I looked over the grandly undulating plain, lovely with its coat of green verdure, with its boundaries of noble woods, heavy with vernal leafage, and regarded the pretty bosky islets amid its wide expanse, I could not but award it its meed of high praise. Daily the country advanced in my estimation, for hitherto I felt I was but obeying orders, and sickly as it might be I was duty bound to go on,' he wrote. 'But day by day the pall-like curtain had been clearing away and the cheerless perspective was brightening.'

In the days that followed, Stanley continued coming to terms with Africa. It wasn't the place of nightmares at all, but a populous, sprawling country of previously unimagined splendour. It was the island he dreamed of years before in Aden, a place where no other man controlled his destiny. Even before Aden – since leaving his family behind on a whim and sailing from England as a teenager – Stanley had sought such a place. Finding it was the realization of years of longing, and the hardship was empowering.

As if sensing Stanley's euphoria, Africa tested him again by letting loose her rains. On 1 April a deluge opened the monsoon season. Stanley's infatuation with Africa dwindled, replaced by the reality that the miles to come would be one challenge after another, punctuated by moments of brilliant, though deceptive, beauty. 'Down poured the furious harbinger of the Masika season, in torrents sufficient to damp the ardour and newborn love for Africa I had lately manifested.'

Then Stanley suffered a more serious setback. As he continued to wait in the rain for his lagging fourth caravan, camped in one spot for day after valuable day instead of moving towards Livingstone, Stanley's men began deserting. As they left they stole equipment, cloth and provisions. Others became sick with various ailments brought on by the rains – fever, chills, a mysterious 'weakness of the loins'. Selim had malaria and even sturdy Bombay suffered from rheumatism. Finally, on 4 April, a week after Stanley began waiting, the fourth caravan arrived, joyously firing their muskets to announce their reappearance. Khamisi, the porter afflicted with the loin malady, found the strength to desert in all the hubbub, stealing two goats, supplies from the caravan and the personal belongings of several fellow porters before running off.

Stanley had had enough. He'd been stern with his men, but reluctant to use force. However, the theft and desertion had to stop or he would shortly be impoverished. Stanley ordered two armed sepoys to find Khamisi and bring him back, using all necessary force.

As the searchers for Khamisi trekked east towards Bagamoyo, Stanley ordered the expedition to break camp and march west. The eighth of April was spent fording a jungle that smelled so foul from plants and decay that Stanley was afraid the men would collapse from nausea. The trail was just a foot wide. There were 'thorny plants and creepers bristling on each side, and projecting branches darting across it, with knots of spiky twigs and spike-nails, ready to catch and hold anything in height'.

After enduring thorns, rains, desertion and dense jungle, Stanley finally encountered Africa's darkest demon. On 10 April, 'we met one of those sights common in this part of the world. To wit, a chained slave gang, bound east. The slaves did not appear to be in any way downhearted; on the contrary, they seemed imbued with the philosophic jollity of the jolly servant of Martin Chuzzlewit,' Stanley observed. He went on to note the surprising fact that both the slaves and their captors were African. 'Were it not for the chains, it would have been difficult to discover master from slave; the physiognomic traits were alike – the mild benignity with which we were regarded was equally visible on their faces. The chains were ponderous. They might have held an elephant captive; but as the slaves carried nothing but themselves, their weight could not have been insupportable.'

Stanley was clearly travelling through a landscape unlike any other on earth. And while he regarded the slaves and slavers as a Dickensian curiosity, their stares made it clear Stanley was the more unique sight: he was white, he was alone and he was in charge of his destiny – with all that implied.

SEVENTEEN

SWAMP FEVER

APRIL TO MAY 1871
Makata Swamp
760 miles from Livingstone

APRIL WAS AN OPPRESSIVE COLLAGE OF DOWNPOUR, DRIZZLE, THUNDER, chills, fever, humidity, sweat, exhaustion and death – punctuated by the sucking sound of feet and hooves plodding through mud. The caravan was unable to find its collective rhythm as the monsoons slowed the men's pace to half a mile per hour. The porters were sick so often in April that the caravan marched on only fourteen of the expedition's first twenty-nine days. Stanley could have helped the pace if he had brought enough medicine for the porters, as well as himself – but he hadn't. The only alternative was a full halt when illness struck the caravan.

Ironically, it was Stanley, the African newcomer, who was the titan of the group, impervious to sickness. He attributed his health to a few teenage doses of a malaria-like Arkansas swamp fever that had struck him down after he first arrived in America and began the process of completely changing his identity. Stanley said he was more robust for having endured the 'ague'. So even as the caravan morale plummeted from the rains and disease, Stanley grew more insistent on pressing the chase for Livingstone. As a man with attention-deficit problems, Stanley craved action. Inactivity gave him too much time to think, which gave him the blues. He wrote of being 'more comfortable and lighthearted while travelling than when chafing and fretting in camp at delays no effort could avoid'.

Stanley liked it that every day on the trail was a new adventure. The path to Ujiji was sometimes thin, sometimes the width of a road, but always defined by mud and vegetation. The caravan threaded through forests of tamarind, acacia and mimosa trees. Rivers like the Ungerengi, where banana trees and seventy-foot-tall, thick-trunked mparamusi trees grew along the banks, were swollen by flash flooding. They had to be waded by the entire caravan – not an easy task for a porter carrying seventy pounds. Nights became two-blanket cool as the trail wound its way to an elevation of a thousand feet. Insects became even more common. Horseflies, tse-tse flies, wasps, black ants, white ants, red ants, centipedes and beetles would fill the four enclosed walls of Stanley's tent each night, crawling over his body and flying into the canvas – so many genera of wriggling, buzzing, biting bugs that he bragged in his writings that a scientific insect collection couldn't match the variety and numbers.

Hyenas began prowling the perimeter of the camp at night, scaring the expedition's donkeys by their mere scent, waiting for the unwary expedition member – man or beast – to venture out. As villages stretched further apart, Stanley's most valuable commodity – food – grew scarce. Hunting expeditions resulted in a small assortment of grouse, quail and pigeons, but the small birds hardly yielded enough meat to fuel a caravan.

Morale was tested again when Khamisi, the deserter and thief, was caught, bound and brought before a tribunal of porters and soldiers. They sentenced him to be flogged with the Big Master's donkey whip. Khamisi's 'crying sorrow' as his peers administered the thirteen lashes drained whatever joy remained from the camp.

Then, as if sickness tapped him on the shoulder and entered his body on a whim, Stanley endured his first hectic day of African fever. 'I surrendered to it at once,' he admitted in his journal on 20 April. 'First, general lassitude prevailed, with a disposition to drowsiness; secondly, came the spinal ache which, commencing from the loins, ascended the vertebrae and extended around the ribs until it reached the shoulders, where it settled into a weary pain.' The pain got worse, causing 'insane visions, frenetic brain throbs and dire sickness'. Twelve hours later the sickness passed. Whether it had been a fever or a brisk jolt of malaria, Stanley didn't know. Regardless, he ingested heavy doses of bitter quinine for the next three days. As chills washed over his body each night, Stanley shivered under a heavy bearskin blanket. Unbeknown to Stanley, the caravan was about to enter its greatest obstacle so far. It was vital for the Big Master to be healthy.

They came upon it after a walk through a pleasant forest with light red soil. Most of the year, what lay before them was known as the Makata River. The plodding, muddy tributary measured only forty feet across. But in the monsoon season the Makata exploded. The river carved great chunks of earth from its banks then overflowed them altogether. In some places it measured a mile wide. The low-lying areas surrounding it became engorged with water until the entire plain between the Usagara Mountains and the village of Simbaweni became flooded. The impromptu swamp measured forty-five miles from one side to the other. The Makata Swamp's mire averaged just a foot deep, but the enormous footprints of giraffes, elephants and buffalo created holes five times that depth. The porters constantly plunged into them as they walked. The donkeys, with their heavy loads, did too, and were sometimes trapped underwater.

The endless hours of trudging through the dirty black water were like poison to the caravan's already devastated morale and health. As the end of each day drew near, they searched the horizon for dry mounds protruding from the swamp where they could make camp. The nonstop rain throughout the night, and the lack of bushes or trees from which to build sleeping huts, made the nights miserable as well.

As they travelled deeper into the swamp, conditions worsened. Tall reeds became a new barrier to progress, like slimy fences of vegetation. The water grew deeper, and finding the courage to step each morning from dry sleeping mounds into murky water grew harder. For five days the *Herald* expedition persevered through the Makata. Food was impossible to find and hunting was out of the question. The exhausted, starving porters shifted their burdens from their shoulders onto their heads to keep the precious cloth dry. Simple fevers became of minimal concern as more fatal diseases attacked. 'First the white man Shaw caught the terrible fever of East Africa, then the Arab boy Selim,' Stanley wrote. 'Then the soldiers one by one, and smallpox and dysentery raged among us.' A porter died. The donkeys died in twos and threes. Even Omar the dog got dysentery. He died, too.

Finally it was Stanley's turn to endure dysentery. The illness was brought about by a vicious series of biological factors, and was nearly impossible to avoid in the flooded jungle. Bacteria entered men's bodies through unpurified drinking water and from swamp water infecting open sores. Bacteria lodged in the mucous lining of intestinal walls, and the intestine bled as the bacteria burrowed into it. A bloody, mucus-laden diarrhoea ensued as the body tried to purge the illness. Fever set in, along with nausea and vomiting. The frequent diarrhoea caused dehydration as the men lost fluid. The lack of water made them lethargic. They grew weak because food passed directly through their bodies without providing nutrition. Sometimes dysentery passes in two or three days; sometimes it is fatal.

During the Civil War, languishing in a prisoner-of-war camp outside Chicago, Stanley had watched fellow prisoners from his adopted Confederate cause die from dysentery. He had almost succumbed himself. Now the same thing was happening in Africa. Dysentery plundered his body from the inside, but Stanley did not die. However, in a single week he lost a quarter of his body weight, dropping from a fleshy twelve stone to a skeletal nine – 'a mere frame of bone and skin'.

Stanley had no choice but to press on. He was in the middle of the swamp. But walking through the Makata, trying to maintain the sense of supreme authority even when many of the men were beginning to hate him and were eager to turn back, was exceedingly difficult. Stanley guzzled three entire bottles of a famous bowel medication known as Collis Browne's Chlorodyne, without improvement. He suffered the indignity of alternately vomiting and emptying his bowels on top of the brackish water again and again. The incident in his flannel pyjamas was a trivial embarrassment by comparison.

On 4 May, after five long days, the caravan cleared the Makata. 'The swamp with its considerable horrors having left an indelible impression on our minds, no one was disposed to forget its fatigues or the nausea,' a relieved Stanley wrote. Still sick, he stopped the caravan in the village of Rehenneko to convalesce. Fresh air and a dollop of Dover's powder from his medicine chest fostered a cure for his dysentery.

There, at the foot of the Usagara Mountains, surrounded by bamboo forests and crystal-clear streams, they rested for four days. The entire caravan needed the refreshment, especially the porters: only five donkeys had survived the swamp. Their 150-pound loads would have to be split among the porters.

There was one small reason to celebrate in Rehenneko: the monsoon season had ended. With drier conditions, it was safe to assume that the sequence of sickness and sloth would end as well. This joy was short-lived, however, for in place of the rains came Africa's legendary heat. Two days after the caravan's 'terribly jaded men and animals' began climbing into the granite and red sandstone of the Usagaras, the temperature reached 128 degrees.

EIGHTEEN

PARLIAMENT

5 MAY 1871
London

AS STANLEY LAY IN HIS TENT THE DAY AFTER EMERGING FROM THE FILTH OF the Makata, his body purging its very essence to stave off dysentery, and as Livingstone began his fifth week of waiting for the canoe that would carry him to the Source, British Foreign Secretary Earl Granville rose to address the House of Lords. The ageing earl was dressed immaculately. As he began speaking his voice carried easily through the narrow parliamentary chamber. The peers sat on benches facing one another across the chamber's broad centre aisle. In one end of the rectangular room was the golden throne where Queen Victoria sat while opening Parliament. At the other end a doorway opened onto the long stone corridor connecting the House of Lords with the House of Commons. That door, as Granville prepared his remarks, was closed.

Granville's family had served Britain with distinction for over a hundred years, but he had little foreign policy experience when he became Prime Minister Gladstone's Foreign Secretary upon Lord Clarendon's death in June 1870. At the time, Granville had been concerned that the job might be too much for him. He was reassured when his Permanent Undersecretary, a man with twenty years in foreign service under his belt, swore he had never 'known so great a lull in foreign affairs', and that he was not aware of any important question he should have to deal with.

Three weeks later, Napoleon III, trying to appear strong after diplomatic fiascos in Mexico and Austria, declared war on Germany. German Chancellor Otto von Bismarck called his bluff. In what would become a recurring theme over the next seventy years, Germany invaded France on 2 August 1870. An army of four hundred thousand German troops raced towards Paris. The apathetic French Army numbered half that size and offered minimal resistance. By September, even as the Germans continued their inexorable push towards the French capital, Napoleon III was captured. It was the Parisians who finally fended off the Germans, but only for a time. The City of Lights, so eloquently remade by Haussmann, was besieged for four months. As Livingstone rested, ate and made journal notations in the very centre of Africa, oblivious to the actions of the outside world, the residents of Paris survived on rats and household pets until finally surrendering to German occupation in January 1871. Napoleon III was sent into exile – to Britain, ironically, the same nation that had banished his uncle to one of the earth's most remote corners half a century earlier.

To say the least, Granville's first year on the job had been an ordeal of fire. The delicate task of maintaining the illusion of British power in European affairs while remaining neutral had been his responsibility. But in May 1871, as Granville rose to speak, the world was finally returning to its pre-war lull. Land and monetary details of the French surrender were being brokered in Germany. The Treaty of Frankfurt, which was due to be signed any day, would restore peace to Europe. It also gave Granville a bit of good news to share with his parliamentary colleagues.

Another piece of buoyant news had arrived, unexpectedly, that morning from Zanzibar.

'Your lordships will, I am sure,' Granville began, every syllable carrying easily, thanks to the House of Lords' formidable acoustics, 'be glad to hear that dispatches have been received this day at the British Foreign Office from Dr Kirk, the acting British Consul at Zanzibar, containing information on the safety of Dr Livingstone.'

Granville went on to say that thanks to Kirk's diligence, relief supplies were racing across Africa. Livingstone's 'immediate wants appear to have been met by the Arabs'. The acting British Consul had taken care of the rest.

Salvos of 'Hear, hear' swept the House of Lords. For an instant, France and Germany were set aside. With Baker sweeping down from the north and Kirk controlling matters in Zanzibar, it was clear Britain had the David Livingstone situation under control. If he was alive, it was only a question of who would find him first.

NINETEEN

MUTINY

MAY 1871
The Rubeho Mountains
670 miles from Livingstone

STANLEY'S TOP-SECRET MISSION PRESSED INLAND, HIS AMBITIONS UNKNOWN
to the world, even as dissension among the men continued to escalate.
In the interests of prodding the caravan forward, Stanley was becoming
a minor despot. Though whipped and sexually molested as a child, he
felt no sympathy for the weak. If he was sick the caravan halted. The
days of halting when porters were ill, however, were becoming fewer. If
a member of the caravan other than himself fell ill – whether white man
or black – he left them behind, whipped them, or stopped, then groused
in his journal about the men's malingering. Africa was the first time in
Stanley's life he held absolute power – no one could reject him, no one
could call him a leper. He gloried in his ability to inflict pain, as if looking for excuses to lay his whip across a bare back. In his mind, it was all
part of his quest to better himself. 'Solomon was wise perhaps from
inspiration, perhaps from observation. I was becoming wise by experience, and I was compelled to observe that when mud and wet sapped the
physical energy of the lazily inclined, a dog whip became their backs,
resorting them to a sound, sometimes to an extravagant, activity,'
Stanley wrote proudly.

Porters were whipped for trying to desert, a Hindi cook was banished from camp for pilfering, a soldier was lashed for being too ill to wade the Makata Swamp and caravan tailor Abdul Kader was publicly accused of being the weakest man alive – then lashed. 'The virtue of a good whip was well tested by me on this day,' Stanley bragged. 'And Abdul Kader (and may he carry the tale to all his kith, kin and race), one may make sure, will never accompany a white man again to Africa.'

Stanley had learned his racism during his teenage years in New Orleans, and saw it reinforced when he fought for the Confederacy during the Civil War. He had a habit of modelling his behaviour on male authority figures, and his treatment of the Africans was copied from the infamous arrogance of Generals George Custer and Philip Sheridan during their battles with the Cheyenne Indians in 1867. Custer and Sheridan thought the Indians should be treated like children. Stanley assumed that attitude with Africans. They were tolerated, but it was understood that the indigenous population were second-class citizens, under the authority of white men.

Stanley was not as extreme as Custer or Sheridan. But just like Sheridan, who became more arrogant in his relations with the Indians as he gained power, Stanley displayed an increasing darkness in his character as he penetrated further into Africa. The journalist once content to record the actions of others, the wide-eyed innocent stepping off the *Falcon* in Zanzibar, the excited new leader parading his caravan out of Bagamoyo – all those aspects of Stanley were set aside. In their place was a dogmatic, oppressive ruler. He was willing to do whatever it took to find Livingstone for the New York *Herald*. Even as men died for his cause, Stanley was setting a new standard for adventure journalism. Even veteran war correspondents like *The Times*'s legendary W. H. Russel were almost passive in comparison.

The two men bearing the brunt of Stanley's oppressive behaviour were Bombay and Shaw. Stanley heaped all his frustrations and fears on those two. The famous Bombay – so vital for encouraging the caravan and overseeing the daily routine of cooking, making and breaking camp, and the overall organization of the forward march – could do nothing right in Stanley's eyes. The journalist was aware that Bombay had been awarded a silver medal by the Royal Geographical Society for his epic journeys alongside Burton, Speke and Grant, and thus was exalted by that august British body as a de facto explorer – an honour and designation far beyond Stanley's most outlandish dreams. It was as if by belittling the gritty Bombay, Stanley was raising himself to the status of

Burton and Speke. Being a racist in an era when it was not just condoned but expected, Stanley had no problem treating the fifty-year-old Bombay, almost twenty years his senior, like an ignorant child. 'Working myself into a fury, I enumerated his sins to him,' Stanley wrote after screaming at Bombay one midnight by the fire, in full view of the entire camp. The list of sins included a lost goat, a fondness for staring into the campfire at night and an inability to locate a deserted cook. Stanley demoted Bombay that night, replacing him with Mabruki, a thief with deformed hands whom Bombay despised.

Shaw was more deserving of Stanley's rage. Since Shaw was a white man Stanley preferred to punish him through subtle disdain rather than public humiliation. The sailor was turning out to be a lazy hypochondriac whose talents as a sailmaker were unnecessary and whose fear of Africa led him to repeatedly threaten quitting. Shaw bullied the porters and soldiers, rode a donkey at all times instead of walking and had venereal disease – though it was unclear whether he brought it with him from his travels at sea or picked it up during one of his many dalliances with African village women. As a sign of his authority, the former mutineer preferred to be called Bwana Mdogo, or Little Master. And even though Stanley afforded Shaw luxuries like a tent and an occasional servant, the sailor's fear of Africa was at odds with Stanley's success-at-all-costs mission. Shaw had lost his temper earlier in the journey, calling Stanley a fastidious ingrate and a slave driver. He swore he'd leave Stanley and join the first caravan they met heading east.

Stanley, who maintained the detached air of a ruler with Shaw, reminded him about his salary advance back in Zanzibar – the one he'd drunk away the morning they sailed. Unless Shaw fulfilled the remainder of his contract, Stanley promised to keep the sailor's personal belongings.

Shaw backed down, but he never stopped maintaining Stanley was a madman. It was only a matter of time before the two would clash again and before Farquhar would re-enter the picture. Mutiny is most often a conspiracy of the unhappy rather than a solo act, and as long as Shaw's only peer had been Stanley, his rage had had no outlet. Shaw couldn't speak Swahili or Hindustani, the two primary languages of the porters and soldiers. But when Stanley and Shaw's fifth caravan caught up with Farquhar's third caravan, everything changed.

The third caravan had come to a halt when Farquhar contracted elephantiasis, a form of leprosy caused by microscopic filarial worms invading the body. The parasites blocked his lymphatic system, causing an enlargement and thickening of Farquhar's bodily tissue. Elephantiasis can cause men's testicles to swell to a foot or more in diameter, and legs and arms to grow until they look like overstuffed sausages. Once the swellings began Farquhar was barely able to walk, and his swollen testicles made riding his donkey an exercise in pain management. His body felt drained of strength. Unable to travel onwards, Farquhar had made camp outside the village of Kiora, and remained in his tent for two weeks until Stanley arrived.

When Stanley first met Farquhar on the barque *Polly*, travelling from Bombay to the Seychelles, he had been awed at the way Farquhar had beaten a fellow sailor. His physical strength was daunting. When the journey into Africa began, Farquhar was broad-shouldered and bellicose, still exuding power. His belly and nose showed the years of drinking, but he was squat and strong and very much a presence to be reckoned with.

But as Stanley stopped before Farquhar's tent in Kiora and called out to his second in command, he was shocked at the corpulent mass wandering forwards. Farquhar, like Stanley and Shaw, was bearded. But he was plump in a way no man should be in a land where food was so precious. 'As he heard my voice, Farquhar staggered out of his tent, as changed from my spruce mate who started from Bagamoyo as if he had been expressly fattened,' Stanley wrote in amazement, 'as we do geese and turkeys for Christmas dinner.'

The navigator was undoubtedly sick. But his dirty little secret was that he'd also been living like a king in Kiora, so uncaring about Stanley's crazy desire to see Africa's wildlife that he'd bartered almost all the third caravan's cloth for a daily banquet of goats, eggs and chickens. Farquhar's new girth was all the more obvious because Stanley was a walking cadaver. 'I saw and regarded, not without wonder, the bloated cheeks and neck of my man Farquhar. His legs were also donderous, elephantine,' Stanley wrote. It seemed incongruous that a man could claim to be so weak and sick but have such a massive appetite. Stanley was sure Farquhar was nothing more than a sensate monster, wasting the New York *Herald*'s money.

That night, Stanley had four porters carry an exhausted Farquhar into his tent to account for all the spent cloth. He demanded an accounting for the waste of time, money and manpower. Farquhar, forced to defend himself while spread-eagled on the thin carpet of Stanley's small field tent, couldn't think straight. His answer was circuitous and convoluted. 'What he did do, what he did not do, what he had expended on cloth and beads, what he had not expended,' an exasperated Stanley wrote, 'were so inextricably jumbled up together that I felt myself drifting towards helpless insanity.'

Stanley had no choice but to relieve Farquhar. 'An Arab proprietor,' he noted, 'would have slaughtered him for his extravagance and imbecility.' Ideally, Farquhar would have been left to find his own way home. Instead, the third and fifth caravans were combined and Farquhar was placed on a donkey. With the trail towards Ujiji leading up through a steep mountain, the ride would be a hell all his own for the swollen Farquhar. Each bump, each sway of the donkey that would pitch Farquhar helplessly to the ground, would be his penalty for incompetence.

The Rubeho Mountains became the caravan's newest nemesis. Sir Roderick Murchison once theorized that Africa's centre was a trough ringed by a mountain plain. And though Stanley was a thousand miles east of the depression forming the Congo's swampy centre, the Rubeho proved the truth of the second part of the theory. Running north by north-east, roughly paralleling the Eastern African coast, the Rubeho and its eight-thousand-foot peaks were a prime, though jagged, example of the geographical term known as 'uplift'.

The first third of Stanley's journey was complete. Jungle terrain was now a memory, replaced by 'wilderness of aloetic and cactaceous plants, where the kolquall and several thorn bushes grew paramount'. Even villages would become few and far between as the caravan entered a moonscape of red sandstone. For Shaw and Farquhar, the mountains were a symbolic point of no return – beyond them lay the centre of Africa. Quitting the caravan would be far more difficult. Thoughts of mutiny passed through their heads.

Shaw tested Stanley's authority the first night in the Rubeho. Too ill to walk, he'd been travelling by donkey cart over the mountains. The rugged trail was impossible to surmount in such a bulky vehicle. Stanley sent word back for Shaw to abandon the cart and catch up with the caravan as quickly as possible. When Shaw showed up four hours later one of the porters was carrying the cart on his head, while Shaw followed behind on a donkey. His stooped body, topped with a conical hat like something from China, was a sorry sight. The bare-chested porters, whose only clothing was cloth tied around the waist like a skirt, didn't look half as tired. Many of them were also sick, but had to either keep up or be left behind for the hyenas and lions – the donkey cart wasn't an option. Shaw, Stanley wrote, was 'riding at a gait which seemed to leave it doubtful on my mind whether he or his animal felt most sleepy'.

Stanley angrily ordered the porter carrying the cart to fling it into a gully, then berated Shaw in front of the men. Shaw, Stanley commanded, was to dismount and walk. The donkey was needed for carrying supplies.

Three tense days later, Shaw worked up the courage to confront Stanley. He and Farquhar arrived at breakfast in a dark mood. Stanley's greeting got no reply. He'd noticed the two engaging in heated conversation over the previous few days, and suddenly realized he was their topic. 'Selim,' Stanley said to his servant. 'Bring breakfast.'

Liver, roasted goat, pancakes and coffee appeared. Then, after scorning the food as 'dog's meat', Shaw aired his grievances. Since the death of most of the caravan's donkeys in the Makata Swamp, he and Stanley had been forced to walk. 'It is a downright shame the way you treat us,' Shaw said. 'I thought we were to have donkeys to ride every day and servants to wait on us. Instead of which I have now got to walk every day through the hot sun, until I feel as if I would rather be in hell than in this damned expedition.'

'Do you know,' Stanley replied coolly, 'that you are my servant, sir, and not my companion?'

'Servant be damned.'

Stanley's punch came out of nowhere, reaching across the camp table and knocking Shaw to the ground. He ordered the soldiers to confiscate Shaw's rifle and pistol, strike his tent and throw all his possessions two hundred yards outside the boma.

Shaw could only watch as Bombay and four of the soldiers took down his tent, brought Stanley the weapons and gathered his belongings. 'Now go, sir,' Stanley told the young sailor. 'These men will escort you outside of the camp, and there leave you and your baggage.'

Shaw stayed determined to get the best of Stanley. He followed Bombay and his men outside the camp. When they returned, Stanley noticed that Shaw wasn't with them. But as he and Farquhar resumed their breakfast inside the tent, with Stanley trying to find a delicate way to tell Farquhar it wasn't in the best interests of the New York *Herald* expedition for the afflicted sailor to travel with them any more, Bombay appeared in the doorway. 'Mr Shaw would like to speak to you.'

'I went out to the gate of the camp, and there met Shaw, looking extremely penitent and ashamed,' Stanley wrote. 'He commenced to ask my pardon and began imploring me to take him back, and promising that I should never find fault with him again.'

The two shook hands. 'Don't mention it, my dear fellow,' Stanley replied. 'Quarrels occur in the best of families. Since you apologize, there is an end to it.'

But Shaw wasn't as penitent as he pretended. The rest of the day passed as usual, and all seemed well that night as the camp lay down to sleep. In the morning they would push on to the village of Mpapwa, which made Stanley happy. With the donkeys all dead or dying, Mpapwa would be a perfect spot to hire new porters.

Stanley entered his tent and climbed into his hammock. There was no mosquito netting to keep away insects. He brushed them away and stared at the canvas ceiling of his tent as he drifted off to sleep. Suddenly, a gunshot. A bullet tore through the tent's canvas and whistled past Stanley's head, missing him by inches. He roared from the tent in his bare feet. 'Who fired that gun?' he barked at the porters huddled around the fire. The mountain air was cold at night. They sat very close.

'Bwana Mdogo,' came the answer.

Gripping a pistol in each hand, Stanley stalked to Shaw's tent and threw back the flap. Shaw was breathing hard, as if sound asleep. His gun lay nearby. Stanley picked it up and felt the barrel – it was still hot. 'I would advise you in the future,' he said to Shaw, who was stirring, 'not to fire into my tent. I might get hurt, you know.'

Stanley never mentioned the incident to Shaw again. He was confident the tension would dissipate when the caravan finally reached Mpapwa, a traditional Arab caravan stopover in a forest at the base of green hills, 160 miles from the coast. To a great extent, Stanley was right. The deprivation and fatigue of the trail – which had caused some of the mutinous tension – was alleviated by Mpapwa's abundance of comfort and, more important, food: eggs, milk, mutton, honey, beans. 'Thank God!' Stanley wrote in his journal that night. A plague of earwigs buzzed around inside his tent, making it hard to concentrate. 'After fifty-seven days of living upon matama porridge and tough goat, I have enjoyed with unctuous satisfaction a real breakfast and dinner.' For Shaw, there were the comforts of women to go with the food – an Arab caravan numbering almost one thousand men and slaves was in

Mpapwa, on the way back to Bagamoyo. The women were being offered as prostitutes.

Abdullah bin Nasib, leader of the large caravan Stanley encountered in Mpapwa, claimed to know Livingstone's location. 'Abdullah,' Stanley wrote of the tall, nervous man, 'gave me information on L. He had gone to Maurieria, which was a month's march from Ujiji. He had shot himself in the thigh while out hunting buffalo. As soon as he gets well he would return to Ujiji.'

If Bin Nasib was being truthful, Livingstone was alive and on his way to Ujiji. Mpapwa was turning out to be a very providential town, indeed.

Stanley was mesmerized by the land around Mpapwa, with its verdant slopes thick with forests of sycamore, acacia and mimosa trees, notched here and there by tumbling streams. As caravan life had not offered much chance for solitude or reflection beyond the functional, he took advantage of the opportunity to slip away for a few hours. He hiked up one hill to the summit to enjoy the view of all he had travelled through. 'One sweep of the eyes embraced hundreds of square miles of plain and mountain, from Ugombo Peak to distant Ugogo, and from Rubeho and Ugogo to the dim and purple pasturelands of the wild, untameable Wahumba,' Stanley wrote of the view.

Then his eye turned to the arid land westward, through which the caravan would pass next. 'The plain of Ugombo and its neighbour of Marenga Mkali, apparently level as a sea, was dotted here and there with "hillocks dropt in Nature's careless haste", which appeared like islands amid the dun and green expanse. Where the jungle was dense the colour was green, alternating with dark brown. Where the plain appeared denuded of bush and brake it had a whity-brown appearance, on which the passing clouds now and again cast their deep shadows. Altogether this side of the picture was not inviting. It exhibited too plainly the true wilderness in its sternest aspect. But perhaps the knowledge that in the bosom of the vast plain before me there was not one drop of water but was bitter as nitre, and undrinkable as urine, prejudiced me against it.'

After three serene days, the caravan marched from Mpapwa. It was 21 May. Stanley had hired new porters in Mpapwa to carry the load once given to the donkeys and had resupplied foodstuffs, then pointed the group 'westward, always westward'. The entire caravan was refreshed by the stop.

The only man in the New York *Herald* expedition who had been unable to enjoy the respite of Mpapwa was Farquhar. The elephantiasis was killing him. He couldn't walk, and he was so heavy that two donkeys had died from carrying him. So when it came time to push on, Stanley was through with Farquhar. Leaving him alone in the middle of Africa was an extreme solution but there was no other choice. He explained to Farquhar 'it would be better if I left him behind, in some quiet place, under the care of a good chief who would, for a consideration, look after him until he got well'.

Just in case Farquhar's condition got worse, Stanley copied the name and address of Farquhar's next of kin, a sister living in Edinburgh, inside his journal. An English-speaking porter named Jako was ordered to stay and protect the dying sailor. Stanley gave Jako cloth, tea, a carbine and three hundred rounds of ammunition for protection and currency. Nobody but Shaw, who was losing his only ally, was unhappy about Farquhar's abandonment. The porters loathed the Scot for his rants and cruelty, and mimicked the former sailor so well that even Stanley couldn't help but laugh. Stanley, who despised weakness in himself and so was hypercritical of it in others, rationalized that Farquhar was worthy of the abuse. 'Farquhar had become the laughingstock of the caravan from his utter helplessness to do anything at all for himself,' Stanley wrote. He was glad to be rid of Farquhar and racing on to Ujiji.

Five days later Farquhar fell down and died as he tried to get out of bed. The locals, not knowing how to dispose of the white man, dragged his naked body into the jungle for the hyenas. 'There is one of us gone,' Stanley told Shaw after hearing the news from some Arab traders. 'Who will be the next?'

The taunt would prove eerily prescient. Only one of them would live to see Zanzibar again.

TWENTY

GONDOKORO

26 MAY 1871
Gondokoro, the Upper Nile
730 miles from Livingstone

STANDING ON THE EDGE OF THE NILE, ROWS AND ROWS OF POLISHED soldiers standing to attention on his new parade ground, Sir Samuel White Baker had every reason to be proud. It had taken him nearly a year and a half, but he had successfully travelled almost the entire length of the Nile and established a British presence in Gondokoro. His position was four degrees north of the equator. Ujiji, by coincidence, was four degrees south.

The winds were light and variable, and the temperature was nearly eighty degrees. As local Bari tribesmen looked on from a distance, naked and curious about the squat bearded man speaking so gravely, Baker pronounced to all assembled that the new outpost was now a colony. Its name was Equatoria. He was now poised to solicit any and all information about Livingstone's whereabouts.

There had been times on the long journey upriver when Baker doubted he would ever reach Gondokoro. The Sudd, for instance, nearly broke him. Located five hundred miles south of Khartoum, the swampy section of the Nile was the most confounding stretch of river on earth. Papyrus ferns and the detritus swept downriver from Lake Victoria clogged the Nile's flow in the Sudd, so effectively bringing it to a standstill that the river stagnated. The banks, which were almost impossible to discern from the choked river, were nothing but unstable mud and impenetrable jungle for a hundred miles in either direction. Crocodiles and hippos loitered in the stinking miasma. Snakes moved without a sound through the reeds and trees. The sun hovered glowing and hot, like the tip of a lit cigar. The Sudd was not land, and not river, and Baker's expedition had been stuck for weeks.

A smaller expedition could have found an alternative route, perhaps hacking through the undergrowth alongside the river. Baker, however, was driving an army. Under his command were 1,700 Sudanese and Egyptian soldiers. Forty-eight sharpshooters protected his and Florence's every movement. He had a personal assistant, a doctor, two engineers, a shopkeeper, an interpreter and a shipwright to consult in times of indecision. He also had an entire fleet. It had taken fifty-five sailboats and nine steamers to transport Baker's men the 1,500 miles from Cairo to Khartoum. The largest steamboat was a hundred feet long and weighed over 250 tons.

Baker, his wife, his assistants, his army and his armada lit the boilers in Khartoum, on 8 February 1870. Their intent was to travel through the Sudd, then five hundred miles beyond it to the abandoned Austrian mission station at Gondokoro. There they would claim the land, establish a military presence and explore. Finding Livingstone, as Baker promised Murchison, would be a primary objective.

Baker was no stranger to adversity or exotic conditions. Before becoming an explorer he had spent 1859 to 1860 supervising the construction of a railway between the River Danube and the Black Sea. He had gone to Africa in 1861 to hunt big game. Searching for the Source was just a sideline. Travelling with Florence, a blonde Hungarian dynamo fifteen years his junior who would later become his second wife, Baker had worked his way upriver from Cairo on an earlier Nile expedition. He crossed paths with Speke and Grant in Gondokoro in March 1863. Though disappointed to hear that Speke had hypothetically confirmed Lake Victoria as the Source, Baker and Florence pushed on in the hope of discoveries of their own. On 14 March 1864 the pair discovered a lake just north of Victoria. Appropriately, they named it Albert, for the Queen's late husband.

Queen Victoria, however, was chagrined to learn that Baker and Florence were unmarried. And, worse, that the Hungarian was a

Catholic. Though Florence converted to Anglicism upon their return to England and the Bakers became husband and wife shortly after, the bohemian tone of their trek to Lake Albert was a stark difference from the spiritual glow in which, for the British public, Livingstone's journeys were imbued.

It was Baker, however, who had the most compassion for Livingstone's plight and who had quickly taken up his pen to write to Murchison on 8 March 1867 when reports of Livingstone's murder surfaced. 'I would rather die thus,' he wrote of sudden death by the Mazitu, 'than be slowly poisoned by a doctor; and the hard soil of Africa is a more fitting couch for the last gasp of an African explorer than the down pillow of civilized home. Livingstone's fate seems to have cast a gloom over African travels, and the papers appear to taunt African travellers with running quixotic risks. If England is becoming so cowardly and so soft that travel shall cease in dangerous countries because some fall victim to it, then it is time to roll up the English flag and admit the decline of the English spirit. In all humility,' he concluded, offering his services as an explorer to Murchison once again, 'I am ready.'

Baker's straightforward letter was a showcase of his complexity. In his renaissance-man lifetime, Baker had founded an agricultural community in Ceylon, shot tigers in India, hunted bears in Russia and undertaken his first Nile exploration just for the thrill of seeing somewhere new. Once, when an African king who was holding the Bakers hostage suggested he and the rugged Englishman exchange wives, Baker boldly pressed a revolver into the king's stomach and told him exactly how little he thought of the idea. For good measure, Florence then charged forward and berated the king in Hungarian.

The Sudd, however, was to prove a year-long obstacle in 1870–71. Hundreds of men died in the back-breaking, futile attempt to clear a channel. So when Baker finally got men and material through the quagmire by building an impromptu dam that raised the water level high enough for his ships to float through, he was mightily relieved.

The celebration was saved for Gondokoro. On 26 May 1871, just five days after Stanley marched from Mpapwa, Baker ordered his remaining twelve hundred soldiers to assemble in clean uniforms. The tiny settlement lay on a hill overlooking the Nile. Lake Tanganyika – and, more important, Ujiji – was just a few hundred miles south. The ruined red-brick Austrian mission huts and sheds had been repaired. A fort consisting of three main buildings and a living area of African-style conical-roofed mud and stick huts were built adjacent. A fence surrounded the settlement, starting at the Nile and running inland around the complex. Vegetable gardens were planted. Baker's vessels were docked along the shore, parallel to the bank, except for the biggest steamship, which parked nose first into a small inlet. Baker, showing he hadn't forgotten his roots as an engineer, even concocted a still.

That balmy May evening, the Bakers dined on roast beef, Christmas pudding and rum. The celebration was an acknowledgement that their goals were being accomplished one by one – slowly, but accomplished nonetheless. Baker had the premier British presence in the interior. He was the new tip of the African spear, hoping to build commerce in the interior and stamp out slavery. He was also poised to go in any direction to find Livingstone, and had already begun the habit of interviewing any and all passing travellers for signs of the elusive explorer.

Unknowingly, that night Sir Samuel White Baker and his lovely wife Florence were almost exactly the same distance from Ujiji as Stanley.

III

TEN HUMAN JAWBONES

Sir Samuel White Baker

TWENTY-ONE

TEN HUMAN JAWBONES

24 MAY 1871
Nyangwe

AS LIVINGSTONE ENJOYED THE SPLENDOUR OF LIFE IN NYANGWE, HE developed a favourite pastime: visiting the village market. Thousands upon thousands of Africans came from surrounding villages to take part. Most were women, though he did observe the comings and goings of the local men, all of whom considered themselves to be chiefs. Livingstone, then, enjoyed the marketplace from both an anthropological and a masculine point of view. 'With market women it seems to be a pleasure of life to haggle and joke, and laugh and cheat: many come eagerly and retire with care worn faces; many are beautiful and many old; all carry very heavy loads of dried cassava and earthen pots, which they dispose of very cheaply for palm oil, fish, salt, pepper and relishes for their food.'

Day after day, waiting for the people to trust him enough to rent him a simple canoe, Livingstone observed the comings and goings of the market. Ultimately, in a way he could only foresee if he shrugged off the trusting nature that allowed him to travel through Africa unscathed, his marketplace observations would come between him and the Source.

The 24 May 1871 entry in Livingstone's journal was yet another marketplace observation. He was still too feeble to walk any sustained distance, and the rainy season made travel difficult. He was also still

175

without a canoe. 'The market is a busy scene – everyone is dead earnest – little time is lost in friendly greetings,' Livingstone wrote. 'Each is intensely eager to barter food for relishes, and makes strong assertions as to the goodness or badness of everything. The sweat stands in beads on their faces. Cocks crow briskly even when slung over the heads hanging down. Pigs squeal.'

Though the only white man for hundreds of miles in any direction, the people had finally got used to Livingstone's presence. He had been able to sit undisturbed, or, when the opportunity arose, make the occasional bit of conversation. On 27 May 1871, Livingstone remarked in his journal, 'A stranger in the market had ten human under-jawbones hung by a string over his shoulder. On inquiry he professed to have killed and eaten the owners and showed with his knife how he cut up his victims. When I expressed disgust, he and others laughed.'

Livingstone, however, had little to fear from the cannibals of Manyuema. Their parameters for eating human beings were narrow: opponents conquered in battle, and fellow tribesmen killed by disease. The bodies were not cooked before eating, but soaked in running water for several days until bloated and tender. Male flesh was considered preferable to that of female, so women were consumed only when no other food was available. As a result of their cannibalistic tendencies, and also from a tendency to consume animal carrion, the people of Manyuema had a powerful body odour. The Nyangwe marketplace, as a result, with thousands of Manyuemans crowded together, carried a strong aroma.

Livingstone was not an enemy, nor was he a fellow tribesman, so he would not be set upon and made a meal of. The cannibals, then, posed no threat to his being. As a result, he passed his days in the bustling village, waiting for the chance to rent a canoe and continue his journey downriver. It was an idyllic time, marked by prolonged periods of marketplace observation and journal entries about the beautiful women of Nyangwe. Livingstone assumed that neither he, nor the people of Nyangwe, were in any danger.

He was wrong.

TWENTY-TWO

REBIRTH

31 MAY 1871
The Marenga Mkali
600 miles from Livingstone

IN EAST AFRICA, ALONG THE TRADE ROUTE BETWEEN BAGAMOYO AND UJIJI, the portal between the coastal lowlands and the high-altitude grasslands of inner Africa – in essence, the entrance to Africa's beating heart – was a barren strip of hell known as the Marenga Mkali. Thirty miles wide, defined by heat, dust and an utter lack of water, it advertised to one and all that journeying into Africa was not going to get any easier. Temperatures reached 120 degrees at midday. White ants, red ants and scorpions made each night's camp a festival of irritation. The smallest insects worked their way into food, bedrolls, clothing and ears. A scalding wind blew across the land, too, forcing sand into eyes and noses. 'Not one drop of water,' Stanley wrote, 'was to be found.'

Stanley began his journey across the Marenga Mkali on the last day of May. For safety, he combined his expedition with six Arab slave and ivory caravans travelling in the same direction. His once mighty caravan had been diminished by a third through desertions and death and he needed the extra company as he travelled through hostile territory. Also, the Arabs were experienced traders who would know the fastest routes. Through them Stanley learned that extreme heat and lack of water meant the three-hundred-man contingent must cross the Marenga Mkali in a single march. Moving mostly at night, they would compress three days into seventeen hours of brisk travel.

Early in the crossing, malaria attacked. Stanley's former presumptions of immunity to Africa's illness were mocked as the alien presence in his body made itself known again. One minute he was riding his donkey across the plain, wishing the distant herds of wildlife were close enough to shoot, the next he was as somnolent as a lion after a night of hunting. His body temperature spiked. Pain coursed through his gut. 'A dangerous fever attacked me which seemed to eat into my very vitals. The wonders of Africa that bodied themselves forth in the shape of flocks of zebras, giraffes, elands or antelopes galloping over the jungleless plain, had no charm for me. Nor could they serve to draw my attention from the severe fit of sickness which possessed me,' he wrote. 'I lay in a lethargic state, unconscious of all things.'

Too weak to ride his donkey, Stanley's boots and spurs were removed. He was placed in a litter and carried by Bombay's soldiers. The Arabs graciously sent doctors to tend to their fellow traveller. The scene mirrored Livingstone's travails.

In that barren expanse, borne on strong arms into inner Africa, Henry Morton Stanley was as helpless as a child. It was oddly appropriate, for Stanley was undergoing a rebirth in Africa. In an environment where the only truth was survival, the crutch of lies supporting his life had no place. Instead, accomplishments, training, setbacks, neuroses, hopes and dreams were all coiling together like a mighty rope – a lifeline to cling to throughout his journey.

Stanley had carried a portfolio of lies through his adult life, drawing upon it to create himself in the image he desired. The greatest lie of all was his name. The second was his nationality. Though only a select group of people knew either truth, as his journey pressed forward, and through Bennett's publication of his stories, it would all be revealed.

His real name was John Rowlands. He was Welsh, born in the village of Denbigh, just south-west of the international port of Liverpool. His nineteen-year-old mother was Betsy Parry, the local whore. His father, after whom he was named, was the town drunk. 'John Rowlands', read the entry for Saint Hilary's Church on 28 January 1841, 'bastard'. No middle name was given.

Betsy immediately pawned the child off on her father. When young John Rowlands was five, kindly old Moses Parry fell over dead while working in the fields and Rowlands was sent to board with an older couple, the Prices. But taking care of a five-year-old was beyond their ken. In a scene straight out of Dickens, their son, Dick, came to get Rowlands one day, telling him they were going to see an aunt in a neighbouring village.

Instead, he was being abandoned. 'At last Dick set me down from his shoulders before an immense stone building and, passing through tall iron gates,' Stanley wrote later, 'a sombre-faced stranger appeared at the door who, despite my remonstrances, seized me by the hand and drew me within, while Dick tried to soothe my fears with glib promises that he was only going to bring my Aunt Mary to me. The door closed on him, and with the echoing sound, I experienced the awful feeling of utter desolateness.'

The St Asaph Union Workhouse was home to forty boys and thirty girls, lorded over by a psychotic former miner named James Francis who had no left hand. Stanley later said that for 'the young it is a house of torture'. The children slept two to a bed, with adolescents paired with the youngest children. 'From the very start,' said an 1847 Board of Education investigation into life at St Asaph's, the children 'were beginning to practise and understand things they should not.' To the despair and confusion the child felt over his unexplained abandonment was soon added the powerlessness of being fondled and violated by teenaged boys as he tried to sleep. A lifetime of sexual ambivalence – a deep longing for women combined with a proclivity for dubious friendships with adolescent boys – sprang from those years.

If Rowlands had any doubts that he was effectively an orphan, the appearance of Betsy Parry at the workhouse when he was twelve put them to rest. She was tall, with an oval face and long dark hair which she'd piled on her head in a bun. The occasion for the visit was to consign two of her other illegitimate children to the workhouse, too.

When told that the woman was his mother, Stanley shyly gazed upon her. Parry glared back, as if checking the boy for defects. 'I had expected to feel a gush of tenderness towards her, but her expression was so chilling that the valves of my heart closed, as with a snap,' he wrote of the day.

By the time Rowlands was released from St Asaph's at fifteen, he had been given a rudimentary education in reading, writing and arithmetic, and had a reputation as being Francis's pet. Young Rowlands was chubby and short and emotionally needy, and had no friends in the outside world. Attempts to communicate with his mother's family were mostly rebuffed. The one time he was successful, an aunt in Liverpool invited him to stay the night. The next morning, after Rowlands left to look for work, she sold his only suit.

Reading became the teenager's escape. 'I became infected with a passion for books. And for eighteen hours out of the twenty-four I was wholly engrossed with them.'

Rowlands found short-term jobs in a haberdasher's and as a butcher-shop delivery boy. But his past hadn't prepared him for a life beyond menial labour. He seemed fated to continue scrabbling hand-to-mouth for whatever table scraps the British Empire saw fit to toss to lower-class men like him. If the averages applied to him, there was a good chance he would be dead by thirty.

But one day, while making a delivery for the butcher shop, seventeen-year-old Rowlands found himself at Liverpool docks. They were a teeming, exotic place. Hundreds of ships' masts poked above the horizon. Boys his age clambered up the ratlines into the rigging. The sailors wore their hair in pigtails, and walked with a splay-footed waddle necessary for keeping balance on decks. Accents, aromas and attitudes from around the world shot through the seaside air and through the doorways of crowded waterfront pubs. For a boy who learned of the world from books but had never ever been to London, the salt and tar of Liverpool's docks stimulated his imagination like a drug.

One ship in port was the American merchantman *Windermere*. Its regular route was delivering cotton from New Orleans to Liverpool, then returning home with finished goods from British textile plants. The captain, a man by the name of David Hardinge, had an ingenious way of decreasing his overheads: young men were hired as hands for the Atlantic passage, with the promise that they would work as cabin boys for five dollars per month. Though he was charming and paternal during the recruitment phase, Hardinge was lying. The boys wouldn't work in his cabin, but below decks and up in the freezing, bucking rigging. The newcomers would work beyond exhaustion, and be subject to sadistic thrashings by the ship's master and mates. Once *Windermere* arrived in port the plan would reach its completion. The young hands would be so eager to flee the floating gulag that they would jump ship without collecting their pay.

Hardinge cast his eye on the butcher's delivery boy and offered him work as his personal cabin attendant. 'But I know nothing of the sea, sir,' Rowlands replied.

'Sho! You will soon learn all that you have to do, and in time you may become captain of a fine ship,' Hardinge promised.

Eager for adventure and not knowing that he was about to endure seven weeks of seasickness, severe cold, brutality and molestation, Rowlands signed on. He quit his job at the butcher's after just two weeks of employment, and, just seventeen, sailed three days later for New Orleans.

The position as cabin boy was forgotten before the *Windermere* had sailed down the Irish Sea into the North Atlantic. Rowlands was cast into the dank, mildewed hold with the rest of the crew. That area below decks, scarcely larger than the living room in a large home, was where all his off-duty time was spent. As he would in Africa, Rowlands slept in a hammock. He had been unfortunate enough to join *Windermere* in December, a time when high seas and constant storms caused the closing of the hold's portals. Fresh air was minimal. The men rarely bathed, and many spent their off-duty hours drinking rum, so the crew's quarters smelled like one of Liverpool's oceanfront taverns – dirty clothing, sweaty bodies, alcohol fumes. Rowlands contributed to the smell by getting violently seasick. He spent the first three days of the trip vomiting.

On deck the air was fresh and crisp, but being on deck meant being put to work. The labour was bone-chilling and sometimes deadly. The tar-covered ratlines had to be climbed every time shifting winds or weather conditions demanded a sail change. The smallest boys, like Rowlands, were forced to climb highest into the swaying rigging, then clamber out along the horizontal yards to furl or unfurl the topsails. A slip meant a long fall to the deck, or into the ocean.

Weather conditions gradually improved as *Windermere* moved south, and by the time she sailed around the tip of Florida into the Gulf of Mexico, the air was balmy and the swells gentle and rolling. But Rowlands wanted out. New Orleans was a city of promise, where the air smelled of 'coffee, pitch, Stockholm tar, brine of mess-beef, rum and whisky drippings'. The Mississippi was the first truly massive river Rowlands had ever seen, disappearing into the American hinterlands like a promise waiting to be kept. Everything about New Orleans was surreal in its novelty. When, on his first night in town, Rowlands wandered into a brothel and was shown four girls in lingerie, he fled back to the ship in panic.

Five days later, unknowingly playing into Hardinge's plans, Rowlands answered New Orleans' siren song. He fled the ship without collecting his pay. It was February 1859. He had just turned eighteen. In Africa, Dr David Livingstone was enduring his second Zambezi expedition.

John Rowlands met Henry Hope Stanley during his first week in New Orleans. The British cotton merchant with the flowing beard was reclining in the morning sun outside his warehouse on Tchapitoulas Street, reading a newspaper. It was 7 a.m. Rowlands walked by, in search of work. 'Would you like a boy, sir?' he asked. The young man's earnest demeanour impressed Stanley, who gave him a series of small tasks. One led to another, until Rowlands became a clerk. And while the relationship was merely that of a boss to a worker for Stanley, the middle-aged gentleman represented a surrogate father for Rowlands. He adored the older man so much that in 1859 he impulsively took the older man's name. John Rowlands was no more. He would spend the rest of his life as Henry Stanley. 'Morton' was added years later, after other middle names were tried and found wanting.

The young Stanley began coming around to his employer's house on Annunciation Square, unaware that men of Stanley's class didn't fraternize with their employees. At first, Henry Hope Stanley enjoyed his young employee's company, and was flattered that his young charge had taken his name. But the older Stanley's young wife, Frances, came between them. They had married when she was just fifteen. She was all of twenty-eight in 1859, which made her only ten years older than Stanley. Frances Stanley found the young man annoying, and mistook his flattery for flirtation. However, with one of his adopted daughters dying young and the other eloping, Henry Hope Stanley filled their absence by treating young Stanley as a son. Both men enjoyed reading, and books were a constant in their relationship. Henry Hope Stanley's greatest gift to his young surrogate son, however, was an American attitude towards success. 'I don't know what customs of the Welsh people may be, but here we regard personal character and worth, not pedigree. With us, people are advanced not for what their parentage may have been, but for what they are themselves.'

The words would function as a parting benediction, for the two men quarrelled in 1860. The younger Stanley was banished up the Mississippi. Just in case he was interested in coming back to New Orleans and pestering him further, the elder Stanley told his overeager employee that he and his wife were moving to Havana to escape the coming Civil War.

Stanley was living in Cypress Bend, Arkansas when the war began, working as a dry goods salesman at a general store on the Arkansas River. Cypress Bend was a swampy backwater, and a breeding ground for mosquitoes. Stanley was soon stricken by his first dose of ague, known in those parts as swamp fever. He endured the chills, headaches and fever, even as his body weight dropped below seven stone and he was forced to ingest bitter doses of quinine grains. His only friend was a hard-drinking Irishman named Cronin who was fond of having sex with slave women. When Cronin was found out, and was forced to move on, Stanley found himself alone again. He had come from New Orleans, and thought the people of Cypress Bend were petty, racist and simple. They felt the same about him.

Stanley felt alone and out of place, but he was in no hurry to find new fellowship by joining the crush of local men enlisting to fight for the Confederacy. There was also a more pressing reason for him to stay in Cypress Bend. Stanley was in love. It was a new experience for him. Until then, he had shied away from women, felt awkward in their company. But a local girl named Margaret Goree had caught his eye, and with the men of Cypress Bend rushing off to war, he was on the verge of having her all to himself. Since Margaret seemed interested in him, too, the decision seemed wise.

One day he received a plain package from his newly beloved. In it was a chemise and petticoat. Margaret Goree, in symbolic terms, was calling Stanley a coward. Desperate to prove his manhood, he enlisted shortly thereafter. Stanley never saw Margaret Goree again. By April of 1862, after nine months of training with the local regiment, Stanley was on the front lines in one of the bloodiest engagements in American military history, the Battle of Shiloh. Ten thousand men died on both sides in less than twenty-four hours of fighting.

The battle was held near Savannah, Tennessee, but took its name from a nearby church – 'Shiloh' means 'peaceful place' in Hebrew. The battle Stanley entered that Sunday morning was anything but. Forty thousand Confederate troops surprised forty-five thousand Union troops just before dawn on 6 April 1862. Stanley and the Confederates marauded through the Union's front lines during breakfast, bayonets drawn. 'How the cannon bellowed and their shells plunged and bounded, and flew with screeching hisses over us,' he wrote. 'One man raised his arm as if to yawn and jostled me. I turned to him and saw that a bullet had gored his whole face and penetrated into his chest. Another ball struck a man a deadly rap on the head, and he turned on his back and showed his ghastly white face to the sky.'

Even with men dying around him, Henry Stanley marched forward untouched. He strode at the front of the Dixie lines as they pushed into the thick of the Union Army, proving to one and all that Margaret Goree's intimation of cowardice was dead wrong.

Then a shell fragment tore into Stanley's belt buckle, knocking the wind out of him. He fell to the ground as the Confederate line surged forward. He was tempted to lie still, then noticed that the only men not moving were already dead. Unless he wanted to join them he had to rise up and press the attack.

As night fell the Confederates pulled back to rest and regroup. Stanley had completed his first day of warfare unscratched. Far from being thrilling, war repelled him. 'It was the first field of glory I had seen in my May of life, and the first time that glory sickened me with its repulsive aspect, and made me suspect it was all a glittering lie.'

The next morning, Union General Ulysses S. Grant counterattacked moments before sunrise. The Union's surprise was as overwhelming at the Confederacy's the day before. This time Stanley was not so lucky. As the attack switched from a bayonet charge to close-quarters fighting, he dashed for cover. To his surprise, he dashed in the wrong direction and found himself the only grey uniform in a sea of Union blue. 'Two men,' he wrote, 'sprang at my collar and marched me unresisting into the ranks of terrible Yankees. I was a prisoner.'

He was sent to Camp Douglas, a prison camp just outside Chicago. Fleas, ticks and lice swarmed through the hovels in which men were forced to sleep. The open sewers bred dysentery and cholera. Rations were minimal. Starvation was rampant. When Union officials offered Stanley freedom in exchange for renouncing the Southern cause, he refused. Six weeks later, after watching thousands die and comprehending that Camp Douglas was a death sentence, Stanley changed his mind. In June of 1862, just two months after Shiloh, he became a member of the Illinois Light Artillery. He was shipped to Virginia to fight for the United States of America.

If it was odd that a man could skip sides so easily, the events that followed for Henry Stanley were more incredible. Within three days of being sent to Virginia he was felled by dysentery, sent to a military hospital for four days, then discharged from the service for being too weak to perform his duties. Without a dime in his pockets, owning nothing but the clothes on his back, the former POW was cast out to wander the back roads of West Virginia. 'The seeds of the disease were still in me. I could not walk three hundred yards without stopping to gasp for breath,' he wrote.

Stanley collapsed along a country lane. He would have died if a family hadn't taken him in. Over the next two months the Bakers nourished Stanley back to health, gave him clean clothes and purchased a train ticket to Baltimore so he could start all over again in the big city. By New Year 1863, Stanley was in New York for the first time in his life. After more than a year working at odd jobs, Stanley decided it was time to try his hand at the Civil War again. On 19 July 1864 he enlisted in the Union Navy for a three-year hitch. Stanley was made a Ship's Writer, a petty officer position responsible for keeping the ship's log. He served aboard the USS *Minnesota* as it bombarded Fort Fisher, North Carolina, in the winter of 1864 and 1865. On a whim, he wrote a story about the experience and sent it to a number of newspapers and magazines. Some bought and ran it, marking the beginning of Stanley's journalism career.

One story in particular that fascinated Stanley was that of David Livingstone. He told friends that his ambition was to go to Africa one day and make his fortune. Neither Livingstone nor the call to Africa, however, led him to desert from the navy in February 1865. Just boredom. When the *Minnesota* docked in Portsmouth, New Hampshire, the restless ship's writer jumped ship with a teenage shipmate named Lewis Noe. They soon parted ways, and Stanley fled to the American West. He wangled a job as a stringer for the Missouri *Democrat*, then began the year of travelling that culminated with his arrival in Central City in January 1866. Five months later he quit his job at the *Miner's Daily Register* and took the stagecoach to Denver with Cook on 6 May of that year.

It was on arriving back in America after the ill-fated journey to Turkey that Stanley devoted himself to journalism. He thought it a gallant, romantic profession. 'The more daunting the assignment, the better,' he later wrote of journalism. 'The gladiator meets the sword that is sharpened for his bosom. The flying journalist or roving correspondent meets the command that may send him to his doom.'

Journalism was also the first thing in his life that Stanley had ever been good at. He had failed so completely, so many times, in so many arenas, that he had taken to embellishing his accomplishments. But with journalism he shone, and he drove himself harder to make a name for himself.

When Bennett finally summoned him to Paris in October 1869, there was no doubt Henry Morton Stanley was the ideal man to find David Livingstone. His whole life had pointed to that moment. His re-inventions – name, country, career – gave him the flexibility to adapt and persevere. Travel across Abyssinia taught him the inner politics of travel with a large party, and to be comfortable sleeping outdoors. From the army he learned the power of a gun, marching, the need for organiza-tion. And reaching back into childhood, Stanley knew that failure was not a temporary setback, but a calamitous turn of events. He didn't want to fail again.

Never having known his own father, Stanley had attached himself to a number of older men through his life. At St Asaph's he was the pet of the one-handed headmaster, James Francis. He had fallen prey to Hardinge, the captain of *Windermere*. He pined for Henry Hope Stanley and their brief father–son flirtation. He idolized Hancock, Sheridan and the other US generals during the Plains War so much that he memorized one of Sherman's speeches to the Indians verbatim. And his entire journey in search of Livingstone had been salvaged through the largesse of American Consul Francis Webb – nearly ten years Stanley's senior.

To find Livingstone – whose worldwide reputation was that of a man kindly and paternal – would be to find the ultimate father figure: older, wise, brave, accomplished, even beloved by an entire nation. The poss-ibility of acceptance was counterbalanced by the realization that rejection would have a crushing finality. The rebirth engendered by Africa's austerity and trial was weeding out the insecurity that had governed Stanley since birth.

No longer was he scared of Africa. In fact, with every obstacle over-come, Stanley – the man who'd never had a home – was beginning to feel as if he belonged there, just like Livingstone. 'My black followers might have discerned, had they been capable of reflection,' Stanley wrote, 'that Africa was changing me.'

And even as he suffered through the Marenga Mkali, unconscious and carried, Stanley was growing stronger. His fever broke during the night. At 3 a.m. he asked to be booted and spurred so he could ride the last miles. Soon darkness gave way to light. By dawn the waterless passage was done. So complete was Stanley's relief to have survived the crossing that in his writings he compared himself with Moses. What the rest of the massive caravan saw was the region of Ugogo, with its baobab trees and green hills. But Stanley, whose pre-journey perceptions about Africa produced nightmares, saw 'this Promised Land'.

Stanley bore little similarity to Moses. However, his actions and predicament bore a great similarity to the heroine of a children's book which had just been published in England. Her name was Alice, and she stepped through a looking-glass into a surreal, fantastic wonderland. Everything in that world was off kilter. Stanley, whose malaria reasserted itself as he finished crossing the Marenga Mkali, had just stepped through a looking-glass of his very own. He was about to enter the surreal world of Ugogo.

TWENTY-THREE

INTO THE FIRE

1 JUNE 1871
Ugogo
500 miles from Livingstone

OUT OF THE FRYING PAN INTO THE FIRE. STANLEY HAD HEARD HORROR stories about Ugogo from the moment he began purchasing supplies back in Zanzibar, but nothing had truly prepared him for the first day of June 1871, as the New York *Herald* expedition entered the most bizarre section of its journey. On a map – if Stanley had been carrying one – there was nothing auspicious about Ugogo. It was a hundred-mile-wide interlude between the vast emptiness of the Marenga Mkali and the abundance of Tabora.

The inhabitants of Ugogo were the Wagogo, a group of tribes infamous for rudeness and extortion. The Wagogo were greatly feared by the Arabs, and caravans approached Ugogo with trepidation. Supplies and water were limited in the region and the Wagogo extracted a series of tolls – known as tribute – for permission to pass through and use their resources. Those refusing to pay were ambushed and murdered. It was a queer place, where the weak were strong, a man had to watch his back at all times, and an item that cost one doti in one village cost ten times as much in the next village over.

One well-known story among Arab caravans was the brave trader who made it his mission to subdue the Wagogo once and for all. His plan was to fight his way through Ugogo without paying tribute. He set off from Tabora with a caravan nine hundred strong, making no secret of his intentions.

The Wagogo never even attempted to fight. Instead, they buried their wells, burned their houses and crops, then retreated to the jungle until the Arabs arrived. The enormous caravan was able to pass through the region for free, with no opposition, but there was also no food or water. Seven hundred of the Arabs died. The remainder slinked back to Tabora or tried to push across to Mpapwa. Only ten of the nine hundred original men survived that passage.

Not only were the Wagogo savvy, but they possessed an eccentric quality that was easily visible to the human eye. Their villages were the usual collection of mud and wattle homes with a single low doorway and a conical roof of sticks and straw. They ate the same diet of corn and cassava found in other tribes. They raised cattle and goats, just like other tribes. However, unlike any tribe Stanley had seen, the Wagogo were fond of decorating their bodies. Most noticeably, they pierced their ears, then enlarged the lobes by forcing strips of wood or wire into the opening. Once the ear stretched all the way down to the shoulder it became the Wagogo equivalent of a pocket: gourds carrying personal belongings or snuff were placed inside. A Wagogo could walk from village to village wearing almost nothing as per custom but with massive gourds or ornaments in their ears. If the lobe ever tore, another hole was opened and the process was begun all over again.

The Wagogo also had a fondness for their hair. Some twisted it into spikes, some adorned their heads with brightly polished shanks of copper, some shaved the very top of their heads and let the sides grow long enough to be shaped into a tail. The Wagogo enhanced their singular appearance by smearing their bodies with red clay, and, for an olfactory element, they also lubricated their skin with animal fats and oils.

The peculiarity of the tribe's physical image and rank aroma was counterbalanced by the heft of their armament. The Wagogo were fiends for weapons. They favoured double-edged knives, long spears, bows and arrows, curved Arab-style knives, and a war club known as a knobstick. Their shields were made of buffalo hide, scraped smooth of hair, the taut surfaces painted in bright yellows, reds and whites.

Although Stanley entered Ugogo battling a severe attack of malaria, the region would have been surreal even without his malarial dementia.

Fortunately for Stanley, the anopheles mosquito which had infected him as he marched into his Promised Land of Ugogo had not transferred the most deadly strain of the disease. A mosquito bite in Africa was like Russian Roulette. There are three thousand different types of mosquito, yet only one carries malaria. There are 156 strains of malaria injected by that one breed of mosquito, yet only four cause malaria in humans. Of those four strains, only one leads to death. And while these odds sound favourable, malaria has hovered near epidemic levels in Africa for millennia.

Stanley's case, though not fatal, was debilitating nonetheless. Even his habit of dosing himself with large amounts of quinine did nothing to control it. His misery was obvious. 'The first evil results experienced from the presence of malaria are confined bowels and an oppressive languor, excessive drowsiness and a constant disposition to yawn,' he wrote of his experiences with the disease. 'The tongue assumes a yellowish sickly hue, coloured almost to blackness. Even the teeth become yellow, and are coated with an offensive matter. The eyes of the patient sparkle lustrously and are suffused with water. These are sure symptoms of the incipient fever which shortly will rage through the system, laying the sufferer prostrate and quivering with agony.'

Unfortunately, the sickness came at a time when Stanley needed his wits about him more than ever. The sheikhs in charge of the Arab caravans, emboldened by the presence of Stanley's firepower in their midst, believed they could proceed rapidly through dreaded Ugogo and predicted a doubling of pace. But they were wrong. Ugogo was a hostile, unpredictable land, and not even Stanley's guns could guarantee a smooth passage.

In Ugogo, the Wagogo tribal chiefs, known by one and all as sultans, did as they pleased. The tributes they demanded were nebulous, and payable on the whim of each sultan. In some cases, even those who paid were then ambushed. 'The Wagogo are the Irish of America,' Stanley observed. 'Clannish and full of fight. To the Wagogo all caravans must pay tribute, the refusal of which is met by an immediate declaration of hostilities.'

As difficult as it was for outsiders to accept, the Wagogo controlled trade in East Africa. Stanley was armed with the document Sultan Barghash had bestowed upon him back in Zanzibar, guaranteeing unhindered passage to Ujiji across the land he believed he ruled (between Zanzibar and Lake Tanganyika). In Ugogo, however, this scrap of paper was meaningless. The facade Webb and Kirk were battling to uphold, that America and Britain controlled African trade, was a myth here.

On 1 June Stanley and the Arab caravans encountered their first Wagogo. It was just after eight in the morning. The hot morning sun was drying the dew on the tall matama stalks as the caravans passed scores of titanic boulders lining the approach to Mvumi, the first village of Ugogo. Initially, all went well. But the villagers had already heard about the approaching white man, and soon hundreds clogged the red dirt path. Dazzled by Stanley's strange hair and clothing, and the varying milky and mahogany hues of his unevenly tanned skin, they pressed forward to touch him. The Wagogo fought one another, yelled at one another, jumped up and down for a better view. At first Stanley found the moment triumphant, but soon he was scared by its intensity.

The Wagogo weren't being respectful of his white skin, as Stanley initially supposed. They were laughing at him. To the Wagogo, everything about Stanley was odd: he was haggard, drawn and testy. He was obviously irritated by so many people pushing up against him. He was feeble from illness, with his beard extending in long brown tufts from his cheeks. Stanley's safari outfit was of bright white flannel, a colour which reflected some of the sun's heat, but which could also be seen from miles away against the brick-red soil. Even his rifle and sidearm, which Stanley assumed gave him an aura of power, weren't so impressive. He felt like a monkey in the Central Park zoo, he wrote, 'whose funny antics elicit such bursts of laughter from young New Yorkers'.

No sooner had he passed through town than the fever attacked again. Stanley spent the rest of the day burning and shivering, battling delusions, dosing himself with quinine.

As if part of some continuing malarial nightmare, the next day the Great Sultan of Mvumi refused to accept the paltry six doti Stanley offered as tribute. Instead, came word to Stanley's camp, the Sultan required sixty doti in exchange for passage. Stanley was furious. He felt humiliated. He confided to the Arabs that he was tempted to fight his way through Ugogo. Instead of paying tribute, Bombay and his soldiers would blaze a trail all the way to Tabora with guns and bullets.

The Arab answer was wise and paternal. 'If you preferred war,' they calmly counselled, 'your pagazis would all desert, and leave you and your cloth to the small mercy of the Wagogo.' Put that way, Stanley, a man who was infuriated any time someone got the best of him, couldn't help but agree. He swallowed his pride and paid the tribute.

The impotence felt by Stanley continued with the Sultan of Matamburu, a few days later. Not only did he allow his people to emit 'peals of laughter' at Stanley's appearance, but the Sultan also professed an abiding friendship with the Arab caravans. They weren't forced to pay any tribute at all. Stanley, on the other hand, had to pay four doti. Learning his lesson, Stanley bit his tongue, knowing that an altercation with the Wagogo could be fatal. 'The traveller has to exercise great prudence, discretion and judgement,' Stanley wrote. 'The strength and power of the Wagogo are derived from their numbers.'

The next day the caravan pushed through a thick wood of gum trees and thorns, then lumbered across a barren, burning plain. There was no water. Elephant footprints were everywhere. The hills were steep and the sun 'waxed hotter and hotter as it drew near the meridian, until it seemed to scorch all vitality from inanimate nature, while the view was one white blaze, unbearable to the pained sight'.

In the middle of that burning plain, there was another demand for tribute. The Sultan of Bihawana, whose subjects were infamous for being thieves and murderers, surprised Stanley by asking for only three doti. However, Stanley was alarmed to learn that his fourth caravan, travelling ahead of Stanley by a few days, had engaged in a gun battle with would-be hijackers. Two of the assailants had been killed as they were being driven off.

A few days later, as Stanley was battling malaria yet again, it was the Sultan of Kididimo's turn to demand tribute. His was a foul kingdom, by all accounts. The water tasted of 'warm horse urine', the locals complained of recurring stomach upset, and two more of the New York *Herald* expedition's donkeys died. Yet the Sultan, whose ego was inflated by the presence of a white visitor, still demanded ten doti to pass. Stanley was too sick to care. 'I was not in a humour – being feeble, and almost nerveless,' he wrote of the malaria's effects, 'to dispute the sum. Consequently it was paid without many words.'

The summation of Stanley's surreal malarial journey through Ugogo came in the village of Nyambwa, where yet another crowd ogled the white men. 'Well, I declare,' Shaw sneered as they marched through the village, with its square huts and tobacco drying on thatched roofs. He and Stanley had maintained a truce since Farquhar was left behind. Being the only two white men for hundreds of miles in any direction allowed them the slightest sense of fraternity. 'They must be genuine Ugogians, for they stare and stare,' Shaw said. 'My God, there is no end to their staring. In fact, I'm almost tempted to slap them in the face.'

Just then, a local warrior tested Stanley. He drew near and taunted the journalist. On another day, perhaps when malaria and dehydration were not making his life a series of miseries and delusions, Stanley might have ignored the young man. But the humiliation of paying tribute finally got the best of his temper. Stanley was in no mood to be trifled with, so he snatched at the man, grabbing him by the neck and holding tight. The crowd looked on in disbelief, then pressed in closer to intimidate the explorer. Stanley, much to their surprise, didn't let go. Instead he reached for his dog whip. Stanley thrashed the man severely then cast him to the ground.

The crowd pressed in against Stanley and Shaw, making a threatening guttural noise that sounded like a man preparing to spit. Earlier in the trip Stanley might have cowed or even shown fear. But he was too sick and exhausted and fed up to care. He brandished his whip like a weapon, threatening all who came too close. 'A little manliness and show of power was something the Wagogo long needed, and in this instance it relieved me of annoyance,' Stanley wrote of using the whip. 'When they pressed on me, barely allowing me to proceed, a few vigorous and rapid slashes right and left with my serviceable thong soon cleared the track.'

The next night, as they camped in a grove of palm trees adjacent, Stanley was even able to convince his fellow travellers to take a day's rest so he could dose himself with quinine. He was reluctant to stop when Shaw or the pagazis were the ones suffering from illness, but ignored that policy when he was sick. 'Sometimes,' he theorized about malaria, 'fever is preceded by a violent shaking fit, during which period blankets may be heaped on the patient's form.' The blankets didn't always work, Stanley went on to write, and he would be forced to lie there in agony while his head throbbed as if someone was beating on his skull from the inside with a hammer. His spine and genitals would ache, and even his shoulder blades would become a source of pain.

Since Stanley had little other hope for recovery, he took some medicine and went to bed. Starting just before dawn, when the caravan should have been assembling for the march, Stanley began ingesting the bitter quinine crystals, extracted from cinchona bark. The doses continued for the next seven hours, when his fever began to break. Huddled under a layer of blankets as the temperature outside peaked well over one hundred degrees, the flap to his tent closed, Stanley sweated with a torrential intensity, soaking his clothing and bedding. Hallucinations set in, an assortment of odd shapes and sensations floating about the room. 'Before the darkened vision of the suffering man, floating in a seething atmosphere, figures of created and uncreated reptiles, which are metamorphosed into every shape and design, growing every moment more confused, more complicated, more hideous and terrible,' he wrote later. 'Unable to bear the distracting scene, he makes an effort and opens his eyes, and dissolves the delirious dream, only, however, to glide again unconsciously into another dreamland where another inferno is dioramically revealed, and new agonies suffered.'

By noon, sleep and medicine were doing the trick. The malaria that had manifested itself in his body for fourteen days, with its delusions and chills and fevers, was finally leaving. He clumsily extricated himself from his hammock and groped around the darkened tent, trying to get his bearings. Suddenly, the tent flap whooshed open. A painfully bright shaft of light jabbed Stanley in the eyes. When Stanley looked over, there stood the Sultan of Mizanza, having come to collect his tribute in person. The Sultan stepped inside the tent as if he owned it himself, and dropped the cloth covering his loins. He wore nothing underneath. Tall, aged, regal, the Sultan had once been powerfully built.

Stanley stood mute. He gazed at 'the sad and towering wreck of what must have been a towering form', but didn't signal acceptance. So with a bemused giggle, the Sultan pulled his cloth on again. He stayed a while longer as if nothing had happened, inspecting the inside of Stanley's tent – the portmanteau where Stanley kept his clothes and the nightstand with its books were particular fascinations – firing his Winchester, and wondering aloud about the extent of Stanley's wealth. Then he left. Later that afternoon, having waived demand for tribute, the Sultan sent Stanley a sheep.

The next morning, Stanley and the other caravans fled the Sultan's domain. The tributes and vagaries of Ugogo were becoming a source of irritation for everyone, and it was time to leave the surrealism of the region behind. 'We had entered Ugogo full of hopes, believing it a most pleasant land – a land of milk and honey. We had been grievously disappointed. It proved to be a land of gall and bitterness, full of trouble and vexation of spirit, where we were exposed to the caprice of inebriated sultans,' Stanley wrote. 'The wilderness of Africa proves to be, in many instances, more friendly than the populate country.'

Two weeks later, after marching 178 miles in sixteen gruelling days, the caravan reached Tabora. It was 23 June, almost three months to the day since Stanley left Bagamoyo. He walked 525 (and a half) miles in 84 days – Burton and Speke had taken 134 days to cover the same distance. The second leg of Stanley's march was done.

Stanley threw a party for the men, roasting a bull and providing the banana beer. For the porters, their journey had reached its end. Afterwards, they were paid off and released. For Stanley, it was time to hire new porters and begin the final leg of his Homeric voyage. It was time to make the push to Ujiji, where, hopefully, David Livingstone waited. Even slowing his pace, Stanley knew he could make Ujiji before September – unless, of course, some incredible catastrophe forced him to turn around and go home.

TWENTY-FOUR

THE AMERICAN TRAVELLER

26 JUNE 1871
London

AT SIXTY-ONE, GENTLE AND URBANE SIR HENRY CRESWICKE RAWLINSON HAD led a fascinating life. He had served in the army in India, deciphered ancient cuneiform tablets in Persia that told of Darius the Great's rise to power in 519 BC, been a political agent at Kandahar in Afghanistan and served as the British Consul to Baghdad. His knowledge of Persian and Oriental languages was matched by few Englishmen. It was only late in life that he abandoned adventure and intrigue and returned to Britain to settle down and start a family.

It was Rawlinson whom Murchison handpicked as his successor after the stroke. He was the sort of globetrotter and intellectual the RGS presidency demanded, able to see the world beyond Britain as a three-dimensional realm of scientific possibility. The transition was awkward because of Murchison's partial paralysis. The frail former geologist and Livingstone apologist was making a miraculous recovery from his stroke, but he was incapable of running the RGS. Hence, the time had come to make a change. Rawlinson, who enjoyed sitting his children on his knee to tell them stories of tigers in India, was two decades younger than Murchison. The world was still fresh in his mind, unlike Murchison, who had been unable to travel abroad for some time. Clearly, the RGS needed Rawlinson.

June was unusually cold in 1871. It was a cloudy, fifty-degree evening when Rawlinson gave his first presidential address in the lecture theatre at Burlington Gardens. Hundreds of RGS members and their wives packed into the room as Rawlinson sat behind a large desk on the speaker's platform and began his first-ever rundown on the state of the Society. There was curiosity in the air. After nine straight years of Murchison's larger-than-life presidential speeches it would be strange having another man deliver the address.

Rawlinson was a polished speaker, and spoke with the confidence of a man who was no stranger to public elocution. His words rose and fell for emphasis. He diverged from his text now and again to speak from the heart. He lacked Murchison's showmanship, which turned out to be a blessing. The audience warmed to him, and over the course of his speech it became clear that the presidency was in able, visionary hands.

Eventually, it came time to get around to Livingstone. 'With regard also to our other great African explorer, Dr Livingstone, we are still kept in a state of most painful suspense,' he began. From then on, however, Rawlinson's statement ventured far beyond mere update. To his lifetime of exciting moments, Rawlinson added one of the most memorable: he broke the news to the RGS that Stanley was looking for Livingstone.

Referencing a letter from Kirk, dated 30 April, in which the Consul proudly announced that the caravan of relief supplies he'd coaxed out of Bagamoyo had passed through Tabora successfully and was almost to Ujiji, Rawlinson told of an odd American adventurer who had secreted himself into Africa. Apparently, the American wanted to say hello to Livingstone then continue touring Africa. 'This gentleman,' Rawlinson noted, 'who is said to be of the true exploring type, left Bagamoyo on the coast for Ujiji in February last, and intended to communicate with Livingstone before proceeding further into the interior, so that we must receive before long from this, if not from any other quarter, some definite intelligence of our great traveller's present condition and his plans for the future. Those who know Mr Stanley personally are much impressed with his determined character and aptitude for African travel. His expedition is well-equipped, and he enjoys the great advantage of having secured the services of Bombay, the well-known factotum of Speke and Grant. He is entirely dependent, I may add, on his own resources, and is actuated apparently by a mere love of adventure and discovery.'

Exclamations of sensation and 'Hear, hear' filled the chamber. While it was a relief that someone was striving to make contact with Livingstone, it was also rather startling that an amateur adventurer – an American – was accomplishing a feat that had taken its measure of Britain's lions.

What no one noticed, because Kirk hadn't mentioned it, was that Stanley was a journalist – the same journalist who had turned London upside down with his Abyssinia coup. If the minor upstaging of the British press had elicited such howls, there was no telling how Britain would react if the American upstaged the RGS, the British Government and the entire cult of British exploration. In Rawlinson's eyes, however, the most important priority was Livingstone's return. His rescuer's background was secondary.

'I need hardly say,' Rawlinson summarized, 'that if he succeeds in restoring Livingstone to us, or in assisting him to solve the great problem of the upper drainage into the Nile and Congo, he will be welcomed by this Society as heartily and warmly as if he were an English explorer acting under our own immediate auspices.'

Nonetheless, the London papers weren't informed of Rawlinson's announcement. The presence of the strange American in Africa remained a secret from the British public. Once again, it would be left to the American press to break that bit of news.

TWENTY-FIVE

MIRAMBO'S KINGDOM

23 JUNE 1871
Tabora
480 miles from Livingstone

STANLEY HAD FINALLY REACHED TABORA, ALMOST THREE MONTHS TO THE day after departing from Bagamoyo. The sprawling village on the savannah, with its large houses and lavish gardens occupied by the wealthiest Arab residents, was one of three primary Arab enclaves in East Africa. The first was Zanzibar. The second was Tabora. The third was Ujiji. All had large Arab populations, harems and thousands of slaves, and existed solely for the purpose of exporting raw materials – mostly slaves and ivory – from Africa, while importing not just cloth and beads, but also coffee, tea, sugar, soap and curry powder. Luxuries like butter were de rigueur.

Of the three enclaves, Tabora was the crown jewel. Set among dun-coloured hills in the heart of the East African countryside, refreshed by clear streams and pockets of forest, surrounded by fruit orchards and well-tended fields of wheat, onions and cucumbers, it possessed a beauty and abundance of resources that made it the African equivalent of an oasis. Many Arabs came to Tabora to trade, then liked it so much they lived out their lives there. The only real drawback to life in Tabora was the enormous population of poisonous snakes – more varieties of the region's serpents could be found in and around Tabora than anywhere else.

Technically, it was Sultan Barghash in Zanzibar who ruled Tabora. He had sent a man named Said bin Salim to act as governor. But Bin Salim was an ineffective leader who clashed repeatedly with local traders. Even the commander of Tabora's three-thousand-man militia ignored Salim and deployed troops at his whim. As long as there was no war, the issue of troop mobilization was moot. Tabora was its tranquil self, an oasis of trade and sensual delights in a sea of dead grass and thirst. But there lived in the village of Urambo, twenty-two miles north-west of Tabora, an African chieftain named Mirambo who despised the Arabs and their claims of sovereignty over Tabora.

Mirambo was a handsome, powerful man who spoke in a quiet voice and was known for his generosity. He greeted visitors with a firm handshake and looked them directly in the eyes, inspiring confidence and a feeling of camaraderie. As a boy Mirambo had worked as a porter in the Arab caravans and had adopted their manner of dress. The turban, cloth coat and slippers he wore in his home gave him a cosmopolitan air.

The scimitar snug in the scabbard dangling from Mirambo's waist was also Arab, and hinted at the more ruthless side of the charismatic young leader's personality. His date of birth was hard to pinpoint, but he was born the son of the Unyanyembe region's mightiest king sometime in the days shortly after the Arabs opened the first Bagamoyo-to-Ujiji slave route in 1825. The Arabs had slowly stripped power from his father, stealing his lands and cutting him off from the ivory trade that ensured his wealth and kingdom. When his father passed on and Mirambo assumed the throne, the Arabs refused to recognize him as the premier African ruler of the region. Instead, they backed a puppet of their choosing named Mkasiwa.

To make matters worse, Mkasiwa was so emboldened by the recognition that he considered Mirambo to be a far-flung vassal. This made Mirambo furious. He didn't immediately wage war on the Arabs, but expanded his kingdom among his own people, capturing village after village. He was a military genius and warred incessantly, excelling at the pre-dawn surprise attack on an opponent's weakest flank. His army of teenage conscripts – married men and older men were considered less aggressive and were discouraged from fighting – would open fire with their single-shot muskets, then switch to spears as they overran villages in relentless waves. Once a village was conquered, Mirambo celebrated the victory by looting the huts and splitting the booty with his army. The goats, chickens, women and cloth were a reward for a job well done and a fine enticement to wage war the next time Mirambo was in a warlike mood.

After the booty was split Mirambo would round up the residents of the village and behead the village chief with his scimitar. Then he would anoint a favoured and loyal warrior as the replacement. If, over the course of time, the new man failed to follow Mirambo's directives to the letter, or attempted to rebel and form his own kingdom, a lesson was quickly taught. Mirambo would travel to the village and gather the citizens together. Then the warrior would be forced to kneel, and the scimitar would flash again. A new puppet would be installed, one who was more clear that Mirambo would tolerate no usurpation of his power. With this combination of battle, booty and beheading, Mirambo rebuilt his father's kingdom. The growth of his kingdom slowly squeezed the lands surrounding Tabora, until the only corridor the Arabs controlled was the trade route between Tabora and Ujiji.

By the summer of 1871, just as Stanley arrived in Tabora, Mirambo's strength was greater than ever – and still ascendant. Tabora was in a state of wartime preparedness as tension between Mirambo and the Arabs ratcheted upwards. Both parties knew full well that the last African chieftain who'd confronted the Arabs, a man named Mnywa Sere, had been beheaded six years earlier. With a lifetime of inequity to avenge, it made no difference to Mirambo that he was outnumbered three to one. The time had come to wage war.

Mirambo began by harbouring runaway slaves. It was a passive move, a taunt that got the attention of the Arabs. The second act of war, however, attacked the Arabs where it hurt them most: trade. Mirambo blocked the route from Tabora to Ujiji. Caravans trying to run the blockade would be plundered and murdered. Immediately, the Arabs called a council of war and made plans to attack. Fifteen days, they predicted, was all the time they would need to crush the infidel.

Stanley knew nothing about the hostilities seething around him. He was simply relieved to be in Tabora, reunited with the other segments of the New York *Herald* expedition's massive caravan. He was overwhelmed when the Governor himself, Sheikh Said bin Salim, sashayed out to welcome him wearing clean white robes. The two men shook hands like old friends, then walked through town to the Governor's home for tea and pancakes, meeting the aged puppet Mkasiwa on the way.

Tabora was not a jewel to Stanley, but dusty and spartan, with that hostile air of repression common to crossroads and border towns. The stares of the local population made Stanley uneasy, a reminder of Ugogo. He was glad they did not attempt to speak to him or approach him in any way. 'All,' he wrote of the silent stares, assuming it was respect, 'paid the tribute due to my colour.'

It was a relieved Stanley who walked the three miles outside town to the home where he and his men would live during their short visit. Though Burton and Speke had spent five weeks in Tabora, Stanley didn't plan to rest for more than a week before beginning the last push to Ujiji.

'There was a cold glare of intense sunshine over the valley,' wrote Stanley of Tabora, rethinking his earlier opinion that it was 'of a picture without colour, or of food without taste'. He wrote of looking up into 'a sky of pale blue, spotless and of an awful serenity'.

The building, which was made available to him by a local Arab merchant, was more like a fortress than a home. The ceiling was made of heavy wooden beams covered with tightly woven bundles of sticks. The walls were made of mud bricks and mostly windowless but with ventilation holes. The veranda faced out onto an open plain. Donkeys were tethered to the sixteen pomegranate trees in the courtyard. There was a kitchen, a gun room, a four-seat indoor toilet, a store room for the bales of supplies, and quarters for Shaw, Bombay and all Stanley's men. Suddenly, after months of being a loose confederation, it was obvious that Stanley and his men were a team. Members of the various caravan segments renewed friendships and swapped stories of the trail. Stanley, who had come to consider himself their master and friend, was cheered by the men.

The housewarming was complete when the Arabs sent over a mini-caravan from town, laden with bowls of curried chicken, rice, pancakes, pomegranates and lemons. Then came more slaves, leading five oxen for slaughter, twelve chickens for plucking and a bowl of a dozen fresh eggs. 'This was real, practical noble courtesy,' Stanley wrote of his Arab hosts. 'Which took my gratitude quite by storm.'

Stanley admired the Arabs' looks, their character, their polish. They were mostly from Oman, he noticed, and handsome. Since Bagamoyo Stanley had strived to keep his mind free from impure thoughts, in keeping with his focus on self-improvement. But the chance to step away from the trail for a while and lower his hardened facade led him to be titillated by the Arabs' practice of keeping concubines. Stanley's normally chaste journal entries spoke of lust and want. He burned with desire for the local women, finding them far more attractive than white women, something he'd once thought himself incapable of. 'The eye that at first despised the unclassic face of the black woman of Africa soon loses its regard for fine lines and mellow pale colour. It finds itself ere long lingering wantonly over the inharmonious and heavy curves of a Negroid form, and looking lovingly on the broad unintellectual face, and into jet eyes that never flash with the dazzling love lights that makes poor humanity beautiful.'

If Stanley took his sexual fantasies a step further, he didn't mention it in his journal. Regardless, a seduction of sorts was taking place – and Stanley was the man being seduced. The highest-ranking Arabs of Tabora travelled the three miles over a dusty, rutted road to pay Stanley a visit, treating the journalist like royalty. When they spoke of their loyalty and attachment to this white stranger, Stanley took their words at face value. They asked about his health and congratulated him on his travels, impressing Stanley with their hospitality and etiquette. It seemed a fine reward for three months of deprivation since Bagamoyo.

The reason for their courtship became clear four days after Stanley's arrival. Stanley's hosts invited him to a luncheon feast. At the appointed time, he rode into town escorted by eighteen soldiers. The first stop was for a palate-tantalizing light hors d'oeuvre at the home of Sultan bin Ali, a colonel in Tabora's army. 'From here,' wrote Stanley, 'after being presented with mocha coffee and some sherbet, we directed our steps to Khamis bin Abdullah's house, who had, in anticipation of my coming, prepared a feast to which he had invited his friends and neighbours. The group of stately Arabs in their long white dresses, and jaunty caps, also of a snowy white, who stood ready to welcome me to Tabora, produced quite an effect on my mind.'

The Arabs had made the desired impression on Stanley. They were not actually holding a dinner for him, they were holding a war council. Their goal was to convince Stanley to join them in fighting Mirambo. The infidel was the biggest threat to Tabora's wealth they had ever known, and the evening was aptly filled with stories about the warrior-king's arrogance, and their desire to put him in his place once and for all. Stanley was told of Mirambo's bloodthirstiness and love of war. The Arabs spoke in outraged tones about Mirambo halting a caravan bound for Ujiji, then demanding gunpowder, guns and cloth in exchange for passage. When the caravan paid, Mirambo accepted the loot, then ordered them at gunpoint to turn around and go back to Tabora.

The Arabs wanted Stanley to know that the Governor, sitting on a pillow on the floor, was a peace-loving man, and had tried every means possible to appease Mirambo. War, they concluded, was the only solution. Speech after speech followed, talking of the Arab right to control the trade routes and lamenting the days when a man could walk along with his caravan using just a walking stick for protection.

'Mirambo,' raged the group's bravest man, Khamis bin Abdullah, 'shall not stop until every Arab is driven from Unyanyembe, and he rules over this country in place of Mkasiwa. Children of Oman, shall it be so?'

Stanley listened quietly, knowing he should stay away from a conflict that wasn't his own. He knew in his heart that war was imminent, and Stanley wanted no part of war. His time wearing Confederate grey had shown him the stupidity of fighting a war to defend someone else's cause.

But the search for Livingstone could not proceed until Mirambo was stopped. Hoping that the Arab prediction of a short war was correct, Stanley rationalized that he could expedite the victory, and thus resume the race to Ujiji. He volunteered himself and his men to join the Arab army. 'The Arabs were sanguine of victory and I noted their enthusiasm,' he observed as great platters of rice, curry and roast chicken were served.

Then Stanley was struck by a terrible thought. What if Livingstone was on his way to Tabora from Ujiji? What then? Was Livingstone prepared for war?

The thoughts of Livingstone's vulnerability were set aside as the party moved to a third house. But as Stanley began walking back to his house outside town, thoughts of Livingstone and the palpable evidence of his need for relief were graphically juxtaposed on the streets of Tabora. For there, in the heart of town, was Kirk's relief caravan. Despite what Kirk was writing to the RGS, the caravan had never proceeded to Ujiji. Stanley was furious. It was Mirambo's war that was preventing the caravan from getting through, but Stanley vented his wrath at the acting British Consul. For if the supplies had left Bagamoyo during November instead of February the war wouldn't be a factor – the relief supplies would have preceded Mirambo's uprising and would already be in Ujiji.

Fuming, Stanley ordered the caravan to place itself under his command. Livingstone's supplies and mail – neither of which had been plundered on the journey to Tabora – would travel with the New York *Herald* expedition to Ujiji. 'Poor Livingstone! Who knows but he may be suffering for want of these very supplies that have been detained so long within easy reach of the British Consulate,' Stanley wrote.

Before Tabora Livingstone had been a distant apparition to Stanley. But the closer he came, and the more he heard the Arabs talk of Ujiji as if it were just an incidental one-month journey, the more the search for Livingstone crept into Stanley's thoughts. His journalistic instincts rekindled, he sat down on 4 July to write his first dispatch to the New York *Herald*. It was written in the form of a letter to James Gordon Bennett, Jr, and ran to almost five thousand words – enough to fill the entire front page of the *Herald*. Stanley's first paragraphs were a justification for all the money he'd spent, reminding Bennett of his specific commands to go and find Livingstone without care for cost. 'I was too far from the telegraph to notify you of such an expense or to receive further orders from you,' Stanley apologized, choosing words that would ensure Bennett paid the bill when presented. 'Eight thousand dollars were expended in purchasing the cloth, beads and wire necessary in my dealing with the savages of the territories through which I would have to traverse.'

Then, his anxieties committed to paper, Stanley moved on to describing the heart of his journey. His travelogue of life in Africa was thorough and complex, speaking to the average reader instead of Bennett. He spoke of his fears and hopes, and even his contemplation of suicide. Farquhar's death was barely mentioned. Shaw was portrayed as lazy and insolent. Selim was praised for being worthy and hardworking. The reader learned that Stanley's caravan was moving twice as fast as Burton and Speke's, and had made it to Tabora at a pace almost as fast as the speediest Arabs. 'I should like to enter into more minute details respecting this new land,' he wrote, 'which is almost unknown, but the very nature of my mission, requiring speed and all my energy, precludes it. Some day, perhaps, the *Herald* will permit me to describe more minutely the experiences of the long march, with all its vicissitudes and pleasures, in its columns, and I can assure your readers beforehand that they will be not quite devoid of interest. But now my whole time is occupied in the march, and the direction of the expedition, the neglect of which in any one point would be productive of disastrous results.'

Stanley saved the information his audience wanted most for the final few pages. Livingstone, he told them, had gained quite a bit of weight. He was also being described by the Arabs who'd seen him as 'very old', with a long white beard. Most important, he was alleged to be on his way to Ujiji. 'Until I hear more of him or see the long absent old man face to face, I bid you a farewell,' he signed off. 'But wherever he is be sure I shall not give up the chase. If alive you shall hear what he has to say. If dead I will find him and bring his bones to you.'

TWENTY-SIX

FATHER FIGURE

7 JULY 1871
Tabora
480 miles from Livingstone

THE ROADS LEADING BACK TO BAGAMOYO WERE STILL OPEN. STANLEY SENT his *Herald* dispatch with a caravan going east. It would be hand-carried by two messengers, men named Ferrajjii and Cowpereh, directly to the American Consul, who would then send it along to New York on one of the Salem merchant ships. Then Stanley, his professional duties temporarily done and the road to Ujiji blocked, allowed himself the luxury of rest. For the next three afternoons he indulged in relaxation on his warm porch, dreaming of Livingstone. The view outside was of hills shaped like lion's paws, mango trees, sycamores and a dried stream bed. It was secluded and quiet, perfect for napping.

On the hot afternoon of 7 July, Stanley sat in the shade as drowsiness washed over him like a drug. He didn't sleep, but found himself wandering through the many rooms of his subconscious. 'The brain was busy. All my life seemed passing in review before me,' he wrote. 'Reminiscences of yet a young life's battles and hard struggles came surging into the mind in quick succession, events of boyhood, of youth and manhood. Perils, travels, scenes, joys and sorrows; loves and hates, friendships and indifferences. My mind followed the various and rapid transition of my life's passages. It drew the lengthy, erratic, sinuous lines of travel my footsteps had passed over.'

Then the orphan dreamed of a father, and remembered the man whose name he'd taken. 'The loveliest feature of all to me was of a noble and true man who called me son.'

Stanley floated through memories of the Mississippi, boat men, Spain, Indians, gold fields, and wandering through Asia Minor en route to Africa. The purge was thorough and unrestricted, a catharsis Stanley didn't expect, but embraced. In his thirty years of life he had been beaten down time and time again. But against all odds Stanley was leading a column of men into the heart of Africa, poised to take a flying leap at glory should he find Livingstone and return to tell the tale. He was beginning to think once again of travelling the length of the Nile, making his triumphant return to civilization in Cairo, as Speke and Grant had done. After a 'hot fitful life', Africa had become Stanley's playground, a continent he wandered at will, overcoming all obstacles through the judicious exercise of perseverance and a Winchester. No man was his boss. No man stood in judgement.

Stanley's intense visions that day welled up to touch him and remind him of emotions he'd long forgotten – 'when these retrospective scenes became serious, I looked serious; when they were sorrowful I wept hysterically; when they were joyous I laughed loudly'. In fact, Stanley's visions signalled something even more telling. He was suffering from dementia brought on by a severe case of cerebral malaria.

TWENTY-SEVEN

THE MASSACRE

15 JULY 1871
Nyangwe

THE MIDDLE OF THE EQUATORIAL SUMMER SAW LIVINGSTONE ANXIOUS TO leave Nyangwe. He was 'reduced to beggary', for the small amount of goods he possessed were back in Ujiji. The people of Nyangwe continued to refuse to rent him a canoe. And finally, many of his questions about what lay further downstream were answered when an Arab trader and his men attempted to paddle north up the Lualaba in search of ivory, along the route Livingstone wanted to follow. Livingstone was in Nyangwe when the news came back that the Arab trader died four days' paddle from Nyangwe, drowned when his canoe got sucked into a rocky, slender rapid. 'Hassani's canoe party in the river were foiled in the narrows after they had gone down four days,' Livingstone wrote of the tragedy. 'Rocks jut out on both sides, not opposite, but alternate, to each other. And the vast mass of water of the great river jammed in, rushes round one promontory to another, and a frightful whirlpool is formed, in which the first canoe went and was overturned, and five lives lost.' Upon further reflection, Livingstone came to the conclusion that his inability to rent a canoe was divinely inspired. 'In answer to my prayers for preservation I was prevented from going down the narrows,' he wrote.

Livingstone changed his plans accordingly. Possessing no beads or cloth in Nyangwe, but hearing reports from the Arabs that a fresh batch of supplies might have made it overland to Ujiji from Zanzibar, Livingstone gambled. Instead of following the Lualaba through the rapids, he would follow it by land. He made one of the Arab slavers a desperate all-or-nothing proposal: a caravan would take Livingstone across the Lualaba to Katanga, which Livingstone believed to be the home of the fountains; in return, Livingstone would sign over his four hundred pounds' worth of food, medicine and cloth thought to be waiting in Ujiji.

The trader's name was Dugumbe bin Habib. The leader of a large group of slavers camping along the Lualaba, he had virtually held Livingstone hostage since the explorer's arrival in Nyangwe. Livingstone had been given food and a house was built for him. But his mail wasn't sent and the simplest of necessities – such as a canoe to cross the quarter-mile-wide river to continue his exploration – had been denied. Dugumbe didn't want Livingstone wandering back to civilization to tell about life inside the slave trade. However, the offer of such a lucrative quantity of supplies was hard for a businessman like Dugumbe to turn down. He had asked Livingstone for time to think it over.

On 15 July 1871, Livingstone took his usual seat in the shade to observe the marketplace. There was controversy as the market opened that afternoon. All morning long Livingstone had heard the sounds of gunshots from the far side of the Lualaba, and could see the smoke of huts being set afire as Arabs burned, enslaved and murdered. As he hobbled into the marketplace he noticed that only about fifteen hundred people had come that day. He blamed it on the fires, remembering that many of those who normally came to market lived in those villages.

At the time, Livingstone didn't look anything like the man Murchison and England knew. In addition to being toothless and bearded, a combination of inactivity and the food provided by the Arabs had made Livingstone chunky and round. His clothes barely fitted him. The Arabs marvelled that Livingstone could eat a pot of rice and saucer of butter and still have room for a pot of porridge. The weight would come off as soon as he began travelling again, but in the meantime, Livingstone's gait was a slow waddle and he had trouble breathing. He plopped down slowly in the shade to watch people and write in his journal.

Livingstone had observed many things from that perch over the previous months. The locals paid little attention to Livingstone, or to the Arabs mingling among them. It was understood that the slavers would not raid Nyangwe, instead using it as a base to raid other villages. The only rule was that guns were not allowed in the market-place.

Even as the citizens and Arabs mingled in the market square, the subtle awareness that the Arabs had the power to enslave them made for a palpable distance between the two groups. The Arabs contributed to the feeling. Despite having mingled with the African populace for centuries, Arabs still held themselves apart, and viewed the people with disdain.

'It was a hot sultry day,' Livingstone wrote later. 'And when I went into the market I saw Adie and Manilla, and three of the men who had lately come with Dugumbe. I was surprised to see the three with their guns, and felt inclined to reprove them, as one of my men did, for bringing weapons into the market.'

Livingstone chalked up the newcomers' faux pas to ignorance of local customs, and got up to leave the market. He noticed two of the Arabs haggling with a vendor over a chicken then trying to grab it without paying for it. The market was always a frantic place, with raised voices and misunderstandings common. For two men and a vendor to disagree was nothing unusual.

But in the next instant, Livingstone's opinion of the slavers changed for ever. 'The discharge of two guns in the middle of the crowd told me the slaughter had begun: crowds dashed off from the place, and threw down their wares in confusion, and ran. At the same time the three men opened fire on the mass of people near the upper end of the market place, volleys were discharged from a party down near the creek on the panic-stricken women who dashed at the canoes. These, some fifty or more, were jammed in the creek and the men forgot their paddles in the terror that seized all.'

Though the Lualaba was broad, the creek feeding into it where the canoes were kept was thin and slow. The mass of people rushing to the boats clogged the narrow outlet, allowing the Arabs to conduct target practice on the men, women and children of Nyangwe. 'Wounded by balls,' Livingstone wrote, they 'poured into them and leaped and scrambled into the water shrieking'.

As the Arabs stood along the river bank, calmly aiming and firing, then reloading quickly so as not to miss the opportunity to kill again, the locals left their canoes behind. Splashing into the Lualaba, they began swimming for the far shore. The game became a test of skill for the Arabs; instead of shooting legs and torsos, they had only heads sticking above the water to aim at. The sun glinted off the languid green river, silhouetting those heads, making them appear as bobbing melons. 'It was the heads above water showed the long lines of those that would inevitably perish,' Livingstone wrote. He had run out of paper, and was penning his journal on any scrap he could find – old bills, magazine pages. Livingstone's supply of ink was done, too. He had made a new batch by pressing roots until a red dye oozed forth. Its colour brought a ghostly realism to the tales of murder.

'Shot after shot continued to be fired on the helpless and perishing. Some of the long line of heads disappeared quietly, whilst other poor creatures threw their arms high, as if appealing to the great Father above, and sank.'

The carnage was relentless and began taking on the chaos of a battle-field. The wounded who managed to make it across wailed in agony on the far bank. In midstream, one native who'd got a canoe out into the river attempted to save others, while another who'd got a canoe fled, alone. The local women knew the river well from their years diving for oysters. Many of them were able to hold their breath long enough to ride the current downstream underwater, resurfacing for a quick snatch of air, then submerging until they were out of rifle range. Then, on the far bank of the Lualaba, a place where Livingstone would never explore, the women slipped ashore into the jungle. Some never made it any further, though, as the abundant population of crocodiles was picking them off one by one.

The shooting and burning continued for twenty-four hours. As the Arabs were setting fire to the grass-roofed huts and sending canoes of their own into the river to enslave the stragglers, they learned they had killed two of their own in addition to almost four hundred locals. Another slaver was drowned on the river, done in by his own greed when his boat capsized.

Throughout the carnage Livingstone was impotent, enraged. What began as a commonplace market dispute over a chicken had become a catastrophic display of Arab brutality. The attack had not been planned, and there was no greater Arab objective, which made the slayings all the more senseless. A righteous rage coursed through him, but there was nothing Livingstone could do to stop the slaughter. The British in him convinced Livingstone he was somehow in charge, however, and cried out for propriety. From his cargo he extracted the Union Jack he was entitled to carry as a British consul. He sent his men forth showing the flag, demanding a ceasefire. Only then did Dugumbe get a grip on his men. The shooting stopped temporarily, and in the eerie aftermath the only sounds were the wounded begging for help.

Livingstone pulled his pistol and advanced on the killers, prepared to do something he had never contemplated – commit murder. He never even came close. Dugumbe stepped forward to stop him, well aware that his renegade employees wouldn't hesitate to shoot the chubby old man. All Livingstone could do to vent his anger was to retreat into his journal and rededicate himself to the anti-slavery cause. For almost five years he had looked the other way, compromising his principles for the sake of exploration and the comforts provided by his Arab hosts. It was as if he had sold a part of his soul in the name of ambition. And what had he accomplished? He was sicker than ever, impoverished, and had no hard evidence that his theories about the Nile's source were accurate. True, he had some very good ideas and a vast amount of circumstantial evidence backing it up, but the Source had been as elusive in the summer of 1871 as it had been the day of the Nile Duel.

'As I write I hear the loud wails on the left bank over those who are there slain, ignorant of their many friends who are now in the depths of the Lualaba. Oh, let Thy kingdom come!' his words cried to God. 'No one will ever know the exact loss on this bright sultry morning. It gave me the impression of being in hell.'

Livingstone spent the rest of that day helping the survivors find their spouses. Later, when the instigators had the gall to blame the slaughter on Livingstone, the explorer knew it was time to leave. Forsaking thoughts of crossing the river to find Herodotus's fountains, he decided to return to Ujiji. The local chiefs, who had secretly thought Livingstone a slaver, were so impressed by his intercession during the massacre that they begged him to stay and help them consolidate several of their villages into a Manyuema nation, of which Livingstone would be ruler. 'But I told them I was so ashamed by the company in which I found myself that I could scarcely look the Manyuema in the face. They had believed that I wished to kill them – what did they think now? I could not remain among bloody companions, and would flee away.' He would return to Ujiji and claim the supplies that should be waiting. Then he would hire new men and search anew for the fountains.

Even as Livingstone prepared to leave, the stress caused his health to worsen. His bowels loosened and he lost a serious amount of fluid and blood. 'I was laid up all morning with the depression the bloodshed made – it filled me with unspeakable horror,' he wrote. '"Don't go away", said the Manyuema chiefs to me, but I cannot stay here in agony.'

Livingstone fled Nyangwe a few mornings after the massacre. Just to show there were no hard feelings, the Arabs came to see him off. They had, however, little hope that Livingstone would accomplish the three-month march to Ujiji safely. Hostilities between the Arabs and local tribes were now at a fever pitch. Livingstone had no Arab guns or numbers to protect him. A tribe would be just as likely to kill Livingstone – a man known to travel in the company of Arabs – as let him pass.

Making matters more dangerous, the path Livingstone would follow to Ujiji was one he'd never travelled before, through virgin jungle and country populated by cannibals. The bright red waistcoat he was wearing was cut like the Arab garments, in honour of his hosts. Unfortunately, the natives would think he was one of them.

Livingstone's journey went well for five days. He, Chuma, Susi and a handful of porters walked carefully, trying to make time and avoid attention. On the sixth day of travel, Livingstone came over a ridge and saw a most beautiful green countryside below. As he trudged through it, he saw the land was devoid of people. The Arabs had taken them all hostage. All that remained were the burned-out ruins of their villages. Livingstone was outraged, thinking it an act of 'sheer wantonness'. There seemed to be nothing he could do to protect Africa from the slave trade. When, a few days later, a small group of African porters asked if they might travel with him, he readily agreed. They were headed for Ujiji, too. His group now numbered almost eighty. After helplessly watching the destruction of the Nyangwe massacre and then witnessing the ghostly sight of villages emptied by the slave trade, Livingstone was actually finding a way to preserve African lives – even if the potential killers were other Africans. He revelled in the added safety the new men provided as they travelled 'among the justly irritated' local tribes.

Two weeks into the journey, Livingstone and his men walked through more burned-out villages. They slept in the remains of one village, protected by a fence of sharpened sticks. Livingstone was sick in the morning but he pressed on. At the next village the people took note of his red jacket. He was still unaware of its implications. 'The people all ran away and appeared in the distance armed and refused to come near,' he wrote of the villagers. 'They threw stones at us and tried to kill those who went for water.'

That night, Livingstone slept in a small hut, protected within the cocoon of mosquito netting he travelled with at all times. But with the locals more and more sure Livingstone and his men were slavers, Livingstone tossed and turned with worry, despite his sickness. Unlike in Nyangwe, the cannibals of this new region of Manyuema considered Livingstone an enemy. Not only would they relish killing him, but, as with all enemies killed in battle, the cannibals would happily soak Livingstone's body in water until tender, then make a meal of Britain's brave, beloved, overdue explorer.

The next morning Livingstone's foreboding was justified. While marching through a jungle trail so narrow that leaves brushed against their faces, they were stopped abruptly by a blockade of felled trees. The vegetation was thick to the point of being impenetrable on either side, and triple-canopy deep overhead. Livingstone had been in Africa long enough to spot an ambush, and when he peered up into the trees he saw black shapes poised to pounce.

Hemmed in on the sides, watched from above, unable to turn around, Livingstone and his small caravan were easy targets as they climbed over the logs. Livingstone went last. 'I was behind the main body, and all were allowed to pass till I, the leader, who was believed to be Mohammed Bogharib,' Livingstone wrote. 'A red jacket they had formerly seen me wearing was proof to them that I was the same that sent Bin Juma to kill five of their men, capture eleven women and children, and twenty-five goats.'

Without warning, spears rained down from the trees, and from out of the dense foliage along the trail. Livingstone's caravan had been funnelled into the ideal killing zone. They could only proceed forwards or backwards down the thin trail, but either way the enemy was all around them. 'Another spear was thrown at me by an unseen assailant, and it missed me by about a foot in front,' Livingstone wrote. 'Guns were fired into the dense mass of forest, but with no effect, for nothing could be seen. But we heard the men jeering and denouncing us close by.' As Livingstone hastened forward down the trail with all the speed he could muster, he walked past two porters, spears jutting from their dead bodies.

For five long hours, Livingstone and his men scampered down the trail, constantly under attack. The unseen enemies mocked him from above. 'I can say this devoutly now, but in running the gauntlet for five weary hours among furies all eager to signalize themselves by slaying one they sincerely believed to have been guilty of a horrid outrage, no elevated sentiments entered the mind,' he wrote later. 'The excitement gave way to overpowering weariness, and I felt as I suppose soldiers do on the field of battle – not courageous, but perfectly indifferent to whether I were killed or not.'

At one point Livingstone thought he was safe, only to stumble into another ingenious killing zone. 'Coming to a part of the forest cleared for cultivation, I noticed a gigantic tree, made still taller by growing on an anthill twenty feet high. It had fire applied near its roots,' Livingstone wrote. The massive tree, the base of its trunk weakened by fire, was perfectly positioned to fall down on the trail and crush him and his men. Livingstone, however, 'felt no alarm'. His unseen tormentors toppled the tree. The trunk snapped. In the silence of the jungle the sound was like the crack of a rifle salvo. Livingstone looked up in horror as the tree came straight down towards him, unsure which way to run. With its thick trunk and profusion of branches, the tree would crush a wide area of the trail when it landed. 'I ran a few paces back and down it came to the ground one yard behind me and, breaking into several lengths, it covered me with a cloud of dust. Had not the branches been previously rotted off, I could scarcely have escaped.'

At the end of the day, Livingstone crossed a small river known as the Liya and entered a section of land cleared for cultivation. He entered a farming village known as Monanbundwa, where he was welcomed, and lay down to rest. The chief came to his side, unarmed. Livingstone explained the mistake about his identity, assuring the chief that he was not the slaver named Mohammed Bogharib and that he had no wish to kill men. The chief was reassured, and allowed them to stay the night. Livingstone, to prevent further animosity, temporarily stopped wearing the offending jacket.

Without his knowing, Livingstone had seen the first stage of a full-scale native revolt against the Arabs from the citizens to the west of Lake Tanganyika – a revolt coincidental to Mirambo's. The Manyuema set Arab encampments ablaze in the months that followed, and the slavers' people were fired upon. Using bows and arrows judiciously, the Manyuema could fire and reload faster than the Arabs with their archaic single-shot muskets. 'This is the beginning of the end,' Livingstone wrote. 'Which will exclude Arab traders from the country.'

Livingstone trekked away from the heart of cannibal country, but the stress of the day he had endured under attack had frazzled his immune system. Dysentery returned. He lost his appetite. Dust got in his eyes, making him temporarily blind. Even in the dangerous country, he was forced to rest most days. On the days he marched it was through mountainous wilderness, in a thick equatorial heat. His French-made shoes were too tight because his feet had swollen. The soles were falling apart and the uppers were rotting. Worse, the trail crossed a mountain path of sharp quartz. 'The mind acted on the body,' he wrote. 'And it is no overstatement to say that every step of between 400 and 500 miles was in pain.'

TWENTY-EIGHT

MORE WAR

21 JULY 1871
Tabora
350 miles from Livingstone

SHAW WAS STANDING OVER STANLEY AS THE MALARIAL JOURNEY THROUGH his subconscious came to an end. Two weeks had passed, Shaw told his incredulous boss. The journalist had been sick in bed the entire time. It was cerebral malaria this time – *Plasmodium falciparum* – and Stanley had almost died. But Shaw nursed him back to health. He had fed Stanley gruel and forced him to sip brandy. Stanley remembered nothing of it. Just the emotions and memories, surging through him, reminding him where he'd come from and preparing him for the battle ahead. 'I remembered the battlefields of America,' he wrote, 'and the stormy scenes of rampant war.'

A new set of stormy scenes was added to those over the next six weeks. Flying the American flag, Stanley marched his men into battle against Mirambo, alongside the Arabs. The warfare was unlike the disciplined marches of the Confederates on Shiloh, or even the British Army's determined assault on Magdala. Rather, Arab sultans trekked into the bush hunting their enemy. Their slaves – men without any training in military tactics – were forced to fight their fellow Africans because their owners commanded it. Mirambo, however, foresaw the attack. He had cleverly concealed his forces in the woods and tall grasses. Stanley, meanwhile, marvelled at the military tactics of the uneducated chief. He found them genius – and savage. He even wrote a dispatch to the *Herald* calling Mirambo 'the African Bonaparte'.

On the morning of 4 August, the men daubed their bodies with a combination of flour and herb juice that they believed would protect them in battle. Stanley's malaria was flaring again, shooting fever and weakness through his veins. Fear of the battle added to his miseries, and he was experiencing serious misgivings about the terms of his alliance with the Arabs. Instead of commanding his own men, Stanley and his group would march into battle under the leadership of the fiery Khamis bin Abdullah, who was serving as the campaign's de facto commander in chief. Just before noon the Arab force of almost 2,500 surrounded the wooden fence of Mirambo's village and prepared to attack. 'Khamis bin Abdullah crept through the forest to the west of the village,' Stanley wrote. 'Suddenly a volley opened on us as we emerged from the forest.'

To Stanley, the battle was comical. The Arabs and their slaves had no concept of taking cover or advancing on the enemy under fire. Instead, they lay in the grass to load their guns, then leapt up and fired, then jumped into the grass again and again. 'Forward, then backward, with the agility of hopping frogs.'

Despite their inadequacies, the Arabs routed Mirambo's forces with ease. When the Arabs finally took the village the only things left behind were ivory tusks, slaves, piles of grain and twenty dead bodies. The Arabs set fire to the village so Mirambo and his men would have no refuge, then set fire to two neighbouring villages and the surrounding grasslands for good measure. When one of Mirambo's men was caught sleeping in the forest he was grabbed by the hair, had his neck stretched as far back as it would go, then had his throat slashed clean through to his spine.

Stanley had been an active participant in the battle on 4 August, but two days later a relapse of his malaria prevented him from accompanying the Arabs as they pressed forth the manhunt for Mirambo. He stayed behind in the war camp, shivering under a blanket on the morning of 6 August. Half of his men had left for the day to join the forces of a fiery Arab, Soud bin Sayd. The Arabs were determined to exterminate Mirambo once and for all, making him an example for future generations of potential rebels. It was obvious from the Arabs' easy victories that Mirambo wasn't the military genius of his reputation.

Just as the sun was setting, the first stragglers of the battle returned.

Stanley was sleeping under a pile of blankets, trying to sweat out his fever, when he learned that Soud bin Sayd had been killed in an ambush, along with five of Stanley's sepoys. Mirambo had allowed Soud bin Sayd to take the village of Wilyankuru, pretending to flee. However, as the Arab forces marched back to their camp laden with tusks, hundreds of slaves and sixty bales of cloth, Mirambo and his men sprang from the tall grass along the road. Soud bin Sayd was reloading his shotgun when a spear pierced him 'through and through'. Every Arab member of his convoy was captured and killed in the same manner.

'The effect of this defeat is indescribable,' Stanley wrote. 'It was impossible to sleep, from the shrieks of women whose husbands had fallen. All night they howled through their lamentations, and sometimes might be heard the groans of the wounded who had contrived to crawl through the grass unperceived by the enemy. Fugitives were continually coming in through the night, but none of my men who were reported to be dead were ever heard of again.'

That single defeat crushed the Arab resolve. The morning of 7 August was spent bickering with one another, pointing the finger of blame. Khamis bin Abdullah raged that his compatriots were cowards, and preferred peace and subjugation to seeing their mission carried out in its entirety. The tent where they held the latest war council was hardly soundproof, and as the screams and rants were heard, soon everyone in camp was privy to the accusations. Stanley, saddened by his men's deaths and more sure than ever about the folly of fighting the Arabs' war, went back to bed in another attempt to overcome his malaria.

But Mirambo was not resting. He pressed forth his advantage. At one thirty in the afternoon, Selim shook Stanley from his malarial daze. It was imperative, Selim shouted, that Stanley get up. The camp was being evacuated. Mirambo was on his way. Even Khamis bin Abdullah was running, with no intention of stopping to help Stanley. 'With the aid of Selim I dressed myself and staggered towards the door,' Stanley wrote. He saw the Arabs and their slaves retreating in terror. There was no order, simply pandemonium. Worse, except for Bombay and three of his soldiers, Stanley's men were fleeing – including Shaw, who 'was saddling his donkey with my own saddle, preparatory to giving me the slip and leaving me in the lurch to the tender mercies of Mirambo'.

Stanley ordered Shaw to give him back his saddle. Then Stanley organized his men into a single unit and led them in a disciplined military retreat. For eleven long hours, well into the night, they stayed together as they fled Mirambo and his men. Finally, just after midnight, he rendezvoused with the Arab forces.

Stanley had had enough. After a fitful night's sleep he lambasted the Arabs for their cowardice. He was insulted that they'd planned on leaving him behind, and even more insulted when they casually greeted him in the morning as if nothing had happened. He lectured the council of war for deserting their wounded and their 'every man for himself' policy. The war was just between them and Mirambo, he scolded them, and their habit of running away at the slightest setback was a solid indicator that the war could drag on for years – years Stanley didn't have. 'I know something about fighting, but I never saw people run away from an encampment like ours at Zimbizo, for such slight cause as you had.'

Stanley paused to look hard at the Arabs, making sure his next sentence struck home. 'By running away you have invited Mirambo to follow you to Unyanyembe. You may be sure he will come.'

In the morning the Arabs continued their retreat to Tabora. But a disappointed and disheartened Stanley was through with their war. As the Arabs marshalled their forces within the city, he gathered his men and returned to his rented home outside town to regroup. He had done his duty to the Arabs, repaying their kindnesses with service during their war. Now he was free to go. The question haunting him, however, was to where? Once the caravan route reopened, the Arabs had told him, Ujiji was just a month's march. But judging by the way the Arabs were fighting, that reopening looked to be a long time in the future. On the other hand, if Stanley tried to run Mirambo's blockade, especially in light of the hostilities, Mirambo would not only demand all Stanley's cloth and beads in tribute, he would butcher each and every member of the New York *Herald* expedition.

Mentally, Stanley began making a case for turning around and going home. He rationalized he had done all that was humanly possible to find Livingstone. No reporter could have done more. Certainly Bennett would understand that.

Stanley had prevailed through swamps, sickness and warfare. His porters had been released, so he had no men to carry his cargo. Many of his men had died, his goods had been stolen by deserters, and certain death waited if he went forward. For as powerful as a Winchester repeating rifle would appear in the short term, in the long run Mirambo's large force would be overwhelming. 'My position is most serious,' he finally wrote. 'I have a good excuse for returning to the coast.'

The determining factor was the same brute reality behind the entire expedition: money. Stanley pictured himself returning to civilization without finding a scrap of evidence about Livingstone's whereabouts. He would be seen as a failure, and would probably lose his job. More pragmatically, he had run up an enormous tab with the Arab merchants. Bennett would refuse to pay, on the grounds that Stanley hadn't done his duty. Legally, Webb was liable, but Stanley had given his word. The pre-Africa Stanley might have run off and left Webb to pay, considering the episode to be another of life's little failures. But now Stanley knew he had to push on. 'So much money has been expended, and so much confidence has been placed in me,' he concluded. Fuelled by more Arab reports that Livingstone was alive but destitute somewhere near Lake Tanganyika, he developed a mental picture of Livingstone trapped in Ujiji, unable to move due to war and lack of supplies. Stanley was the cavalry, riding to the rescue. 'I feel I must die sooner than return.'

It was 11 August. It had been seven weeks since Stanley had first set foot in Tabora. Counting Bombay, the soldiers and Shaw, he was down to his last thirteen men. The time had come to do something ingenious and even a little stupid, for that's what it was going to take to reach Ujiji.

Stanley's salvation came from the man he had denigrated the most: Bombay. The short former slave with the flat teeth told Stanley of a little used trail to the south of Tabora. It was the long way to Ujiji, adding two hundred miles to the trip by giving the traditional caravan route the widest possible berth. It was a path the porters feared, leading through thick woods of sycamore and scrub, filled with giraffes and a smallish breed of elephant. In addition to his own caravan, Stanley would also need to bring along the lazy members of Kirk's relief expedition, overseeing them for the final march to Ujiji to ensure Livingstone's supplies didn't get spent in Tabora, as in past years.

The Arabs tried to convince Stanley to stay. His mind, however, was made up. The expedition had spent almost as much time in Tabora as they had getting there. The time had come to go, and as soon as possible. Even as Shaw fell ill with what he claimed was malaria but what Stanley suspected was venereal disease, Stanley began hiring the necessary porters and preparing his men for the trail once again.

Then, as Stanley predicted, Mirambo attacked Tabora. The Arabs could look out across the plains surrounding the town from their roofs and see the vast African army spread across the bleached white grass. Mirambo's massive tent was pitched in the rear, fully visible and out of rifle range, protected by his men. If he chose to attack Tabora there was nothing the Arabs could do to prevent the annihilation of their town, the rape of all their women and the enslavement of their children.

Stanley armed his men once again, and accepted any refugees who came to his encampment seeking security. But this time he refused to fight alongside the Arabs. Khamis bin Abdullah, the volatile merchant who had instigated the war in the first place, hatched a plan. Alone, except for a gunbearer and eighty slaves, Abdullah would approach Mirambo's encampment under the pretext of peace. When the two were alone, he would kill the African, bringing an end to the war.

Assembling his forces, Abdullah marched his men to the edge of town and approached Mirambo. The African, of course, didn't rise to power through gullibility. He saw through his spyglass that Abdullah's eighty armed slaves looked far more like a party of war than men seeking peace. Mirambo hastily ordered his men to retreat. Abdullah marched forward, unaware he was walking into Mirambo's trap. 'Khamis,' Stanley wrote of his friend, 'rushed on with his friends after them. Suddenly, Mirambo ordered his men to advance upon them in a body.'

Abdullah's slaves turned around and ran, but the Arab and his young gunbearer stood their ground. The first bullet that felled Abdullah was through his leg. As he dropped to the dirt in agony, blood spurting from the wound, he became aware that his slaves were no longer at his side. Then his eyes shifted to Mirambo's warriors. He rose to his knees as they strode forward. He knew what was about to happen to him.

'Khamis bin Abdullah,' Stanley wrote that night, 'who was a fine, noble, brave, portly man, was found with the skin of his forehead, the beard and skin of the lower face, the forepart of the nose, the fat over the stomach and abdomen, the genital organs, and lastly, a bit from each heel, cut off by the savage allies of Mirambo.'

As Stanley pondered the awareness that his dead friend's body was being stewed and eaten by Mirambo's men as a potion for greater strength in battle, he fortified his citadel. Every man who came to his home was armed, until 150 riflemen were stationed along the walls, waiting for Mirambo. 'I hope to God he will come,' Stanley concluded that night's journal entry. 'If he comes within range of an American rifle, I shall see what virtue lies in American lead.'

TWENTY-NINE

INTO THE WOODS

26 AUGUST 1871
Tabora
300 miles from Livingstone

MIRAMBO NEVER ATTACKED STANLEY. HE LOOTED AND BURNED TABORA, raping and killing and enslaving until Arab opposition finally forced him to pull back. But his main objectives had always been control of the caravan route and a show of force, not driving the Arabs from their indefensible trading outpost. Having accomplished his goals, Mirambo and his men melted back into the woodlands on the night of 26 August. The Arabs, who had frantically marshalled their forces for a counter-attack, woke up the next morning to find him gone. Once again Mirambo had got the better of them. All they could do was lament the missed opportunity and argue about ways to reopen the trail to Ujiji. Many of the most prominent Arabs even began making plans to leave Tabora for good, preferring to do business in Zanzibar.

Stanley became consumed with getting out of town as quickly as possible. It seemed adversity blocked his every move towards Livingstone. If it wasn't Mirambo forcing a two-hundred-mile detour it was a lack of local porters to carry the bales of supplies, or the lack-adaisical air of African life, where 'tomorrow' might mean 'a month from now'. An infuriated, frustrated Stanley became convinced he was fated to while away his life in Tabora, constantly in search of porters.

He began scaling back the expedition, deciding to leave sixty of the bales and almost all of his personal luxuries in Tabora. He and his men would travel light and fast – if they ever got out of town.

Stanley's greatest vexation, however, was Shaw. He'd signed on at a salary of three hundred dollars per year, which had sounded astronomical back in Zanzibar, when he was a sailor without a ship or prospects. The image of travelling into Africa to explore the headwaters of the Rufiji River had been rather swashbuckling. However, there was no glamour about the reality of life in Africa. Stanley still hadn't told him they were searching for Livingstone, so Shaw was beginning to think his boss was crazy for being so adamant about reaching Ujiji. Stanley had told Shaw that their goal was to measure the depth of Lake Tanganyika, though Shaw didn't see how it was worth risking his life and the lives of all his men to get there. Africa wasn't what he'd imagined it would be, and Shaw desperately wanted to turn around and go home. He begged Stanley to release him from his contract.

Stanley wouldn't allow it. His excuse was that Shaw, as a white man, had to provide a good example for other members of the caravan. If he showed fear, so would they. But the real reason had nothing to do with race or exploration or leadership, for Shaw was proving himself inept, clumsy, lazy and sometimes just plain stupid.

The real reason Stanley wanted to keep Shaw nearby was because he liked his company. Stanley had been aware of race since Ugogo. Shaw represented another white face in a sea of Africans and Arabs. They shared a frame of reference. They spoke the same language. For all his bluster, Stanley was alone in Africa. He had no one to counsel him, no one to whom he could open up emotionally. In a strange way, merely having Shaw around – as sly as the sailor could be – was comforting. Stanley would not have crumbled if Shaw left, but he certainly would have felt more isolated. There would be no one to watch Stanley's back in case of trouble.

Even as Stanley berated and mocked Shaw during August, making sarcastic remarks about his laziness and insatiable sexual appetite, it was Stanley who returned the favour and nursed Shaw back to health when a strange illness almost killed the sailor. He dosed Shaw with cinchona bark and made him drink tonics of brandy, sugar, raw eggs and lemons. Sadly, nothing worked. Despite brief recoveries, Shaw repeatedly relapsed. 'Shaw will not work,' Stanley wrote on 30 August, convinced his charge was feigning sickness because his symptoms were different from malaria. In fact, Shaw was suffering from smallpox. 'I cannot get him to stir himself. I have petted him and coaxed him. I have even cooked little luxuries for him myself.'

Desperate, Stanley unveiled the truth about why they were in Africa, hoping it would spark excitement in Shaw. 'I sat down by his side,' Stanley wrote, 'in order to encourage him. And today, for the first time, I told him the real nature of my mission. I told him I did not care about the geography of the country so much as I cared about finding Livingstone.'

Shaw's eyes lit up for the briefest of instants, then became dull again. 'It is to find Livingstone I am here,' Stanley continued. 'Don't you see, old fellow, the importance of the mission? Don't you see the reward from Mr Bennett if you will help me? I am sure, if you ever come to New York, that you will never be in want of a fifty-dollar bill. So shake yourself, jump about, look lively.'

Shaw's eyes stared into space. Stanley grew desperate. Looking at his young friend, he implored him to go the distance. His previous taunts about death were forgotten. 'Say you will not die,' pleaded Stanley.

Shaw didn't. But whereas Stanley enjoyed reprieves from malaria, Shaw – and many of the soldiers, too – couldn't shake the highly infectious smallpox. When Stanley finally attracted a corps of porters by offering three times the going salary rate, Shaw was still too ill to travel. Stanley's thoughts and words were filled with speculation on whether the Cockney was truly sick, or merely pretending so he could stay behind and steal back to Zanzibar. 'If I took a stick I could take the nonsense out of him,' Stanley fumed.

Shaw saw through Stanley's facade. Their relationship could never be termed a friendship, but trial had given it depth. Time had given understanding. They had become like a cantankerous couple who know each other's strengths and weaknesses all too well, mocking one another most of the time while occasionally letting a ray of warmth shine through.

Shaw began opening up to Stanley as he lay in bed in the house outside Tabora, where the rooms were small and rectangular and the sounds of donkeys and of pans rattling in the nearby kitchen could be heard outside his door. He had plenty of time to reflect on his life. Shaw told of a life as the son of a captain in the Royal Navy, and how as a child he had met Queen Victoria on four occasions. Then Shaw spoke warmly about Stanley and looked back in awe on all they'd been through. Characteristically, Stanley laughed in the sailor's face and dismissed him as a 'sentimental driveller'. But when Shaw became angry at the rejection, Stanley didn't lash out caustically, as he had when Shaw rebuked him in the past. Instead, he rolled his eyes and complained of wanting to 'cry out with vexation', then continued to encourage Shaw to rise from his sickbed and prepare to travel.

Shaw, however, did not. And as Stanley contemplated the enormity of the challenges he was facing, depression set in. 'The Apostle of Africa,' he wrote of Livingstone on 13 September, 'is always on my mind. And as day after day passes without starting to find him I find myself subject to fits of depression. Indeed, I have many things to depress me.' If only to snap out of his gloomy mood, Stanley was desperate to get out of Tabora, no matter how sick Shaw, Selim or some of his other caravan members happened to be.

The Arabs, who thought Stanley was suicidal for attempting the south-west loop towards Ujiji, didn't understand Stanley's mania. They could only see that Shaw was in the throes of a great sickness. They scolded Stanley for being so cruel as to make a dying man travel through the hard country, with its dense forests, bad trails, wildlife and warring tribes. 'You will find the people will be too much for you and that you will have to return,' one particularly unsavoury slave trader told Stanley. 'The Wamanyar are bad, the Wakonongo are very bad, and the Wazavira are worst of all. You have come to this country at a very bad time. There is war everywhere.'

Rumours that those tribes were either preparing for an expected invasion from Mirambo or travelling north to join Mirambo increased their perception of Stanley's lunacy. And though Stanley wasn't frightened, his new porters were losing heart and grumbling about the mission they'd signed on for. Even Bombay, veteran of so many African expeditions, told Stanley that turning back for Bagamoyo and trying again later was the smart thing to do. Instead of listening, however, Stanley hired two local men to act as guides. He was particularly impressed with the one named Asmani, who was broad shouldered and over six feet tall. He would be protection against the warring tribes, a hulking Goliath marching at the front of Stanley's small army. Between the flag of the United States and the stature of Asmani, Stanley would present an intimidating presence to the Wakonongo and Washenshi tribes. 'If vastness of the human form could terrify anyone, certainly Asmani's presence is well calculated to produce that effect,' Stanley marvelled.

Stanley hired Asmani and his friend Mabruki on 16 September. His caravan, with its reduced size so perfect for a speed march, was complete in Stanley's mind. It was finally time to leave Tabora. What had once seemed idyllic had been tarnished, and he was eager to get on the trail. He threw a massive feast for the caravan, and urged the new porters to invite their families. A pair of bulls was slaughtered, chickens and sheep were grilled on a spit, five gallons of the native beer were purchased. Everyone in the caravan except he and Shaw drank and danced into the night. Stanley sat on his porch and stared into his now familiar hills and dried streambeds, smoked a cigar and wrote in his journal. The date of departure would be 19 September, he decided. The morning after next.

But on the morning of the nineteenth, Stanley was struck by a wave of fever. He piled on the blankets and lay in bed, thinking it just a 'slight' attack that would pass in a few hours. But the fever raged on through the day. Shaw even got out of bed to gloat that Stanley would die 'like a donkey'. When that happened, Shaw said, he planned to take charge of Stanley's journals and trunks then head straight back for Bagamoyo.

'Who would you like me to write to, in case you die?' Shaw cooed to Stanley that night, standing over the journalist's bed. 'Because even the strongest of us may die.'

'Mind your own business,' Stanley snapped. 'And don't be croaking near me.'

Shaw left the room, leaving Stanley to sweat out the fever. Finally, at 10 p.m. the fever broke, and Stanley woke to a quiet compound. A single candle flickered in his room. The night air smelled of dry grass and earth, and the only sounds were an occasional snore from the soldiers' room. Fever or not, he decided, in the morning he would leave, venturing into a region that terrified even the natives and Arabs. He felt alone, lying there in the dark, and the sadness of being without a friend in the world washed over him. He had always been afraid of this sadness, and tried to chase it away with positive thoughts as he had done for years.

Writing had become a catharsis on the journey and his journal was the only place he could freely admit his emotions. So he got up and began describing what he felt. 'An unutterable loneliness came on me as I reflected on my position and my intentions, and felt the utter lack of sympathy with me in all around,' he admitted. 'It requires more nerve than I possess to dispel all the dark presentiments that come upon the mind.'

The Arabs' warnings haunted him as he wrote, and he began to wonder if they were trying to deceive him in an attempt to keep him in Tabora. Mirambo had recently been driven back with great losses, but was still too close for Stanley to attempt the main caravan route. Stanley grew defiant in his writing, imagining the Arabs were trying to take advantage of him, just as others had throughout his life. He grew righteous in his desire to prove the Arabs wrong. He heaped contempt upon them for underestimating him. The Arabs had placed themselves squarely in the path of his mission to find Livingstone, depriving him of a job and a future by trying to make him fail. He could see that clearly.

Stanley had grown to hate Tabora. It represented disease in his mind. The taste of medicines like calomel, colycinth, rhubarb, tartar emetic, ipecacuanha and quinine made his stomach turn just thinking of them. Calling it 'inane' and 'repulsive', he was anxious to be going and to leave behind the place that had begun to feel like a jail.

Stanley rededicated himself to his mission. 'I have taken a solemn, enduring oath; an oath to be kept while the least hope of life remains in me,' he railed, 'never to give up the search, until I find Livingstone alive, or until I find his dead body. And never to return home without the strongest possible proofs that he is alive, or that he is dead. No living man, or living men, can stop me. Only death can prevent me.'

It was almost midnight, and Stanley felt weak again from the malaria. He would leave in the morning, no matter how badly he felt. He turned to his journal one last time and wrote emphatically, 'FIND HIM! FIND HIM.' A wave of calm filled Stanley. 'I feel more happy. Have I uttered a prayer? I shall sleep calmly tonight.'

THIRTY

ESCALATION

19 SEPTEMBER 1871
Fort McPherson, Nebraska

THE CAT WAS OUT OF THE BAG. JUST AS LIVINGSTONE REACHED THE WESTERN shore of Lake Tanganyika and Stanley spent his last nights in Tabora, the New York *Herald* printed a Livingstone rumour from its London bureau. The date was 19 September 1871. 'Advices from Zanzibar announce to the receipt of positive intelligence about the fate of Dr Livingstone. The authority of the statement is unquestionable. A party of Americans is hurrying into the interior with the object of rescuing the doctor from his perilous position,' the intentionally vague piece read. As with the byline and source of the information, the rescuer's name was notably missing.

Until then, James Gordon Bennett, Jr had mentioned nothing about Stanley or a rescue mission in the *Herald*. But Henry Rawlinson's 26 June RGS address had broken the secret. The rigid class divisions of Victorian England, which precluded a member of the aristocracy from speaking informally with members of the lower classes, kept Rawlinson's admission within the upper class domain of those attending the meeting. But Livingstone gossip was too delicious to remain secret for long. Maids, butlers, footmen and grooms weren't deaf to their employers' conversations. The rumours about a non-English rescue expedition spread like smoke. When they wafted Bennett's way via his bureau he had no choice but to run the brief mention. Otherwise it was only a matter of time before British papers broke the story. The identity of the 'party of Americans' became a much-discussed mystery in New York and London.

Bennett had a crisis on his hands. There were many layers and tangents to the situation, all of which would have to be handled as a whole for the news leak to be resolved to his advantage. In simplest terms, however, the crisis was about money. For all his free-spending ways, Bennett could be miserly if his bottom line was threatened. The only way he would sell more newspapers was by controlling the news cycle. That would be done by exposing minimal details about the rescue until it actually took place. Mentioning the *Herald*'s involvement or Stanley's name before that time would allow other publishers to cover the story, or open the *Herald* up to ridicule if Stanley failed. And Bennett certainly didn't want a premature leakage of the news to cause Baker to begin racing towards Livingstone.

The greater dilemma was Stanley: Bennett didn't know if he still had the journalist's loyalty. The first bill for the expedition had reached New York in late March. An outraged Bennett took one look at the enormous sum and instructed I. F. Lockevon, a *Herald* accountant, to reject it. 'Please take notice,' Lockevon's letter to Stanley read, 'that a draft drawn by you on James Gordon Bennett Esquire, Jr at Zanzibar January 17, 1871 for 3,750 gold dollars is protested for non-acceptance and that the holders look to you for payment thereof.'

The dismissal, written on 29 March 1871, made sense at the time. The Gould-Fisk Gold Crisis of 1869, the catalyst for Stanley's search, was long forgotten. Bennett and President Grant had become very dear friends. Bennett was the commodore of the New York Yacht Club. The *Herald* was flush. It didn't make sense to pay an outrageous bill by an overzealous correspondent who would likely die somewhere in Africa, thereby wasting thousands of dollars of Bennett's money.

But Stanley was alive, on his way to Livingstone. If Stanley returned safely to Zanzibar he would need to come up with those thousands of dollars in a hurry. The obvious way to accomplish that was selling his stories to the highest bidder – or, in keeping with freelance tradition, to several of the highest bidders. Bennett's great commission would fill the headlines of every paper but his own.

Just like his flight to Paris in 1869, Bennett escaped New York to think. He headed for Nebraska to hunt buffalo at the invitation of the obese General Philip Sheridan, whom Bennett met at President Grant's summer home in Long Branch, New Jersey. Recreational hunting was a fashionable new pastime among the wealthy, copied from the British aristocracy. By hunting on the prairie, Bennett and his cronies were again imitating the British. For in addition to traditional big game expeditions through Africa and India, British sportsmen had become fond of the American West. The first British hunters came as far back as 1855, when Sir George Gore's party killed three thousand buffalo and forty grizzly bear.

Bennett assembled a coterie of New York's most powerful men for the trip west. By coincidence he even brought his own Livingstone – the stockbroker Carol, a member of the New York Livingstons, related to the explorer in name only. Another friend making the trip was Leonard W. Jerome. The 'King of Wall Street' was President Grant's emissary to Germany's Otto von Bismarck. He had just returned from observing the Franco-Prussian War with Sheridan. They even visited Bismarck at Versailles during the siege of Paris in February 1871.

On the night of 16 September, Bennett's band of financiers, generals and executives chugged out of New York's brand new Grand Central Depot in a special railway car – but Bennett himself was not with them. The Stanley crisis needed to be resolved. He waited a day, ordered the story to run, then began the thirty-six-hour train trip to Chicago.

Bennett arrived in Chicago on the morning of Tuesday the nineteenth, at roughly the same time the 'American traveler' story reached New York newsstands. In all, the buffalo caravan numbered seventeen shooters, equally divided between Bennett's peers and Sheridan's. Five greyhounds came along to flush jackrabbits. A French chef prepared all meals. Waiters served the food on china and silverware.

Bennett's caravan moved into the Union Pacific Railroad's superintendent's private car after switching trains for the journey's final leg. The tracks paralleled the north banks of the cottonwood-lined Platte, which was nothing more than a trickle after the summer heat. The prairie was flat and spare. Miles passed without change. As the others read and smoked, Bennett left to ride on the cowcatcher. Wind in his hair, smoke stack just behind him, Bennett's first glimpses of true wilderness came from that steel perch on top of the v-shaped forward tip of a Union Pacific locomotive, squinting into the afternoon Nebraska sun. It was the same territory Stanley had travelled five years earlier in search of glory. Now, nine thousand miles east, Stanley crawled across Africa in a state of near starvation, while Bennett skimmed west across the America frontier like a sultan.

On 22 September 1871 the hunting party disembarked near Fort McPherson, a cavalry outpost at the convergence of the North and South Forks of the Platte. This was where Stanley had nearly been arrested while rafting the Platte with Cook five years before, but the place had changed dramatically. During the Transcontinental Railroad's construction it had become a boomtown, with saloons and brothels and the Railway Hotel springing up. Even after the railroad construction crews continued their westward push, the area remained vibrant – if not so raucous.

Sixteen wagons of provisions awaited Bennett and his companions, including one wagon specially designed to keep champagne iced. They would travel to Fort Hays, ten days' journey south in Kansas. The terrain was sprawling grassland creased by a handful of muddy rivers. There were few settlers. For protection, just in case the Cheyenne and Pawnee violated their peace treaties, 350 soldiers from Company F of the US 5th Cavalry would ride alongside.

As Stanley walked or rode a donkey, fretting about every doti of cloth and watching his subordinates die from malaria, smallpox and elephantiasis, Bennett's caravan proceeded under the guidance of legendary Indian scout Buffalo Bill Cody. 'Tall and somewhat slight in figure,' wrote General Henry Davies in describing Cody, 'possessed of great strength and iron endurance; straight and erect as an arrow, and with strikingly handsome features.'

Cody wasn't impressed by the easterners. The scout with the Vandyke beard and flowing blond hair made fun of his charges by wearing a white buckskin suit fringed in white leather, complete with a white sombrero, a blood-red shirt and a flashy white horse. 'As it was a knobby and high-toned outfit,' Cody wrote, 'I determined to put on a little style myself.'

Bennett wasn't a very good shot. His journey through the wilderness was more a social interlude than an adventure. Every day the caravan rose at three thirty, Cody would lead the 'dudes' in a shot of pre-breakfast bourbon, and the hunting would begin. The drinking began again late each afternoon when the tents were pitched and the waiters began the first course of the evening's seven-course meal. 'Claret, whiskey, brandy, and ale' were staples of the daily menu. So many bottles of champagne were consumed that Cody called the easterners

'The Mumm Tribe' and commented many years later that settlers 'recognized the sites upon which these camps had been constructed by the quantities of empty bottles which remained behind to mark them'.

The caravan reached journey's end at Fort Hays on 2 October 1871. They had travelled 194 miles, and killed six hundred buffalo and two hundred elk. They had eaten prairie dog and fillet of buffalo *aux champignons*, broiled cisco, fried dace and stewed jackrabbit. They had seen the Platte and forded the Republican; hunted along Beaver Creek and Medicine Creek, the Solomon and the Saline. But at Fort Hays they reached the end of the wilderness. It was a land once as wild and untamed as the Africa Stanley was trudging through, but had become civilization.

Fort Hays was the home of Indian fighter General George S. Custer and his 7th Cavalry. It would become the epicentre of the diminished American frontier in a few short years, the original 'wild west' town. Cattle drives from Texas would conclude at the local railhead. Wild Bill Hickok would become sheriff – and would be run out of town for arresting Custer's brother. Legendary showman P. T. Barnum would be suckered out of 150 dollars by local card sharks on his one and only visit, when he came west in search of 'wild men' to populate his circus. However, though bawdy, anarchic and unromantic, Hays was under the governance of a single nation. Its growing pains would form a cohesive national identity once the transition from wilderness to civilization was complete. Africa in 1871, already being nibbled and divided by the British and Germans and Portuguese and Arabs and Italians and French, was being robbed of that potential for a singular identity.

It was near Fort Hays where the caravan's railroad car waited. They rode the Kansas Pacific locomotive home via Kansas City and Chicago. There the men shaved their ten-day beards and bathed, completing their return to civilization. They didn't see the journey as a farce, but as a legitimate adventure. In fact, the *Herald* ran dispatches from Bennett's great journey on 23 and 28 September. Despite the fact that other newspapers lampooned the trip as 'New Yorkers on the warpath', General Davies published an adventure book about the intrepid foray, *Ten Days on the Plains*.

In typical Bennett fashion, the Stanley and Livingstone crisis was solved during his time away from New York. Bennett needed Stanley on his side, and knew the financial rewards from the circulation boost brought on by the exclusive story of Stanley finding Livingstone would outweigh the expedition's exorbitant cost. Also, with the New York *Times* gaining readership through their groundbreaking investigation of deep-seated crime and corruption in New York's Tammany Hall, Bennett couldn't afford to be cautious. If Bennett refused to pay Stanley's bills there was a real possibility Stanley could compound the New York *Times*'s advantage by selling the Livingstone story there.

On 22 September, from Fort McPherson, even before climbing into the saddle to begin the hunt, Bennett sent a wire to New York authorizing payment for all of Stanley's expenses. The telegraph was relayed to London, where the message was passed on to Zanzibar on 25 September. Bennett could only hope Stanley received the news before selling the Livingstone story elsewhere.

Then, taking charge of the Livingstone news cycle, Bennett began a build-up to the day he would, he hoped, publish Stanley's stories. The *Herald*'s editorial columns began running news about East Africa. The writing was informative, introducing the public to men like Kirk and reacquainting them with Livingstone.

When it came to Stanley, however, Bennett hadn't received a word of copy since the reporter sailed from India a year earlier. He could only pay the bills and hope for a return on his investment.

THIRTY-ONE

THE UNKNOWN

20 SEPTEMBER 1871
Tabora
250 miles from Livingstone

STANLEY CONTRACTED SMALLPOX IN THE MIDDLE OF SEPTEMBER, BUT HE WAS determined to leave Tabora, regardless. After a brief few days of fever and bed rest, Stanley finally marched his lean caravan from Tabora on 20 September. His route from Tabora to Ujiji was simple on paper: 150 miles south-west from Tabora, then 150 miles north-west, 90 miles north, then 70 miles slightly north-west again – 460 miles in all. Most important, it would theoretically be outside of Mirambo's reach. The only thing Stanley knew about the terrain itself was its reputation for being forested and sometimes swampy, and he also knew that the Arabs predicted his death.

Stanley mounted his donkey and led his men out of Tabora. The Stars and Stripes were flying, guns were fired, the men were laughing and shouting, all happy to be on the move. Only the Arabs and Shaw were distraught to see the caravan's three months in Tabora come to an end. As a show of their displeasure, and to reinforce their belief that Stanley's precious cloth and beads would be wasted when he died, the Arabs commandeered Livingstone's relief supplies. They forbade the bundles of cloth and the porters from leaving Tabora. Stanley, though outraged, was also eager to leave Tabora. Rather than let the issue delay his departure, he merely argued that denying Livingstone his mail was inhumane. The Arabs agreed. A single porter was allowed to join Stanley's march, carrying nothing but Livingstone's letters.

Looking on with dour expressions, remonstrating with him for forcing Shaw to travel, the Arabs stood to one side and said goodbye to Stanley. The temperature on the shadeless plain was over one hundred degrees.

'Farewell,' Stanley cried to the Arabs, tipping his hat. Shaw, who had relapsed in the night, could barely stay on his donkey. It was with reluctance that he spurred his animal forward. With that, the New York *Herald* expedition moved from the safety and luxury of Tabora back into the wilderness. For the first time in their entire journey, they were marching into a place no other caravan or expedition had ever travelled to.

Before they had even left the Arabs behind, however, Mabruki, one of the new guides, playfully goosed Shaw's donkey with a stick. The animal bolted and tossed the hapless sailor into a bush with inch-long thorns.

The Arabs rushed forward to help Shaw, running across the dusty flat field in their flowing white robes, verbally abusing Stanley for making a sick man travel. And though they called him cruel and stubborn, Stanley was through with listening to them. He dismounted, lifted Shaw off the ground and hoisted the dying sailor onto his donkey once again. 'Pluck up,' Stanley cried sarcastically as he walked back to his donkey, ignoring Shaw's moaning and the Arabs' accusations. 'Courage.'

All went well most of that first day. Instead of pushing the pace up front, Stanley rode at the rear to help Shaw. The rest of the caravan surged ahead on their forced march and they made good time. But as Stanley came over a small ridge and spotted the night's camp in the distance, his American flag flying in the midst of a grove of rice paddies and plantains, his fever returned. He collapsed into his hammock at the campsite and covered himself in his bearskin. Caused by the variola virus, smallpox's incubation period is twelve days. Thirty per cent of all people who develop the fever, fatigue, headaches, backaches and lesions brought on by smallpox die. Interestingly, it is spread from one person to another by the spray of infected saliva during face-to-face contact. Stanley most likely contracted it in those moments with Shaw, standing over the bed and berating him to rise.

That night, as Shaw nursed his wounds from repeatedly falling off his donkey and Stanley went to bed with fever, the remaining porters sat around the campfire discussing what the next day would bring. There was much quiet talk of desertion. Though Tabora was just a few miles behind, the broad, sunny plains were about to be replaced by the thick and dismal forest they had heard so much about. Stanley had paid a portion of their inflated salaries before departure, and given out guns and ammunition, so if they deserted they could run back home with a small amount of wealth. On the other hand, the law stipulated that Stanley would be able to exact a punishment on his way back from Ujiji when he stopped in Tabora once again.

The scared porters argued silently. Stanley wasn't likely to be coming back, they guessed. He would die for certain. Not even a massive man like Asmani could protect a fifty-four-man caravan if a tribal force of a thousand attacked. Deserting before the journey went on too much longer seemed almost prudent compared with becoming another set of bleached bones whose meat had been picked clean by hyenas.

Twenty porters ran off that night. Stanley found out the next morning when he rose, determined to ignore his fever and continue forward. He flew into a rage. Selecting twenty of his most faithful men, he dispatched them back to Tabora to round up the deserters. Selim the servant was also sent back to Tabora and told to buy a slave chain from the Arabs. 'Towards night my twenty detectives returned with nine of the missing men,' Stanley wrote. 'Selim also returned with a strong chain capable of imprisoning within the collars attached to it, ten men. Kaif-Halek also appeared with the letter bag which he was to convey to Livingstone under my escort. The men were then addressed, and the slave chain exhibited to them. I told them I was the first white man who had taken a slave chain with him on his travels. But, as they were all so frightened of accompanying me, I was obliged to make use of it, as it was the only means of keeping them together. The good never fear being chained by me – only the deserters, the thieves, who received their hire and presents and guns and ammunition and ran away.'

Nevertheless, two more men tested Stanley that night. After standing around in 108 degree heat waiting for Bombay to hunt down the deserters, Stanley had the men flogged and chained.

Morale in the camp had plummeted fast in the few short days since leaving Tabora, and Stanley seemed to be losing control. Men begged Stanley to be released from their contracts. Some, like Kasegra Saleem, were released on grounds of sickness (Saleem was vomiting from one end and passing worms out of the other). Another, Abdul the tailor, had been a burden since Bagamoyo. He was allowed to leave because Stanley had grown tired of his whining. Finally, Stanley wondered whether it was time to turn around and go back. 'The fates had determined on our return,' he wrote.

But Stanley struggled on. When the caravan reached the village of Kigandu on 24 September, four days into the trek, he was taunted by the natives for his refusal to fight Mirambo and called a coward. The villagers demanded cloth in exchange for permission to pass through their territory. Stanley wouldn't pay, so he and his men were forced to sleep in an area a mile outside the village infested by rats. There, Shaw fell hard getting off his donkey, but was so weak from the sleeping sickness that he simply dozed off where he hit the ground rather than rise to go to his tent.

Stanley looked at this friend, and finally felt pity. 'Do you wish to go back, Mr Shaw?' he said wearily.

'If you please,' Shaw replied. 'I do not believe I can go any farther.'

'Well, Mr Shaw, I have come to the conclusion that it is best that you should return. My patience is worn out.' Stanley warned Shaw that he would die if he returned to Tabora, for there would be no one to take care of him, but the sailor's mind was made up.

'I wish I had never ventured to come,' Shaw admitted. 'I thought life in Africa was so different from this.'

The travellers' last night together was spent mournfully. Sitting around a campfire while Shaw played 'Home Sweet Home' on a cheap accordion he'd carried since Zanzibar, they celebrated their friendship. 'We had mutually softened towards each other,' Stanley wrote. He was sure Shaw would die, and it was hard saying goodbye. Shaw, on the other hand, was planning on recovering and marching back to the coast. His heart was light. 'Home Sweet Home' wasn't a lament, but anticipation.

The next morning, Stanley gave Shaw a canteen of tea, a leg of lamb and a loaf of bread, then placed him in a litter to be carried back to Tabora. It would take two men to carry him. Their regular loads would be carried by Shaw's donkey. Stanley ordered the trumpet sounded and the flags raised then formed the men into two lines. His good friend Shaw was leaving, and he wanted it done in style. The sailor was carried between the two rows in a sign of respect and farewell. He and Stanley said a solemn goodbye, wishing each other well. Then they went in opposite directions to meet their fates.

After all was said and done, their parting was a relief to Stanley, too. 'Shaw was borne away to the north, while we fled to the south, with quicker and more elastic steps as if we felt a great incubus had been taken from us,' Stanley wrote.

Even before Shaw's departure Stanley had imagined what it would be like to emulate Livingstone in his travels. 'With the illustrious example of Livingstone travelling by himself before me, I was asking myself, Would it not be just as well for me to try to do the same thing?'

Without Shaw, Stanley ignored his own weakened condition and fairly raced for Ujiji. His pace increased from one mile an hour to three. The journey was into its seventh month. In Stanley's mind, Livingstone was most definitely in Ujiji. He wasn't thinking beyond that. He couldn't. He barely had the resolve to make it to Ujiji. Finding the strength to go further into Africa, or to wander indefinitely searching for the good doctor, was unthinkable.

As it was, the new trail was a challenge unlike any other Stanley had faced so far. The danger of Africa had increased by increments since leaving Bagamoyo, but in the wilderness south-west of Tabora it was as if a Pandora's box of Africa's most violent hardships was opened. Clouds of tse-tse flies and sword flies had the men constantly swatting the air and flapping their arms. The heat was relentless in its intensity, like a flame being applied to the men's skin. Rotting vegetation was sometimes poisonous when inhaled. Dead bodies of natives who had died of smallpox littered the side of the trail. Guerrilla warriors roamed the countryside, and villages were fortified for war, surrounded by fences of three-inch-thick wooden poles lashed tightly together, with special platforms for sharpshooters to see over the top.

Yet in the hardship, Stanley knew a strange peace. Africa became him, despite its dangers. Stanley took a proprietary interest in Africa, and thought of the land as his own. 'I felt momentarily proud,' he admitted in his journal after revelling in a 'romantic' vista, 'that I owned such a vast domain.'

He embraced that sense of ownership, and like the need to find Livingstone, it gave him courage. The porters were born and raised in Africa, yet were uncomfortable in the wilderness and pressed forward reluctantly. But Stanley rejoiced in each day's march, and in merely being in Africa. Unable to procure cigars, he had taken to smoking a white clay pipe at the end of each day to watch the sun set. 'Colours of gold and silver, saffron and opal, when its rays and gorgeous tints were reflected upon the tops of the everlasting forest, with the quiet and holy calm of heaven,' he wrote of the sunsets.

In those hours, listening to the men smoking their gourd pipes around the campfire and hearing the chirp of crickets, Stanley also became anxious about Livingstone. 'We are both on the same soil, perhaps in the same forest – who knows? – yet he is so far removed from me,' Stanley wrote.

The worries disappeared during the day, especially when in early October the thick forest gave way to a grassland where game of all variety waited to be felled for the cooking pot. On 4 October the expedition began a three-day halt along the Gombe River to hunt and regroup. After two weeks of travel, they had walked over two hundred miles but were still unable to shake their fear of the land through which they were walking. That its beauty and providence were equal to its dangers made no difference.

The men didn't like it that Stanley's demand for a brisk pace left them exhausted at the end of each day, and Stanley hoped rest and fresh meat in their stomachs would rekindle the men's morale. Buffalo, zebra and antelope fed the caravan, and the porters were briefly happy. Stanley found himself in conflict over the killing, however. Fresh meat was a precious commodity, for protein was hard to come by on the trail. But he marvelled at the animals' beauty and majesty, and it pained him to shoot a zebra and see it rear up on its hind legs in shock, then collapse and have its head sliced off by the natives. 'Ah, it is such a pity. But hasten, draw the keen sharp-edged knife across the beautiful stripes which fold around the throat. And – what an ugly gash! It is done.'

Immediately after that particular kill, Stanley walked alone to the banks of the Gombe and stripped for a swim. He was in a pensive mood and wanted to be alone. The Gombe meandered slowly past, its waters green and languid. Lotus leaves floated on the surface and it reminded Stanley of something from a summer dream.

He relaxed as he stepped into the warm water. There wasn't an ounce of fat on his body any more, just sinewy muscle. Stanley stretched then brought his hands together in front of him to dive into the deep waters. 'My attention was attracted by an enormously long body which shot into view, occupying the spot beneath the surface that I was about to explore. Great heavens, it was a crocodile!' he wrote that night. Africa had soothed him and calmed him and made him feel as if he were its master. But it was a myth. The continent had no equal. He took the crocodile as a reminder to 'never again be tempted by the treacherous calm'.

His heart beating, Stanley hastily grabbed his clothes and retreated from the river bank to dress. He walked back to camp slowly, composing himself, then ate a hearty meal of zebra steak as the moon rose. He hunted again the next day, and the next. By the time their three days had come to an end, Stanley and his men had killed two buffaloes, two wild boar, a hartebeest, a zebra, an impala and several birds. The bounty was so overwhelming that it couldn't all be eaten before breaking camp. Stanley selected a group of porters to cut and dry the uneaten meat for the miles ahead. The new guides, Asmani and Mabruki, told of over one hundred miles of barren wilderness to come, where game would be hard to find and there were no villages for purchasing food. The crocodile encounter had been a grim reminder that Stanley needed to be prepared for anything. Loading up on food stores could save their lives.

On the morning of Saturday, 7 October, the New York *Herald* expedition broke camp and prepared to leave the hunting ground behind. They faced three more days of long marches to the south-west before turning north and making haste for Ujiji, and the men were deeply unhappy. They had liked their three-day rest and loathed the idea of pressing forward. They wanted to stay near the game one last day, continuing their hunting, feasting and relaxation.

Just as the march was to begin, Bombay approached Stanley. He had been designated the group's spokesman and would now break the news that the men refused to march. The short man was unafraid of Stanley, and had shown it repeatedly throughout the journey by silently absorbing the lashings Stanley inflicted upon him with a dog whip. Bombay requested the extra day of rest, and without hesitation Stanley berated him for even broaching the subject. There would be no rest, he furiously stated. At that, Bombay's face, normally the picture of accommodation, turned mean. He shoved his lower lip out in a display of contempt then turned his back on Stanley and delivered the news to the men.

The entire camp watched them in silence. As Bombay walked off, Stanley barked for the horn to be blown, signalling the start of the march. More silence followed, though some of the men were obediently stooping down to pick up their loads. Asmani's voice wafted across the campsite, shouting to Mabruki that he was sorry he'd taken on the journey.

Insolently, angrily, the porters shouldered their loads and their bare feet padded down the trail. Fearing desertions, Stanley rode at the rear of the caravan when it finally got under way. Selim was nearby with a shotgun and pistols, should Stanley need them.

Only a mile later, the men threw their bales to the ground. The caravan lurched to a dead halt. The men formed into small groups and began arguing, as if contemplating something sinister. Stanley dismounted. 'Taking my double-barrel gun from Selim's shoulder, I selected a dozen charges of buckshot and, slipping two of them into the barrels and adjusting my revolvers in order for handy work, I walked on towards them. I noticed that the men seized their guns as I advanced,' he wrote that evening.

The soldiers were there to protect Stanley, but there was no telling how they might behave after Stanley and Bombay's falling-out. The soldiers, however, ceased being the centre of Stanley's concerns. He spied two men trying to hide behind a set of earthen ramparts, but the hiding place was too small – their heads and the barrels of their guns stuck out. 'Come forward and talk to me or I will blow your heads off,' Stanley shouted. He levelled his shotgun in their direction and took careful aim.

To Stanley's shock, Asmani and Mabruki rose and began walking towards him. Asmani smirked as he walked. The fingers of his right hand tickled the trigger of his rifle.

'Drop your gun or I will kill you instantly,' Stanley shouted.

Asmani dropped the gun, but his smirk remained. 'His eyes shone the lurid light of murder,' Stanley noted, 'as ever it shone in a villain's eyes.'

Stanley was almost a foot smaller than Asmani. He studied the guide's eyes and body language, looking for a sign of what would happen next.

Asmani gave nothing away. But behind Stanley came the sound of a powder being carefully loaded into a musket. He spun around with his gun chest-high, and was shocked to see that Mabruki had crept around behind him. Just four feet away, the guide was preparing to fire. 'Drop your gun instantly,' Stanley demanded, then reminded both men that his smooth bore could fire off twenty-four shots to their one.

As Mabruki complied, Stanley jabbed him hard in the sternum with his own gun. Mabruki flew backwards, buying Stanley the time to confront Asmani, who had bent down to retrieve his gun. 'Put the gun down,' Stanley ordered nervously, fingers on the trigger. Asmani would not. He slowly raised it towards Stanley's face.

Stanley was about to shoot – wanted to shoot, if only to set an example. If he couldn't intimidate Asmani, his power was ended. But just as he was about to fire, a soldier came from behind and knocked away the big man's gun. 'How dare you point your gun at the master?' he said incredulously.

Watching this, Mabruki realized his foolishness. He threw himself at Stanley's feet and began kissing them, then demanded that Asmani apologize – which he did. Stanley had them both thrown in chains.

For good measure, Stanley beat Bombay about the shoulders with a spear. Stanley was becoming like Livingstone in so many positive ways – except his inability to treat subordinates with respect.

THIRTY-TWO

KIRK LEARNS THE TRUTH

22 SEPTEMBER 1871
Zanzibar

JOHN KIRK WAS IN A STATE OF PANIC. MESSENGERS FROM THE INTERIOR HAD just arrived, carrying newspaper dispatches written by Henry Morton Stanley. The American, it turned out, was more than a mere traveller; he was a journalist, and in search of Livingstone. American Consul F. R. Webb had gleefully shown Kirk portions of Stanley's initial dispatch. Stanley was reporting that war in Tabora had stopped all caravans – including Livingstone's relief supplies. Once word reached New York, then London, it was inevitable that blame for Livingstone not receiving his supplies would fall squarely upon Kirk. It was vital that Kirk proactively state his case.

'My Lord,' Kirk wrote to Foreign Secretary Earl Granville on 22 September. 'Letters just received by special messengers who left Unyanyembe about a month ago, inform us of a sad disaster . . . I am indebted to Mr Webb, the American Consul here, for some details related in those letters, which will, no doubt, be published in full elsewhere.'

Though Stanley's first story was a nuts and bolts preview of the actual expedition, detailing caravan logistics and apologizing for spending so much of Bennett's money, it was clear that Stanley was leaving no stone unturned. There was a very good chance Kirk's name would eventually make it into print for failure to expedite Livingstone's relief supplies. Even worse, however, was that Mirambo had just closed the trail to Ujiji. Kirk knew that the supplies would have got through if he had done his job properly. In a second letter, written three days later, Kirk assured Sir Roderick Murchison there would be little chance of British embarrassment at the hands of Stanley. 'His prospect of getting on is at present small,' Kirk wrote on 25 September. 'But I cannot really say where he desires to go to. He never disclosed his plans to me,' Kirk wrote. Then Kirk signed off by pleading, 'Believe me.'

Unfortunately for Kirk, Murchison would never receive the letter. The acting British Consul to Zanzibar would have to weather the Stanley crisis on his own.

THIRTY-THREE

THE VALLEY OF DEATH

7 OCTOBER 1871
South of the Malagarasi River
160 miles from Livingstone

A LITTLE WILD-EYED, A LITTLE WEARY, A LITTLE PARANOID, STANLEY WAS IN control. The caravan moved forward. Above the treetops, hills could occasionally be seen on the horizon. When the caravan finally ascended the hills and carefully picked its way down the far side, Stanley noted with pleasure that the slopes were westward facing, and took it as a sign that Lake Tanganyika was getting closer. The vegetation changed from mere woodland trees to thick orchards of mbembu fruit, which tasted like a peach. Tamarind seeds and wild plums were abundant, as were game birds for the cooking pot. Only the sight of shiny white human skulls adorning the gates of a local village detracted from the Eden-like atmosphere.

The terrain changed daily as they pushed further off the beaten path: undulating plains pocked with brackish pools of water; steep mountains; marshes heavy with water, making every step a test of stamina. One forty-mile stretch was nothing but swamp, just like the Makata so many months before.

On 10 October, as Stanley's caravan made camp, a small band of natives came past. When they heard where Stanley was leading his men they shook their heads and guaranteed the group was marching to its death unless it changed course. The land ahead had become Mirambo's latest battlefield, and the warfare was intense.

One of the few times on his journey, Stanley actually took advice. He altered his course to Ujiji once again, choosing to push into rugged country to the north-west. The land was low-lying and riven with streams. Forests of mvule, sycamore and gigantic tamarind trees lined the water. Thick bushes and grass as tall as a man covered the ground. Stanley didn't need to be told that lions and leopards lived in the tall grass. That was a given in Africa. But Africa delivered a reminder anyway. On their first day on the new course, walking a thin trail, a leopard attacked one of the donkeys. It leapt from a place of camouflage and dug its fangs into the donkey's neck. Leopards are known for being fierce fighters, preferring to press an attack than back down. But the donkeys brayed so loudly in panic that the leopard fled.

The big cats came back again that night. As the New York *Herald* expedition sat around the fire, surrounded by their protective fencing of thorn bushes they'd arranged around the camp, a pride of lions surrounded them. All night long their low growls shook the camp. The porters were terrified. 'Our camps by these thick belts of timber,' Stanley wrote with understatement, 'my men never fancied.'

Stanley thought the land was prettier by day than any he'd ever seen, comparing it with the golden hills of northern California. As they pushed on through the woodland, he marvelled that such a vast swathe of land was unpopulated. He predicted that eventually, once everywhere on earth was developed, mankind would return to Africa. He'd seen the same happen in California, and on the Great Plains. There was no reason Africa couldn't be the scene of similar civilization.

That love affair came and went, depending upon Stanley's relationship with his men on any given day. He was tired of yelling at them, of enduring their laziness and always having to watch his back. He was tired, in a word, of being alone. 'It is much the result of fatigue and monotony, every day being such a repetition of previous days,' he wrote. There was an uncertainty to the days, too. Without villages at regular intervals, or a predictable supply of game, finding food was always a priority. Armies travel on their stomachs, and Stanley's caravan was an extreme version of that maxim. His men were travelling great distances, carrying tremendous loads, over almost virgin terrain. Some days they had their bellies full, but sometimes their hunger slowed the caravan's pace.

That was the case as Stanley's men pushed out of the woodlands. They had four days' worth of provisions to reach the Malagarasi River, a wide, powerful flow that fed Lake Tanganyika. Reaching the Malagarasi would be a symbol that their dangerous journey was almost complete.

The problem, however, was that the country was getting too rugged for rapid travel. 'The scenery was getting more and more sublime every day as we advanced northwards, even approaching the terrible. We seemed to have left the monotony of a desert for the wild, picturesque scenery of Abyssinia and the terrible mountains of the Sierra Nevada's,' Stanley wrote.

After four days, the Malagarasi was nowhere in sight. The caravan's mood turned quiet. Many of the men were so weak they lacked the strength to talk. Stanley compared it with being shipwrecked. 'Bleached and bare,' he wrote of the landscape, 'it was cut up by a thousand deep ravines and intersected with a thousand dry water courses whose beds were filled with immense sandstone rocks and boulders washed away from the great heights.' Their only food was the peach-like mbembu they had collected by the bagful. The fruit gave them energy and fibre, but the lack of protein brought forth a breakdown in muscle mass and rapid weight loss. The overabundance of fructose caused an osmotic pull within their bodies, giving rise to severe watery diarrhoea. And that, as the fluids gushed precipitously from their bodies, also brought about dehydration.

There was no more forest to protect them from the heat, and no water sources with which to replenish the lost fluids. Their dehydration grew worse. Thirst ravaged every man. As the crow flew, the New York *Herald* expedition was less than a hundred miles from Ujiji. But with the daunting landscape and their pace slowed by lack of food and water, it might as well have been a thousand.

Stanley pressed the march, sure that the Malagarasi was just over the next ridge. But instead of finding relief, the party found the terrain more and more rugged and geometric – rounded cones of sandstone, loose haematite underfoot, fissures and pyramids of red ochre, long narrow deep ravines with disintegrating rock overhead. There was no vegetation. The soldiers prayed to Allah for relief and lions roared outside camp in the night. Stanley took solace in the notion that, while the caravan's situation was dire, there had been few moments since leaving the coast when it had not been so.

On 29 October, five weeks since leaving Tabora and their seventh day without food, the caravan came upon the deserted remains of a village. A jungle stream flowed nearby. In the shade of a giant sycamore Stanley ordered a halt. 'The people were very hungry. They had eaten every scrap of meat, and every grain they possessed,' Stanley wrote, 'and there were no prospects for food. I had but one pound and a half of flour left, and this would not have sufficed to begin to feed a force of over forty-five people. But I had something like thirty pounds of tea, and twenty pounds of sugar left. And I at once, as soon as we arrived at camp, ordered every kettle to be filled and placed on the fire, and then made tea for all, giving each man a quart of hot, grateful beverage.'

Africa taunted them as they rose before dawn and began the desperate search for food. Rhino tracks and buffalo droppings were everywhere, but there was no sight of any living thing. Their descent down the watershed continued, though instead of vast chasms they were travelling down short steep gullies. The air began to get humid as the terrain took on a greenish hue, and Stanley knew water was close. Two more hours of hiking led them into a long lush valley, with a forest at the far end. Most wondrous of all, the trail took the caravan into the midst of a cornfield. The stalks were bare, but the field's presence meant a village was near. Desperately scanning the ridgeline for some sign of life, Stanley spotted fortifications on top of a nearby mountain. And even before he could make camp and send men upwards with bales for trade, the villagers were rushing down to the expedition laden with meat and grain. Stanley broke out the cloth. Soon 'the men's jaws', Stanley noted with relief, 'were busy in the process of mastication'.

The chief of the village, however, was a sharp trader. His name was Rusunzu. His isolated location left him few opportunities to showcase his skill, but he more than made up for that by extorting as much cloth from Stanley as possible. During an afternoon of haggling, Rusunzu demanded ten doti for the amount of food Stanley purchased. Stanley was ferocious in his refusal. Rusunzu then stated that the cloth wasn't to pay for the food, but tribute for the privilege of continuing through his land.

Stanley had a hard time arguing with that. But he was also running out of cloth, and even small tribute payments needed to be avoided whenever possible. By the end of the day, worn down by Rusunzu's haggling, Stanley agreed to pay seven and a half doti. When it was learned that two tribes were at war in the swampy morass between the village and the Malagarasi, Stanley was also forced to hire two of

Rusunzu's men as guides in order to show him an alternative route.

It was 31 October when Stanley travelled onwards again. In America, Cochise and his Apache warriors were being hunted in the Arizona Territory, Chicago had just been destroyed by fire, and President Grant was about to issue a proclamation making the Ku Klux Klan illegal. In England, Darwin's *Descent of Man* was just days away from publication. In Paris, the first exhibition of impressionist painting was about to get under way. If Stanley were back in the world, he would likely have been covering one of those events for the *Herald* with great gusto and self-importance. But those happenings were just the peripheral sounds of a civilization trying to make sense of itself compared with Stanley's ongoing need to find food and water for himself and his men. His focus was on surviving, not embellishing his existence.

Marching east north-east, the expedition came upon a broad green meadow framed by sheer cliffs. But as they got closer, they found a phenomenon unlike anything any expedition member had encountered. The 'meadow' wasn't land at all. It was a vast bridge of vegetation formed by thick swamp grasses that had knitted together. Beneath the bridge flowed a black river a mile wide and of unknown depth. As Stanley and his men wondered how in the world they were going to get forty-five expedition members plus laden donkeys across, the guides didn't help matters any by pointing out that the bridge of vegetation had once collapsed as a traveller was passing through. The traveller, his donkey, thirty-five slaves and sixteen tusks of ivory fell into the crocodile-filled river and were never seen again.

Stanley stayed back to make sure all of his men found the courage to cross. He marvelled at the odd shapes the grass took when men and material passed over – undulating wave-like in some spots, while another section looked 'like a small lake buffeted by a squall'. More ominous, as Stanley took his first tentative steps onto the grass it sank until water rose above his ankles. The river, it seemed, was not as far below as Stanley had thought.

Carefully, slowly, the New York *Herald* expedition crossed to the other side. He bought goats from a village nearby and slaughtered eight that night in celebration. A week after they supposed they would find it, the Malagarasi was still nowhere to be seen. Stanley sensed, however, that it was getting near.

They came upon the river the next morning. Villages lined its banks, and fish-eating birds could be seen in the shallows. The Malagarasi, it turned out, wasn't a particularly wide river, but it was deep and filled with so many crocodiles that their heads dotted the surface as far as the eye could see. The men and material would have to be ferried across. Knowing this, the local sultan, Nzogera, demanded so much cloth that Stanley feared he would become bankrupt. Fifty-six doti were demanded by Nzogera, and only for the privilege of passing through his land. The cost of ferrying the expedition by canoe was extra. Stanley refused to pay. He sent Bombay and Asmani to negotiate with the Sultan.

All through the night of 1 November, Bombay and Asmani argued. No sooner would an agreement be made and payment be extended, than the Sultan would find another reason to demand payment. Ultimately, Stanley had to pay almost an entire bale of cloth to Nzogera – and still he had to pay the owners of the small canoes that would ferry the expedition across the river, four men to a boat. More beads and cloth were doled out. The river men, after taking one group of men across, then demanded another payment for returning to ferry a second group. After that payment was made, the process continued each of the three times the canoes ferries men across. Finally, at sunset, almost everyone was across except the two donkeys. They would cross one at a time. Knowing they wouldn't fit in the canoes, Stanley's men would sit in the canoe holding the donkey by a halter as the animal swam alongside. The first donkey to attempt the crossing was a favourite of Stanley's, a wild Kinyamwezi named Simba – 'lion' in Swahili. Halfway across, Stanley was horrified to see Simba attacked on the throat by a swarm of crocodiles. Even as Stanley's men fought to drag Simba across the river, the crocodiles clamped down hard on the donkey's face and neck, then dragged it under. Simba never kicked its way back to the surface, never fought free of the crocodile. It simply slipped under and was never seen again. 'We had seen the light-brown heads, the glittering eyes and the ridgy backs, hovering about the vicinity,' a horrified Stanley wrote, 'but we never thought the beast would advance so near such an exciting scene as the vicinity of the ferry during the crossing.'

The other donkey would go across with Bombay the next morning, a time when the crocodiles were traditionally absent from the river.

As they waited for dawn, an uncharacteristic wave of sadness swept over the caravan. Despite their fear and mutinies in the early days, the entire group – animals included – had endured Stanley's wilderness together. The early tensions were being replaced by camaraderie. The end was near, or so it seemed. To watch the gruesome carnage of Simba's death was a reminder that the same could happen to anyone at any time. That sadness stayed with them all night long.

The next morning, however, any trace of melancholy vanished. Stanley received confirmation that a white man was in Ujiji.

THIRTY-FOUR

LOOKING FOR A SAMARITAN

8 OCTOBER 1871
Ujiji

HIS PAIN THRESHOLD WAS INCREDIBLE AND HIS ENDURANCE REMARKABLE, but when Livingstone finally reached Lake Tanganyika on 8 October, his will was shattered. He wrote, simply, 'I was reduced to a skeleton.'

The continued failure to complete his mission was breaking Livingstone. The Source had been left behind. His physical condition and the Arab–Manyuema hostilities meant he would not return any time soon – if ever. 'The mind, sorely depressed, reacted on the body,' he wrote on the lake's bank. All around him slave and ivory traders were heading back to Ujiji, then on to Bagamoyo, crowing about their successful missions. 'I alone had failed and experienced worry, thwarting, baffling, when almost in the sight of the end towards which I had strained.'

He set about finding a canoe for the paddle across to Ujiji, where his stores waited for him. He could purchase food, new shoes and new supplies. He would relax and regroup. After months of being dependent upon the Arabs, then after two long months trekking from Nyangwe to Lake Tanganyika, Livingstone would relish not being beholden to anyone.

As had happened the last time, two years and eight months earlier, there were no stores waiting once Livingstone finally reached Ujiji.

254

Sherif, an Arab trader and friend of Kirk's, had picked through the calico and beads. Most appalling was Sherif's unrepentant attitude. He adorned his slaves in fine clothes purchased with Livingstone's goods. And Sherif 'came without shame to shake hands with me, and, when I refused, assumed an air of displeasure as having been badly treated'. Sherif taunted Livingstone with a good luck salutation twice a day, until Livingstone had had enough. 'If I were an Arab,' the venerable Scot swore to Sherif, 'I would have your hand and both ears cut off for thieving.'

Sherif had given the explorer a wide berth after that, but it didn't matter. Livingstone was destitute. He faced either becoming a beggar or starving to death, and he simply refused to align himself with the Arabs again or rely on their charity. After the massacre, they couldn't be trusted. And though they came to him and offered gifts of ivory for him to sell, Livingstone turned them down. He spent his days in Ujiji inside his small house, praying for deliverance and mentally preparing for the day his food would run out and he would be reduced to begging. He could see the lake clearly, with the fishing boats travelling out each dusk and returning home at dawn. 'I made up my mind to wait until men should come from the coast,' he had written in the hope that the British Consul would send more supplies from Zanzibar. 'But to wait in beggary was what I never contemplated, and now I felt miserable.'

Livingstone had finally admitted something he'd never admitted before: he needed rescue.

That possibility, however, looked bleak. To the west, from where he'd just come, the Arabs and Africans were beginning hostilities. To the east, towards Tabora, Mirambo was waging a massive campaign against the Arabs. No one in Ujiji could ever remember warfare on such an enormous scale. There was no way for supplies to reach Livingstone from either direction.

'I felt, in my destitution, as if I were the man who went down from Jerusalem to Jericho, and fell among thieves. But I could not hope for priest, Levite or good Samaritan to come by on either side,' Livingstone wrote.

Clearly unbeknown to Livingstone, his rescuer was closing in on Ujiji.

THIRTY-FIVE

FOUND

3 NOVEMBER 1871
Isinga
80 miles from Livingstone

'NEAR ISINGA MET A CARAVAN OF EIGHTY WAGUHHA DIRECT FROM UJIJI, bearing oil and bound for Unyanyembe. They report that a white man was left by them five days ago at Ujiji. He had the same colour as I have, wears the same shoes, the same clothes, and has hair on his face like I have, only his is white. This is Livingstone. Hurrah for Ujiji!'

Stanley's ecstatic thoughts on 3 November were a compendium of the haste, excitement and even trepidation beating in his heart. 'This is Livingstone! He must be Livingstone! He *can* be no other. But still, he may be someone else – someone from the West Coast. Or perhaps he is Baker! No; Baker has no white hair on his face, but we must now march quick, lest he hears we are coming, and runs away,' Stanley wrote, suddenly eager to be there instantly. 'I was madly rejoiced, intensely eager to resolve the burning question: is it Dr David Livingstone? God grant me patience, but I do wish there was a railroad.'

Setting aside the impossibility of finding a train to speed him quickly into Ujiji, Stanley brought the men together and asked if they would be willing to march nonstop for that town. The reward for their efforts, he promised, would be an extra doti. To a man, they agreed. Even as he made the offer, Stanley's thoughts were going back to the very start of the journey, when both his bay and his grey Arabian had died within fifteen hours of each other. 'With a horse,' Stanley thought, 'I could reach Ujiji in about twelve hours.'

As close as it seemed, however, Ujiji was still eighty miles away. The terrain was mostly gullied woodland tilting ever so slightly downhill as the watershed searched for Lake Tanganyika. The soil was rich and red. Banana and mango trees grew in small groves. Rocks and marshes littered the trail like so much natural debris. All in all, the roadblocks to his journey's final steps were considerable. But Stanley set aside thoughts of horses and began the final push. The men were uplifted, and marched without fear. If all went well, Stanley estimated they could be there in fifty hours.

Africa, however, had never made the going easy for Stanley. The last leg of his journey would be no different. Just three hours after leaving the Malagarasi River, Stanley passed through countryside that reminded him of the Nebraska prairie. Villages seemed to be everywhere, comprised of mud huts shaped like beehives. The equatorial sun bleached the grass white. It was while travelling through a village so large it had small suburbs surrounding it that the New York *Herald* expedition was halted by a large group of warriors. They were members of the hostile Ha tribe.

'How dare you pass by without paying tribute to the King of Uhha?' Stanley was asked imperiously.

'We have paid it,' Stanley sputtered.

'To whom?'

'To the Chief of Kawanga.'

The Chief of Kawanga, it turned out, had kept the tribute for himself. Stanley was in a new territory. The warriors ordered Stanley to rest his caravan in their village until tribute was paid.

But Stanley was through dealing with the vagaries of tribute and in no mood to stop his caravan until reaching Ujiji. Under the blazing sun that had become such a regular part of his day, he forced his caravan to stand in the middle of the road as he sorted the matter out. After a series of emissaries had challenged Stanley in the name of the King, a regal young man clad in a crimson toga, a turban and an ivory necklace sauntered over. 'The gorgeously dressed chief was a remarkable man in appearance,' Stanley wrote. 'His face was oval in form, high cheekbones, eyes deeply sunk, a prominent and bold forehead, a fine nose and a well-cut mouth. He was tall in figure and perfectly symmetrical.'

The chief was Mionvu, of the Uhha tribe. His turban, Stanley noted with a keen journalistic eye, was made of cloth woven in Massachusetts. Politely but firmly, Mionvu requested that Stanley and his forty-five men come out of the sun. 'Why does the white man halt in the road?' Mionvu wanted to know. His manner exceedingly polite, but firm. 'The sun is hot. Let him seek the shelter of my village, where we can arrange this little matter between us.'

Stanley thought it was a trap. An army of a thousand Ha warriors had assembled around the caravan. Stanley was frightened by how the warriors applauded Mionvu's speech with too much enthusiasm, and noticed with alarm that they were armed with bows, arrows and spears – and fully prepared to use them. The next time he came to Africa, he vowed to himself, he would march through Mionvu's village with one hundred men and punish the man who didn't fear the New York *Herald* or the Star-spangled Banner.

'Will the white man,' Mionvu concluded his speech, 'have war or peace?'

Though Stanley's reply matched Mionvu's oratory prowess – his words were a stirring and lengthy paraphrase of a speech he once heard General Sherman deliver to the chiefs of the Arapaho and Cheyenne Indian tribes on the North Platte in 1867 – it cost him an amazing eighty-five doti to get out of the regal king's territory alive.

The next village was Kahirigi. The chief was Mionvu's brother. He wanted thirty doti and was persistent that there would be no negotiation. 'I saw my fine array of bales being reduced fast,' Stanley wrote. 'Four more such demands would leave me cleaned out.'

Despite the King's mandate, Stanley sent Bombay and Asmani to negotiate. Stanley stewed in his tent all afternoon, smoking his pipe and searching for a desperate solution to a desperate situation. There were five more chiefs between him and Ujiji. All lived within two hours of each other and would already know about the wealth of Stanley's caravan when he passed. The cloth would certainly go. Arriving in Ujiji without any currency for trade would defeat the purpose – he would find Livingstone but would be unable to buy food or medicine, let alone pay his own way back to Tabora. Stanley considered going to war with the various tribes comprising the kingdom of Uhha, but ruled that out. He had come to the conclusion that prudence, not aggression, was the key to remaining alive in Africa. 'How am I to reach Livingstone without being beggared?' Stanley wondered.

Stanley called his guides into his tent. Unveiling his plan immediately, Stanley asked how to get past the next five chiefs without paying tribute. They told him it was impossible. However, they added hopefully, there was another guide in the boma who might know a way.

The guide's name was Mguna. He was the slave of an Arab living in Tabora. When Mguna heard Stanley's plan he didn't reject it out of hand, but he made sure Stanley knew the odds of success were slim. 'You must have complete control over your men,' Mguna told Stanley. 'And they have to do exactly as told.' Failure would mean war and death.

Stanley agreed. For twelve doti, Mguna promised to show Stanley a back road out of town. The caravan would have to leave in the dead of night and observe total silence. Because they would be avoiding villages at all costs, the caravan must be carrying enough food to last at least four days.

As soon as Mguna left, Stanley sent his men out to purchase four days' worth of grain. They returned with six. All seemed to be going in Stanley's favour. 'I did not go to sleep at all last night,' he wrote in his journal the next day. 'A little after midnight, as soon as the moon was beginning to show itself, by gangs of four the men stole quietly out of the village. By 3 a.m. the entire expedition was outside the boma and not the slightest alarm had been made.'

As soon as the caravan was gathered, Stanley whistled softly for Mguna. The new guide appeared out of the shadows and stepped into the light of the moon, which had grown bright. Walking carefully, making sure the donkey and chickens and goats were quiet and the bundles didn't snag on any low tree branches, the New York *Herald* expedition tramped out of the village through a burned-out section of flat ground. They travelled south, away from Ujiji until clear of the village, then turned due west and made a beeline for Livingstone. Their path was parallel to the main road, but four miles off it to avoid being seen. As the sun rose they stopped for a silent breakfast in a jungle clearing. Antelope were clearly visible and waiting to be shot, but Stanley didn't dare risk a single sound. He sipped a cup of coffee and exulted that his escape seemed to have worked.

But as they waded across the swift, knee-deep Rusizi River, a woman who had joined the group to travel with her husband was suddenly overcome with fear. She let out a piercing shriek, as if bitten by a crocodile. Mguna motioned for Stanley to shut her up before the whole countryside knew they were there. 'We would have hundreds of angry

Wahha about us and probably a general massacre would ensue,' Stanley wrote.

Stanley ordered the woman to be quiet, but several of the scared porters were already running off with their loads. Instead of silence, what Stanley got from the woman was an even louder brand of shriek. Like a siren, the sound rose higher and higher. The woman's husband became so enraged that he drew his sword and asked Stanley's permission to cut off her head. Instead, Stanley placed his hand over her mouth. When she fought her way clear and began screaming again, Stanley whipped her across the shoulders ten times and had her gagged and bound.

The exhausted and scared Stanley waded ashore, regrouped his scattered caravan, and resumed his march. Twenty-four exhausting hours later, after being forced to slit the throats of their chickens and goats when Mguna mistakenly led them too close to a village in the middle of the night, the New York *Herald* expedition emerged from a bamboo jungle and found themselves safe. They cheered each other and knew the brotherhood of those who have endured near-death together. Stanley made another estimate of time and distance. They were forty-six miles from Ujiji. He thought they would make it in eighteen and a half hours. 'Patience, my soul,' he wrote that night. The caravan was camped in a thick forest, but a village had been spotted nearby, so no fires were lit or noises allowed. 'A few hours more then the end of all this will be known!'

The world seemed brighter to Stanley. He noticed the smoothness of pebbles that day, the beauty of wildflowers, a grove where wild fruit trees grew. His happiness grew even more when the group turned onto a smooth road and the pace increased. He thought back on all he had been through and it seemed simple in retrospect. 'What cared we now for the difficulties we had encountered – for the rough and cruel forests, for the thorny thickets and hurtful grass, for the jangle of all savagedom, of which we had been the joyless audience. Tomorrow! Ay, the great day draws nigh and we may well laugh and sing while in this triumphant mood. We have been sorely tried, we have been angry with each other but we forget all these now, and there is no face but is radiant with the happiness we have all deserved.'

The men cheered Stanley as Ujiji drew near. He had taken them through a wilderness and boldly past thieving sultans. Now they camped one last night in the village of Nyamtaga, just a short march from town.

Beer was served and goats were roasted. Stanley was nervous about presenting himself to such an important 'Englishman' and laid out the clean set of clothes he'd saved for the occasion: a white safari uniform, a new plaid wrap for his helmet and polish for his boots. 'Hyah Barak-Allah,' the faithful shouted to him. 'Onward, and the blessing of God be on you.'

When Stanley dressed in the morning he was pleased with his appearance, thinking that he looked good enough to parade down the streets of Bombay. The New York *Herald* caravan set forth with the great blow of a horn, on what it hoped would be the last hours of its mission. The path was rugged and steep, leading them to the top of a small mountain, but Stanley didn't care. He was so taken with the idea of confirming that the white man in Ujiji was Livingstone that the miles flew past.

The view from the summit, however, took Stanley's breath away. For the first time, Lake Tanganyika shone below him. It was like a silver sea, bordered by the most amazingly ominous mountains. Stanley couldn't take his eyes off it, even as the caravan descended the mountain's far side. It had been almost exactly two years since Bennett's commission. The pressures and risks of marching across Africa to find Livingstone had been on his mind every day since. Somewhere down there, on the shore of that sparkling lake, lay Ujiji. To finally see the spot where the meeting would take place – and a lovely spot it was, a beautiful reward for all the toils and struggle – was like a dream come true.

As the miles passed, the caravan's trail wound through a field of ten-foot-tall matete grass – elephant grass – which obscured their view of the lake but did nothing to slow the pace. 'In a few minutes we shall have reached the spot where we imagine the objects of our search,' he wrote of the last miles into Ujiji. 'Our fate will soon be decided. No one in the town knows we are coming.'

When the caravan was just a mile outside of town, Stanley ordered the colours raised and the men to begin announcing their arrival. He gave the order for every man to load his guns. 'Commence firing,' he roared, growing more nervous by the minute that he was on the verge of meeting Livingstone. What would happen? Would the veteran explorer run in the other direction? Would he be warm? Was there a possibility, as Kirk predicted, that he knew of their coming and had already left Ujiji?

'The flags are fluttered, the banner of America is in front waving joyfully,' Stanley wrote. The sound of muskets firing and horns blowing filled the air, punctuating the flag's presence. 'Never were the Stars and Stripes so beautiful in my mind.'

The residents of the town came pouring out to greet them. The arrival and departure of caravans was a regular fact of life in Ujiji, but there had been none for months due to the war with Mirambo. Stanley had blazed a new trail for the caravans to travel. He was no longer a journalist, writing about the actions of others. Henry Morton Stanley had become an explorer, with all the fame and glory that implied.

Even as Stanley strode into town, the emotions of surprise and happiness could be seen on the faces of the Arabs and locals alike. The Arabs pressed against him, shaking his hand and asking where he'd come from. 'They were much astounded to find it to be a caravan,' Stanley wrote, 'and led by a white man.'

The whole time, Stanley anxiously surveyed the sea of faces for another white man's. But there was none.

By the time Stanley made it into the heart of town thousands of people were pressed around the caravan. And though it was a triumphant moment, with all the fanfare Stanley's phenomenal achievement deserved, he grew suddenly impatient. Livingstone was nowhere to be seen.

A young black man appeared at Stanley's side and spoke to him in English. 'How do you do, sir?'

'Hello! Who the deuce are you?'

'I am the servant of Dr Livingstone.' It was Chuma, and as soon as he uttered those intriguing lines, he dashed off just as quickly as he appeared.

'Joy,' Stanley wrote in his journal. 'Heart beat fast. I had to keep control over my emotions lest my face might betray them or detract from the dignity of a white man appearing under such circumstances. But what would I have given for a bit of friendly wilderness wherein I might vent my joy in some mad freaks, such as idiotically biting my hand, twirling a somersault, slashing at trees or something in order to purge these exciting feelings before appearing in the presence of Livingstone.'

Everything had come together for Stanley – his years of failure and rejection, his desperate underdog's need to succeed at all costs, his hunger for a loving father figure. Stanley had waited a lifetime for a moment of such appreciation and validation. Now that it had come, the world span off kilter, robbing him of the stern and angry facade with which he had driven across Africa. In its place was a humble young man, desperate to do and say the right thing when meeting one of the world's greatest and most famous men. He wanted to appear smart and genteel, devoid of any pandering tone in his voice.

Minutes earlier, Livingstone had been sitting on the mud veranda of his small house, pondering his woeful future. His seat was a straw mat with a goatskin on top for cushioning. Behind his back, as he leaned against the hut's mud wall, another goatskin was nailed. The skin kept him from getting a chill as he leaned back against the cold mud. Suddenly, he witnessed the unusual sight of Susi racing down the dirt street. 'When my spirits were at their lowest ebb the Good Samaritan was close at hand, for one morning Susi came running at the top of his speed, and gasped out, "An Englishman! I see him!" and off he darted to meet him.'

Livingstone slowly rose. His doorway faced east, the direction from which the caravan was marching. Livingstone could see everything clearly. Above the throngs of people gathered to greet the incoming caravan, he saw the American flag snapping in the breeze. He didn't see a white man, but saw porters bearing an incredible assortment of goods: bales of cloth, huge kettles, cooking pots, tents. 'This must be a luxurious traveller,' Livingstone thought. 'And not one at wit's end like me.'

All the most prosperous Arabs stepped forth to greet Stanley, shielding him from Livingstone. They clamoured for news of Stanley's path and war with Mirambo. But even in their excitement at the prospect of the trade route to the coast being reopened, the crowd began to part. Livingstone was pushing his way through, curious to see who the traveller might be.

What Livingstone saw was a tanned, gaunt young man whose hair was turning prematurely white from stress. His uniform was as crisp as could be expected, given the travel. His boots were well worn. His sun-beaten helmet had been cleaned. All in all, the man had such a formal bearing that, despite the Stars and Stripes, Livingstone assumed he was French. He hoped the traveller spoke English, because Livingstone didn't speak French. He thought that they would be 'a pretty pair of white men in Ujiji if neither spoke the other's language'.

What Stanley saw was a pale white man wearing a sun-faded blue cap and red Jobo jacket like the Arabs. His clothing showed signs of being patched and repaired. The explorer's hair was white, he had few teeth

263

and his beard was bushy. He walked 'with a firm but heavy tread', as if stepping on thorns.

Stanley stepped crisply towards the old man, removed his helmet and extended his hand. Not counting the months between his great commission and the start of his journey, Stanley had come 975 miles in 236 days for the moment. They wordlessly shook hands, each man appraising the other. Livingstone didn't know who the young man was, or what he might want. The Arabs and citizens of Ujiji crowded around.

According to Stanley's journal it was 10 November 1871, a day that would change the world.

Stanley's heart was beating furiously, and he was striving desperately to say exactly the right thing to such a distinguished gentleman. Livingstone's British background, though, gave Stanley great pause. He wasn't sure whether or not he was welcome, how Livingstone would react, or whether he was about to be embarrassed in front of a large throng. But Stanley had not come across Africa to be denied.

With a grave formal intonation, representing America instead of his native Britain but trying to affect British gravity and trying to quiet that singsong Welsh flutter that crept in when he got excited, Stanley spoke the most dignified words that came to mind: 'Dr Livingstone, I presume?'

'Yes,' Livingstone answered simply. He was relieved that the man wasn't French.

'I thank God, Doctor,' Stanley said, appalled at how fragile Livingstone looked, 'I have been permitted to see you.'

'I feel thankful,' Livingstone said with typical understatement, 'I am here to welcome you.'

THIRTY-SIX

BROMPTON

27 OCTOBER 1871
Brompton Cemetery, London

ON A FIFTY-TWO DEGREE AUTUMN MORNING, UNDER A BLACK SKY THAT would threaten rain all day long, Sir Roderick Murchison was laid to rest. A man of his stature could have been buried in Westminster Abbey or St Paul's, but he preferred to be buried alongside his beloved Charlotte in Brompton Cemetery.

The end came into sight just two months earlier, when he suffered a second stroke that made him unable to speak or swallow. 'He got better,' as *The Times* noted, 'and desired a trip into the outdoors.' The man who had ridden to hounds as a country squire, trekked the Alps as a newly-wed and roamed the countrysides of England, Scotland and Russia in the name of geology went for a ride in his open-air carriage. During the drive he caught a cold. The cold became bronchitis. At eight thirty on the night of 22 October 1871, in his Belgrave Square mansion, Sir Roderick Impey Murchison's ambitious life came to an end.

'His zeal and energy in supporting the cause of his friend and fellow countryman,' *The Times* wrote in a two-column eulogy the next day, 'and the persistent faith in his safety which he has always felt and expressed when the most sanguine have been doubtful and down-hearted, will long be remembered.'

A procession of thirteen mourning carriages left Belgrave Square at eleven thirty on the morning of 27 October, destined for Brompton Cemetery. Shortly before noon the procession entered the narrow archway marking the large cemetery's north entrance and drove slowly to the site of the grave. The creak of carriage springs, the soft jangle of bridle and harness hardware, and the *sotto voce* commands of carriage drivers to their horses announced their progress.

When the carriages reached Murchison's burial site, Prime Minister William Gladstone and a host of geological and geographical dignitaries solemnly positioned themselves around the freshly dug grave. Murchison was a Conservative and Gladstone was the day's eminent Liberal, but their mothers had known one another, and the two men had crossed paths for a lifetime. The death of such an old, esteemed acquaintance had a profound effect on Gladstone, making his own mortality more immediate. 'Went to Sir R. Murchison's funeral; the last of those who had known me or of me from infancy,' Gladstone wrote thoughtfully in his journal that night. 'And so a step towards the end is made visible.'

Of Murchison's lions, only James Augustus Grant was at the graveside. Burton was nearly penniless, holed up in Howlett's Hotel at 36 Manchester Street with Isabel, lobbying for another consular position after failing in Beirut. Instead of attending the funeral, Burton wrote a strident letter to *The Times* that ran the same day. Seven years after the Nile Duel, fourteen years after his journey with Speke, Burton ranted that Speke was getting too much credit for the exploration of Africa.

Fulfilling Murchison's last wish, the Royal Geographical Society awarded him the gold medal for excellence in exploration as he lay dying. In his lifetime he had been knighted, made a baron, made a Knight of the Second Class of St Anne by Russia, made a member of the Order of Stanislaus, given the Brisbane Gold Medal from Edinburgh, the Prix Cuvier from Paris and the Wollaston Gold Medal from the Geological Society of London. Sweden, Brazil, Denmark and Italy had honoured him. In all, nineteen stars, crosses and emblems of distinction had been awarded to Sir Roderick, the most ever given a man in modern times by crowned heads of state for purely scientific achievements. The gold medal, however, was the honour he cherished most of all. 'This was the last distinction conferred on him,' Sir Henry Rawlinson eulogized. 'And he assured me that, looking on the Society almost as a child of his creation, he valued our humble tribute of admiration and respect above all the more brilliant trophies which filled his cabinet.'

Murchison did not live to see his favourite lion return. 'With Livingstone his name was so identified,' Rawlinson said in his eulogy, 'that when the great traveller returns – as return he assuredly will – the only feeling of regret will be that Sir Roderick will not be here to welcome him.'

Ironically, later review of the journals of Stanley and Livingstone showed that both men lost track of time due to their many illnesses. Their journals were off by days, and in Stanley's case by as much as two weeks. The date on which Stanley actually found Livingstone was 27 October – the day Murchison was laid to rest. It was two years to the day since Bennett had bestowed the Great Commission upon Stanley.

Most startling, given that Murchison's funeral ran from eleven in the morning until one-thirty in the afternoon, that Stanley met Livingstone late in the African morning, and that a two-hour time difference existed between Brompton Cemetery and Ujiji, Murchison finally rested in peace just after his long-lost friend was found.

Gladstone defined the day best: 'It was a *great* funeral.'

IV

THE WORLD TURNED
UPSIDE DOWN

Sir Roderick Impey Murchison

THIRTY-SEVEN

THE SEARCHERS

NOVEMBER 1871 TO JANUARY 1872
Ujiji

EVEN AS STANLEY TIPPED HIS HAT TO THE ARAB CROWD IN RESPONSE TO deafening choruses of the Swahili congratulatory salute 'Yambo', Livingstone motioned towards his small hut. Stanley and Livingstone walked down the red dirt street together, not knowing one another but with much to talk about. Livingstone offered Stanley his goatskin seat on the veranda, but Stanley refused. Then they sat under the eaves that had protected Livingstone from the equatorial sun as he'd prayed for deliverance, hoping against hope for a Samaritan to emerge from the wilderness and save his life.

The people of Ujiji – Arab and African alike – couldn't stop looking at them. They numbered a thousand strong, and had followed them to Livingstone's house. Stanley wrote of the locals 'filling the whole square densely, indulging their curiosity, and discussing the fact of the two white men meeting at Ujiji'.

'Where,' Stanley began once pleasantries had been exchanged, asking the one question the entire world wanted answered, 'have you been all this time?'

'Yes, that was the way it began,' Stanley wrote later. 'But whatever the Doctor informed me, and that which I communicated to him, I cannot correctly report, for I found myself gazing at him, conning the wonderful man at whose side I now sat in Central Africa. Every hair of his head and beard, every wrinkle of his face, the wanness of his features and the slightly wearied look he wore, were all imparting intelligence to me – the knowledge I craved for so much.'

Stanley's rational mind told him to take out his journal and scribble emotions, thoughts, words and sensations – to be a journalist again, after finally capturing the story of a lifetime. But he was too consumed by Livingstone's words, and by the luminescence of the older man's presence. 'He had so much to say that he began at the end, seemingly oblivious to the fact that five or six years had to be accounted for. But his account was oozing out. It was growing fast into grand proportions – into a marvellous history of deeds,' Stanley remembered later.

The people of Ujiji slowly lost interest and wandered back to their lives. The two men found themselves alone. Remembering himself, Stanley called for Bombay and ordered that Livingstone's letters and the bottle of Sillery champagne from Zanzibar be brought. The champagne was warm after the many miles of African travel, but not flat, and they drank from silver goblets. Livingstone spent the afternoon glowing in the giddy awareness that he had been rescued, a sensation enhanced by the lion's share of the champagne. Then food was brought – meat cakes, curried chicken, stewed goat meat, rice – and Stanley was amazed to see how much the feeble old explorer could eat. 'You have brought me new life,' Livingstone repeated over and over to Stanley as he mashed the food between his gums. 'You have brought me new life.'

Throughout that first afternoon on the veranda, and even after they could see the mountains Stanley had crossed at dawn turn dark, they talked. In that whole time, Stanley never once mentioned his occupation, his employer or his motivations; never mentioned that he had essentially travelled all the way across Africa to profit from Livingstone's mis-fortune. The atmosphere on the veranda was so warm, and their moods so jovial, that Stanley never found the courage to explain that he was far more than just a traveller.

The next morning, Stanley awoke not knowing where he was. 'I woke up this morning with a sudden start. The room was strange,' he wrote. Instead of his hammock in his tent, he lay in a crude bed on a mattress of palm leaves. He rejoiced as his memories of the previous day triggered a wave of relief: he had done the impossible. He had found Livingstone. The truth of his accomplishment – and the ecstasy that knowledge produced – was almost too good to believe.

The nagging of his conscience detracted from his euphoria bit by bit, however, until Stanley had no choice but to confront his duplicity. By not telling Livingstone the truth of why he had come, he had lied. The lie was silent, and perhaps it could be categorized by omission as a half-truth, but Stanley was more than aware he needed to confront the issue immediately. How, though, to reveal his true motives without jeopardizing their incredible new friendship?

Stanley lay in bed, comfortable in the cocoon of palm-frond mattress and his precious bearskin blanket, but anguished. The thread defining his life had once been failure, but now it was lies that wove together the story of the man alternately named John Rowlands and Henry Morton Stanley. From Denbigh to New Orleans to Central City to Zanzibar, he had spent so many years lying to people about his true self that it was impossible to remember the most outlandish misrepresentations. For they were all, if measured against a man like Livingstone, whose life was on public record, enormous.

There was a genius to Stanley's deception: the twisting of words, the massaging of facts and the dodging of blame. A master like Stanley would be able to assemble a simple charade that would fool Livingstone, just like he'd fooled the rest of the world – even the intractable paranoid, James Gordon Bennett, Jr. Stanley merely had to continue pretending he was a traveller: a curious, quirky tourist wandering into Africa to see the sights and plumb the depth of Lake Tanganyika. The lie would harm no one. Livingstone would continue to hold Stanley in high esteem as a modern-day Good Samaritan instead of being repulsed by his mercenary intent.

For the first time in many years, however, Stanley felt lying to be repugnant. Anything but the truth was uncomfortable. Livingstone – the man with *baraka*, the man who trotted through Africa like the Apostle Paul – had effected the moral change Stanley sought since Aden. 'We also rejoiced in our sufferings,' Paul had written in his letter to the Romans in the middle of the first century. 'Because suffering produces perseverance; perseverance, character; and character, hope – and hope does not disappoint us.'

Both Stanley and Livingstone had persevered in Africa. Yet while Livingstone had earned the character and hope of which Paul spoke, Stanley struggled mightily in his soul about making that leap. He was capable, yes. But he was unwilling, fighting the urge to tell the truth and risk rejection. His first thoughts were, as usual, self-preservative. He didn't owe Livingstone an apology for who he was or why he was there. 'I have paid the purchase,' he rationalized, 'by coming so far to do him a service.'

Then he reflected on Livingstone's great emotion when they met, and that he hadn't run in the other direction, as Kirk predicted. Certainly that reflected well on Livingstone's compassion. And, unlike all the other British he'd met, Livingstone certainly wouldn't take issue with Stanley's nationality. The stiffness of Stanley's initial greeting was no doubt due to the subcurrent of American versus British tensions in Zanzibar, London, New York and elsewhere on the globe where the reigning powers clashed.

'Here,' Livingstone noted of Africa the day before, 'Americans and Englishmen are the same people. We speak the same language and have the same ideas.'

Stanley had hastily added that they were like brothers: 'Flesh of your flesh, and bone of your bone.' Livingstone had agreed. It was obvious the man was eager to accept Stanley as a peer.

Stanley still hadn't solved his dilemma as he pushed back the bearskin and lowered his bare feet to the cold mud floor. He dressed quietly as the pale light of dawn shone into his window. Carefully he walked past the hut's only other room and opened the front door. He meant to go outside and slip down to the water's edge. By taking a walk on the beaches of Lake Tanganyika before Livingstone rose, Stanley would find his answer. Stepping onto the veranda, Stanley cringed as the door's hinges emitted an awful creak. Their whine seemed as loud as a siren in the still air.

There, meditating on his goatskin, sat Livingstone.

'Hello, Doctor. Are you up already?' Stanley wrote of the moment.

'Good morning, Mr Stanley,' a rejuvenated Livingstone responded, making room for Stanley to sit down next to him. 'I am glad to see you. I sat up late reading my letters. You have brought me good news and bad news. But sit down.' Stanley arranged himself next to Livingstone as the doctor continued talking. 'Yes, many of my friends are dead. My eldest son has met with a sad accident – that is, my boy Tom. My second son, Oswell, is at college studying medicine and is doing well, I am told. Agnes, my eldest daughter, is enjoying herself in a yacht.' Livingstone's outer peace belied inner conflict. The eldest son who had met with a sad accident was not Tom, but Robert, who died in a Confederate prison camp during the winter of 1864. The same detachment that allowed

Livingstone to spend years away from his children had already distanced him from that tragedy, and mentally reorganized his offspring as if Robert had never been alive at all. Robert's death meant Tom was now the eldest, and Oswell the second son.

Stanley failed to catch the slip of the tongue. He stared at Livingstone, still having a hard time believing the explorer was not a figment of his imagination after all those months on the trail, dreaming of him, striving to find him. 'Now, Doctor, you are probably wondering why I am here,' Stanley began.

'It is true,' Livingstone said, 'I have been wondering.'

'Doctor,' Stanley said. 'Now don't be frightened when I tell you that I have come after . . . *you*.'

'After me?' Livingstone answered in his Glasgow burr.

'Yes.'

'How?'

'Well . . . Have you heard of the New York *Herald*?'

'Oh. Who has not heard of that despicable newspaper?' Livingstone retorted, not understanding the connection between his adventurous new acquaintance and the journalistic scourge of the free world. The paper had been a mere tabloid when he sailed from London in 1866. The transformation to international titan had not begun.

'You will not call it despicable after you have heard what I have to say,' Stanley continued. Then Stanley poured out the story, making certain that Livingstone knew James Gordon Bennett, Jr was the driving force behind Livingstone's rescue. There was honesty in mentioning Bennett, but also a secondary motive: Stanley secretly hoped Livingstone would write a letter to Bennett. At the very least the letter would prove he'd found the explorer. At best, Livingstone might praise Stanley in a way that would boost his career.

Livingstone was not concerned with motives. He was so destitute that any help at all was welcome. 'I am not of a demonstrative turn,' a touched Livingstone wrote later. 'As cold, indeed, as we islanders are usually reported to be. But this disinterested kindness of Mr Bennett, so nobly carried into effect by Mr Stanley, was simply overwhelming. I really do feel extremely grateful and at the same time, I am a little ashamed at not being more worthy of the generosity.' Livingstone did not push Stanley away. Instead, as a gesture of thanks for Stanley's courage, Livingstone wrote a long letter for Bennett to publish, praising the newspaper and Stanley.

In the days that followed, their friendship deepened. Stanley attached himself to Livingstone as a needy child would to a long-absent father. The *Herald* and the *Herald* expedition receded into the background. More relevant discussions of their lives and travels moved to the fore. Livingstone told of an eagerness to go home and see his children again. Stanley described paying tribute in Ugogo and Mirambo's war. He also darkened Livingstone's mood by telling of Kirk's apathy. Livingstone wrote another long letter as a consequence, this one lambasting Kirk as a coward and poseur with 'an eager desire to mix up his name with discoveries which he had too much regard for money to make himself'.

On the surface, Livingstone and Stanley should have been at odds. Both were solitary men, given to following their own paths. Both balanced introspection with showmanship, and seemed oblivious to occasional lapses into temper. They were both stubborn, not suffering fools or hypocrites gladly. In fact, Stanley's initial plan had even acknowledged their adversarial natures: he would find Livingstone, say hello, stay just one day or however long it took Livingstone to jot a letter in his own hand to prove they had linked, then race back to Zanzibar to tell the world. As they grew to know one another through long hours of conversation, however, Stanley's haste evaporated. He longed to stay with Livingstone, basking in the older man's wisdom and grace.

Not that Livingstone was undamaged mentally and emotionally by his travels. He had grown quirky in his time away from civilization, and talked to himself without noticing. He could only sleep on the ground or a native sleeping platform of grass and sticks – attempts to sleep in his bed in Ujiji left him tossing and turning. As for religion, on those Sundays when no Africans cared to join his congregation, Livingstone preached a sermon to himself. But Stanley was willing to overlook any quirks, just as Livingstone had overlooked Stanley's jaded demeanour. 'Dr Livingstone is about sixty years old, though after he was restored to health he looked like a man who has not passed his fiftieth year. His hair has a brownish colour yet, but here and there is streaked with grey lines over the temples. His beard and moustache are very grey. His eyes, which are hazel, are remarkably bright. He has a sight as keen as a hawk's. His teeth alone indicate the weakness of age,' Stanley wrote. 'I grant that he is not an angel, but he approaches to that being as near as the nature of a living man will allow . . . His gentleness never forsakes him, his hopefulness never deserts him. No harassing anxieties, distraction of mind, long separation from home and kindred can make him complain. He thinks "all will come out right at last".'

A week passed. Then another. Stanley observed Livingstone's every movement, just as the explorer had observed so many tribes, animals and geographical features over the years. He noted Livingstone's amazing cleanliness and appetite, and how the explorer quickly became stout from eating the four meals a day Stanley fed him. But more than anything, Stanley revelled in Livingstone's company. 'There is a good-natured abandon about Livingstone which was not lost on me. Whenever he began to laugh there was a contagion about it that compelled me to imitate him,' Stanley wrote. 'The wan features which had shocked me at the first meeting, the heavy step which told of age and hard travel, the grey beard and bowed shoulders, belied the man. Underneath the well-worn exterior lay an endless fund of high spirits and inexhaustible humour. That rugged frame of his enclosed a young and most exuberant soul.'

And just as soon as Livingstone felt capable again, the older explorer suggested that the younger explorer might want to accompany him in his search for the Source. Stanley, who had been prodding Livingstone to return to Zanzibar with him, was flattered, but knew it was impractical.

So they had reached a compromise. They would return to Tabora together, but only after searching the shores of Lake Tanganyika for a river flowing out of its northern end, towards Lake Victoria. That would at least confirm a portion of Livingstone's Source theory.

It was agreed. They canoed from Ujiji on 16 November in a long dugout canoe paddled by twenty of Stanley's men. The canoe was crafted from a mvule tree so wide that the paddlers could sit by side. Fair weather made the journey pleasant. Stanley and Livingstone passed the hours in conversation as the canoe glided over the dark-green waters of Tanganyika. Hippos sported around the boat, coming up for air and threatening to tip the canoe before disappearing back underwater. The shores were heavily wooded and grassy, with some of the trees bursting with startling, bright blossoms. The lake was so vast that Stanley considered it an inland sea.

Their adventures were as dangerous and unlikely as anything Stanley or Livingstone had seen before: a near ambush while camping along the shore, the sight of couples making love along the banks as Stanley and Livingstone paddled past. To Stanley's surprise, Livingstone never whipped or harangued his men, preferring to settle all differences through gentle persuasion. Even more surprising was how Livingstone used the same method with hostile tribes demanding tribute. Not only did Livingstone achieve more through kindness than Stanley had through rage, but by the time Livingstone had negotiated their way out of one problem or another, a hostile tribe or recalcitrant porter was often a new ally.

As Stanley and Livingstone paddled the shores of Lake Tanganyika together, world attention towards Livingstone's plight was escalating into frenzy. It all began when Kirk's letters of 22 and 25 September arrived in London. Murchison was dead, so his letter was passed on to the new RGS president. When a horrified Sir Henry Rawlinson learned that Livingstone was surrounded, without hope of escape, he went public with the truth about Livingstone's predicament. On 27 November, Rawlinson decreed that the RGS would send a search and relief expedition to save Livingstone. 'It appeared to the Council and myself that the hope we had of communicating with Dr Livingstone through Mr Stanley, the American traveller, must for the present be abandoned,' Rawlinson said. 'One plan proposed was to send native messengers, offering a reward of one hundred guineas to whichever would bring a letter back in Dr Livingstone's handwriting to the sea coast. Another, recommended by one of our African travellers, was to organize a direct expedition headed by some experienced and well-qualified Europeans.'

In a follow-up meeting on 11 December, the latter won out. Rawlinson demanded that the RGS go and rescue Livingstone. However, his influence waned outside the RGS. Rawlinson was an articulate man and a true adventurer, but the new RGS president lacked Murchison's political connections. His position was further weakened on 14 December, when James Grant publicly expressed great faith in 'the little American Stanley', whom he had by coincidence met once in Abyssinia.

When Rawlinson formally requested money from the Foreign Office to finance a search, they gave it their official backing and expressed their deep sympathy, but refused to allocate funding. Public outrage was so great that the issue of rescuing Livingstone was taken up on the floor of Parliament. James Grieve, a sixty-one-year-old Liberal Member of Parliament from Greenock, stood in the House of Commons to battle for Livingstone's cause. He demanded that Robert Lowe, the Chancellor of the Exchequer, explain the rationale behind denying funding for a search.

Lowe was not a popular man by any stretch of the imagination. He was enormously disliked by Gladstone, the very prime minister who'd given him his job. Lowe's attention to fiscal restraint at the expense of humanity and warmth even had the charismatic Benjamin Disraeli refusing to shake his hand. Lowe had no intention of changing his manners on account of a wayward African explorer. Having already dealt with the Livingstone issue back in May 1870, Lowe wasn't any more amenable to dispensing funds – unnecessarily, in Lowe's point of view – nearly two years later.

After first telling Grieve that he thought the question was ludicrous, Lowe reminded Grieve that money had previously been allocated to find Livingstone, that Livingstone was nowhere to be found, and that Sir Samuel White Baker was already in the region with a large armed force. 'It is from those armed men,' the Chancellor told Grieve dismissively, as part of a lengthy defence, 'that Livingstone would be most likely to receive relief.'

Grieve was reluctantly forced to accept Lowe's explanation. No governmental monies were allocated to fund a rescue expedition. But in Gondokoro, unbeknown to Lowe or Parliament, Sir Samuel White Baker was giving Livingstone very little thought and none of his assets. He was too busy finding food for his men, trying to motivate his apathetic Egyptian troops, enlisting Florence to keep track of weather and barometer and waging war with the naked Bari. Baker had not forgotten about Livingstone, of course. He was in the habit of questioning the occasional traveller from the vicinity of Lake Tanganyika, and had even heard vague reports of a white man or two in Central Africa, but Gondokoro was not yet stable enough for Baker to leave without risking its collapse. The little fort on the Nile was a bare, dusty expanse hardly capable of sustaining the grain vital to Baker's still. To Baker and the Bari, however, Gondokoro was worth fighting for. Neither group planned on leaving it to the other.

Back in London, in the minds of Henry Rawlinson and the RGS, Baker had become less relevant. They were no longer depending upon Baker's passive search plan – regardless of the British Government's official position. The time had come for action. A public fund-raising drive was begun, led by the Crimean War hero Florence Nightingale. 'If it costs ten thousand pounds to send him a pair of boots, we should send it,' she railed in what would be an overwhelmingly successful public campaign. 'England too often provides great men then leaves them to perish.'

Nightingale's candour rallied the British public, but by then America had appropriated their hero. In New York, James Gordon Bennett, Jr was busy twisting the lion's tail like never before. On 11 December 1871 – the same day Rawlinson belatedly agreed it was time to search for their lost lion, but long before the world became aware that Stanley had found Livingstone – Bennett had run Kirk's letters pleading innocence in the *Herald*. With Stanley elevated from merely the 'American traveler' of the 19 September edition all the way up to a swashbuckling adventurer who was not only racing through Africa, but tormenting the British Consul in Zanzibar to such a degree that letters to officials in London were being written, the stage was set for Stanley's mission to be ladled out to the people of New York, dispatch by dispatch.

The first ran on 22 December 1871. It was the piece Stanley had written on 4 July, the ninety-fifth anniversary of America's declaration of independence from the British. That symbolism gave his published words a patriotic tinge that enhanced the Anglo-American rivalry. The ensuing commotion was so great that Bennett ran a taunting editorial the following day: 'An African exploring expedition is a new thing in the enterprises of modern journalism,' Bennett wrote proudly, 'and in this, as in many other great achievements of the Third Estate, to the New York *Herald* will belong the credit of the first bold adventure in the cause of humanity, civilization and science.'

Then, contradicting Kirk's assertion that Stanley was stuck, Bennett assured the *Herald*'s readers that his reporter would get through. Bennett was 'thus encouraged in hope that this expedition will settle all doubts in reference to Dr Livingstone, and we hope too, that it will accomplish something more than the solution of the Livingstone mystery'.

Bennett was confident Stanley and the *Herald* would be forever linked with 'the names of Burton and Speke and Grant, and of Baker and Burton and Livingstone', then went on to conclude that Britain was 'too slow and too penurious' to find her missing explorer.

Other American papers took up the cause. On 27 December 1871 the Buffalo *Express* called Stanley's expedition 'the most extraordinary newspaper enterprise ever dreamed of'.

Bennett then twisted the lion's tail even harder, puckishly sending a second New York *Herald* expedition to Africa. The *Herald* was now off to Gondokoro to find and rescue Sir Samuel White Baker (completely disregarding the fact that Baker wasn't lost and certainly didn't need to be rescued). Bennett's mocking of British exploration while trumpeting American initiative elevated the rivalry to new heights. *Herald* circulation soared.

Alvan S. Southworth, the journalist in charge of finding Baker, planned to hire a massive steamboat to cruise upriver on the Nile from Cairo. Southworth's published opinion that 'energetic, live, I might say reckless Americans, each with his special mental and physical gifts, could bare this whole continent to the view of anxious mankind', set the table perfectly for the coming publication of Stanley's dispatches. 'The British,' Southworth went on to write, 'are good, hardy, stubborn travelers, but they are like their journalism and ideas – slower than the wrath of Grecian gods.'

Meanwhile, deep in Africa, Livingstone and Stanley were oblivious to the hype and bedlam. The sublime bond growing between the two explorers would become the richest by-product of the New York *Herald* expedition. Stanley was an eager pupil, and basked in Livingstone's paternal influence. Even though Stanley had already proven adept at the fundamentals of African exploration during his travels through Ugogo, dealings with the Arabs in Tabora and circuitous escape from Mirambo, Livingstone was giving him a new kind of tutorial on exploration. On the northern end of the lake, they found the river rumoured to flow from Lake Tanganyika into the Nile – the Rusizi – but it flowed into Tanganyika, not out of it.

The Source lay elsewhere, Livingstone confided in Stanley. He would have to travel south again. In the absence of a river flowing out of Lake Tanganyika, Livingstone was sure that the fountains were somewhere far to the south of his current position – likely somewhere between latitudes ten and twelve degrees south. Livingstone had heard of four fountains, two of which spawned a river that flowed to the north – the Lualaba – and two which begat a river flowing south – the Zambezi. Natives had mentioned them to him time and time again. That put the fountains in the vicinity of a lake called Bangweolo, which Livingstone had visited in 1868. As the crow flew, it was four hundred miles from Ujiji to Lake Bangweolo. But a wanderer like Livingstone never travelled in such a direct manner. For him to walk that far south again and find the Source, he would likely need to wander for a full year.

One thing was certain: Livingstone would not allow Stanley to rescue him. The explorer longed to return to England but, no matter how much he missed his children and friends, and despite physical problems that would have years earlier killed a man of lesser constitution, Livingstone would not leave Africa until his work was done.

On 13 December, after a month-long, three-hundred-mile canoe trip, Livingstone and Stanley paddled back to Ujiji and took up residence at Livingstone's home once again. Livingstone's dysentery had returned, worse than ever. Also, he was showing stronger signs of a hereditary form of manic depression known as cyclothymia, which caused alternating days of low moods with days of euphoria. This chronic bipolar dysfunction was manifest in the way Livingstone communicated with Stanley – one day revelling in endless conversation, and the next shunning the young American with the curious accent – even as they had sat together in the dugout mvule canoe. Despite those illnesses and the constant anaemia and hookworm, the two men's relationship continued to deepen. They spent their remaining days in Ujiji buying supplies with Stanley's dwindling bundles of cloth and girding for the trek back to Tabora. Once they arrived at Stanley's home there, Livingstone would remain in Tabora to rest while Stanley would race back to Zanzibar and purchase supplies so Livingstone could continue his travels. Stanley would then immediately commission a new group of porters to carry the new supplies to Livingstone. The men accompanying the medicine, cloth, food and beads from Zanzibar to Tabora would then remain in Livingstone's employ until he found the Source. In many ways, Livingstone would be starting fresh, as if he was stepping off the *Penguin* once more, as he did back in 1866. The only differences would be the knowledge gained thus far, the fact that his position deep in Africa precluded another journey through the coastal jungles and Livingstone's ever-diminishing health.

Their plan was to leave Ujiji for Tabora some time around New Year's Day, 1872. Stanley purchased goats for the journey so Livingstone would have milk, which was the easiest way for him to ingest calories. A mule was also procured, meaning Livingstone could ride after so many years of walking. Stanley dedicated himself to crafting a comfortable, functional saddle for his mentor. When fever forced Stanley into bed again on 18 December, Livingstone was by his side until it snapped on 21 December. It was then that Stanley noticed that Livingstone's left arm suffered some sort of paralysis, and was shorter than the right. Livingstone explained to Stanley about the lion attack from 1843, then let the young man trace his fingers along the left bicep and elbow to feel how the bones had set improperly.

Livingstone didn't mention the epiphany that transpired as that arm was crushed in a lion's jaws almost thirty years before. 'The shock produced a stupor similar to that which seems to be felt by a mouse after the first shake of the cat,' Livingstone had described the encounter just after it happened. 'It caused a sort of dreaminess, in which there was no sense of pain nor feeling of terror, though I was quite conscious of all that was happening. It was like what patients partially under the influence of chloroform describe, who see all the operation, but feel not the knife. This singular condition was not the result of any mental process. The shake annihilated fear, and allowed no sense of horror in looking round at the beast. This peculiar state is probably produced in all animals killed by the *carnivora*; and if so, is a merciful provision by our benevolent Creator for lessening the pain of death.'

That rendezvous with God's mercy had rendered death powerless before Livingstone. The transcendent ability to walk alone through the wilds of Africa had been born that day in 1843. He planned to continue walking alone long after returning to Tabora, and long after Stanley had gone to England. He approached the coming time of hardship and potentially fruitless exploration without fear.

On 7 January 1872, the New York *Herald*'s London correspondent continued Bennett's anti-British ridicule, writing that 'British munificence at times presents queer aspects. No sum is thought too large to devote to Christianizing the Fiji islanders, or for the purpose of carrying Bibles and warming pans to the benighted heathens of Central Africa or Nova Zambia. But for furthering in comparatively the greatest work of the nineteenth century – that of the discovery and exploration – the British government manifests an apathy and infirmity of purpose singularly at variance with both past policy and with present interest.'

The very next day *The Times* of London ran a story about Livingstone, reporting the new search. Wholly unaware – like all the world outside Ujiji – that the explorer had been found three months earlier, Nightingale had almost single-handedly raised four thousand pounds to fund the Second Livingstone Search and Relief Expedition. The RGS added five hundred more pounds from their own coffers. On 9 February, the expedition left London by train from Charing Cross station. In command was Lieutenant L. S. Dawson, who earned his exploration stripes along China's Yangtze. Lieutenant W. Henn of the Royal Navy was second-in-command.

The third member gave the rescue an emotional heft. Twenty-year-old Oswell Livingstone was off to find his father. He was a timid young man, more comfortable in the city than the wilderness. He hadn't been to Africa since he was a child and had been in the presence of his father fewer than five years of his life, but the time had come to follow in his father's large footsteps – if only to save him.

Bennett, though, didn't let sentimentality interfere with his attacks. The *Herald* mocked the new expedition as a reaction to American intervention, and one whose purposes paled in comparison with Stanley's. 'When the *Herald* equipped an expedition to explore Africa,' a Bennett editorial reported on 13 February 1872, 'it marked a new era in journalism as the ripest phase of modern civilization.' On 14 and 17 February the *Herald* continued its taunts by printing assurances from the RGS and the expedition members that Stanley would fail.

By that time, back in equatorial Africa, Stanley and Livingstone had left Ujiji and were en route to Tabora. Following the southern route to avoid Mirambo, they made good time. By 14 February, they were in the village of Ugunda, just four days' march from Tabora. Word of their coming had already reached Tabora. Ferrajjii and Cowpereh, the two special messengers Stanley had enlisted to carry his early *Herald* dispatches from Tabora back to the coast, had returned from Zanzibar carrying letters and newspapers. Even as the *Herald* dispatches were just beginning their hundred-day voyage by American merchant ship from Zanzibar to New York, the two messengers met the two explorers in Ugunda.

As the mail was eagerly opened, Stanley was stunned to read a letter from a furious Consul Webb, informing him that Bennett had refused to honour Stanley's debts. Stanley, usually so full of bravado, was so staggered by the news that he couldn't open any more of his mail. Even as Livingstone was absorbed in his own letters from home, Stanley merely sat and ruminated about the financial impossibility of repaying Webb. 'There was no doubt of it,' Stanley wrote in his journal. 'Bennett was about to treat me as I had heard he had treated others of his unfortunate correspondents.'

After an hour and a half of worry and fear, Stanley found the strength to sort through the mailbag again. He came upon a letter from the *Herald*, and opened it. Inside was the telegram from London, the one

Bennett had authorized before his hunting trip with Buffalo Bill, dated 25 September 1871 – Bennett had changed his mind. All Stanley's expenses were covered. A relieved Stanley cast off his gloom and spent the rest of the day chatting with Livingstone about all the news from the outside world.

They left Ugunda the next morning, and arrived in Tabora on 18 February 1872. 'Doctor,' Stanley had told Livingstone as they walked into Stanley's old house arm in arm, still unaware of the stir they were creating in the outside world, 'we are at last home.' Livingstone learned that a man named Shaw had died there some months before. His grave was two hundred yards to the left of the front door, in a cradle of trees, dried scrub and low hills.

Stanley remained at Livingstone's side for another month. On the morning of 14 March, they bade one another farewell. Livingstone was devastated, and Stanley had to turn away so Livingstone wouldn't see him crying. When Stanley began marching out of town towards Zanzibar, Livingstone had insisted on accompanying him for a while. They walked side by side, singing. Stanley kept looking over at Livingstone, trying to imprint the aged explorer's features upon his memory. Finally, when he could bear the anguish of parting no longer, Stanley begged Livingstone to go back.

'You have done what few men could do,' Livingstone told his young protégé. In their time together, Livingstone had paid Stanley the ultimate compliment by asking the journalist to return to Africa one day and carry on the explorer's work. It was an implicit acknowledgement that death would likely intrude on Livingstone finding the Source. 'And I am grateful for what you have done for me. God guide you for what you have done for me. God guide you safe home and bless you, my friend. Farewell.'

Livingstone watched Stanley walk into the rising sun, then he walked back to the house in Tabora that had once provided Stanley with refuge and a place to rest, and now would do the same for him. Livingstone was alone once again with the powerful Chuma and lighthearted Susi.

'My Dear Doctor,' Stanley wrote in a letter to Livingstone the next day. 'I have parted from you too soon. I am entirely conscious of it from being so depressed ... In writing to you, I am not writing to an idea now, but to an embodiment of warm good fellowship, of everything that is noble and right, of sound common sense, of everything practical and right-minded ... Though I am not present with you bodily you must think of me daily, until the caravan arrives. Though you are not before me visibly, I shall think of you constantly, until your least wish has been attended to. In this way the chain of remembrance will not be severed.'

The focus of Stanley's mission changed as he turned away from Livingstone. No longer was he racing into the unknown. Africa was not an obstacle in that sense any more. Now it was an impediment to sharing the news about Livingstone. The travails between him and Zanzibar – the Ugogo, the Makata swamp, fevers, thorns and the rainy season – were no less than before. If anything the journey would be more daunting, for Stanley planned to travel at breakneck speed.

He carried Livingstone's journals and a packet of sealed letters from the explorer. They were Livingstone's communiqués to the outside world, and the key to unlocking the mysteries of his whereabouts those many years. To Stanley, however, they were something just as vital and important: proof.

THIRTY-EIGHT

UPROAR

6 MAY 1872
Bagamoyo
525 miles from Livingstone

ON 25 APRIL 1872, WITH STANLEY BEARING DOWN ON BAGAMOYO, MOUNT
Vesuvius erupted in Italy. An immense explosion of lava, mud and
smoke poured from the long-dormant volcano. The eruption continued
for a solid week. Newspapers the world over ran stories about the
thick black plumes billowing from the crater, turning the day into
night.

Then just as Vesuvius grew quiet, another explosion rocked the newspaper world. It was Thursday, 2 May. 'Dr Livingstone,' *The Times*
reported, 'is safe with Stanley.'

Stanley's dispatch about the meeting, sent by special messenger from
Ujiji the previous November, had arrived in Zanzibar in March. By sheer
coincidence, the British steamer *Abydos* was in port, offloading the
Second Livingstone Search and Relief Expedition. *Abydos* then raced
from Zanzibar, eager to be away before the April monsoons. Even as
Webb sent Stanley's dispatches back to New York via merchant ship –
transporting them to either Bombay or Aden for transmittal via the
British-run telegraph network was far too risky – the British steamer
carried the verbal message about Stanley and Livingstone into Bombay.
There news soon flashed around the world by telegraph wire.

Ironically, the *Herald* wasn't alone in breaking the story in America. The New York *Times* pounced on the news out of Bombay. Hidden in a thicket of lengthy stories about the recently concluded Republican National Convention in Philadelphia, where New York *Tribune* owner Horace Greeley was selected to run against President Grant in the coming national election, was a small, hopeful item about Livingstone. 'A telegram has been received in this city from Bombay announcing the safety of Dr Livingstone. The steamer *Abydos*, which carried the Livingstone Search Expedition to Zanzibar, had arrived at Bombay from that place with the intelligence that the great traveler was safe with the American Stanley,' the story declared. 'The report is brought by negroes and believed there.'

The *Herald* soon regained the upper hand, however, publishing column after column boasting about the 'Grand Triumph of American Enterprise'. So many Livingstone stories were published in the *Herald* on 3 and 4 May that one reader – in a letter published on 5 May – asked the paper to let up, suggesting that Livingstone's heirs must have a financial interest in the newspaper.

On the evening of 6 May 1872, the day after the *Herald* printed a brand new Kirk letter (in which Kirk promised British officials that Stanley would fail), Stanley arrived safely in Bagamoyo. Since leaving Tabora, he had marched 525 miles in 52 days – a swift 32 days less than on the outbound journey to Tabora. Thirteen months after marching away to the fanfare of the local people and the *a cappella* singing of his men, Stanley strode into town. He was tanned, thin and toughened by Africa – almost unrecognizable as the unsure young man he was when he left. Against all odds, he was returning alive to the little town on the Indian Ocean with the white sand beach and sensual trade winds. A redheaded Englishman called out to him as he strolled down streets that were muddy and puddle-ridden from the worst monsoon season on record. It was Lieutenant Henn of the RGS's Livingstone Search and Relief Expedition, freshly arrived on the African continent. 'Won't you walk in?' he cried out from the door of a small, fly-infested bar. 'What will you have to drink – beer, stout, brandy? By George, I congratulate you on your splendid success!'

Stanley sat down with Henn and told of Livingstone. Stanley was glad for the drink and thankful for the warm welcome, but he didn't stay in Bagamoyo long. On 7 May 1872, after just one night in the beachfront town, Stanley sailed for Zanzibar. His now-tattered American flag flew high above his dhow as he turned his back on Africa. It was a moment filled with more emotion than he ever could have imagined during those times when he first arrived in Africa, suffering nightmares and pondering suicide. 'Farewell,' he had written in his journal two nights before, thinking of what it would be like to leave the continent behind, 'Oh Wagogo with their wild effrontery and noisy culture. Farewell to you Arabs and your sinful work – your lying tongues and black hearts. Farewell to fever remittent and intermittent, to the Makata Swamps and crocodiles, to brackish waters and howling plains . . . Above all, fare thee well Oh Livingstone, hero and Christian. Be thou healthy and prosperous wheresoever thou goest . . .'

'That bright flag whose stars have waved over inner Africa,' Stanley then wrote of the American flag Mrs Webb had sewn for him, 'which promised relief to the harassed Livingstone when in dire need in Ujiji. Which though not so rich, yet vied in beauty with America's flag. Return once more to sea, its proper domain. Torn it is, but not dishonoured, tattered but not disgraced . . .'

News of Stanley's return to Zanzibar had spread throughout the island and the harbour was awash in celebration as his dhow nosed into port. 'It was certainly a great sight,' reported an eyewitness. 'When the dhow neared Zanzibar, the gun fired and the American colours were soon visible, proudly flying from the gaff. The beach was lined with people, native and white, who testified their delight by increasing discharges of small arms. The guns in the sultan's batteries fired repeated salutes. And, in fact, the enthusiasm was something unparalleled. There was certainly never anything seen like it in Zanzibar. The Americans in particular were joyful in the extreme . . . the English were somewhat chagrined that the Americans had carried off the honours attached to the discovery.'

John Kirk was perhaps the least joyous about Stanley's arrival. The American had placed him in the middle of a controversy that might ruin his career and forever damage his reputation as a valued friend of Livingstone. When Stanley approached the wary British Consul and asked for his help in expediting the shipment of supplies to Livingstone in Tabora, Kirk immediately refused. 'I am not going to do anything more for Dr Livingstone,' he coolly told Stanley.

Stanley pressed Kirk to elaborate, but he merely explained that he was through with being insulted. Knowing that Stanley was eager to race back to England, Kirk told Stanley that if he wished to send new supplies to Livingstone, he would have to stay in Zanzibar long enough to purchase the goods and hire the porters himself.

Stanley did. Three long weeks later, Stanley was done. His last act before leaving Zanzibar on 29 May was to meet with the fifty-seven men who would carry goods inland to Livingstone. Many of them had been with Stanley during his journey into the interior. The moment when they finally went their separate ways was a surprisingly emotional one for Stanley. 'You are now about to return to Unyanyembe, to the Great Master. You know him,' Stanley said to the assemblage. He was standing in front of the American Consulate as he spoke. A dhow bobbed at anchor, waiting to load the men and their supplies on board for yet another journey to Africa. 'He is a good man and has a kind heart. He is different from me; he will not beat you as I have done.'

Then, in a whirl of nostalgia and long-hidden respect, the racist aspect of his character slipped momentarily aside. Stanley paid homage to the men who made his expedition possible. 'There is one thing more,' he said in conclusion. 'I want to shake hands with you all before you go – and we part for ever.'

Stanley wrote later that, 'they all rushed up, and vigorous shake was interchanged with each man'.

On 29 May, aboard the German ship *Africa*, Stanley finally sailed from Zanzibar, en route to London.

He envisioned a glorious return to England, but it was not to be. In London, even before Stanley sailed, the first seeds of doubt about his accomplishment were being sown. In a 7 May letter to *The Times*, the RGS's expert on Ethiopia, Charles Beke, publicly professed his scepticism that Stanley had truly found the missing explorer. Less than a week later, at an RGS meeting on 13 May, Sir Henry Rawlinson joined the anti-Stanley chorus, scoffing at the journalist's supposed accomplishment. 'It had been generally inferred that Mr Stanley had discovered and relieved Dr Livingstone,' the Manchester *Guardian* quoted Rawlinson the following day. 'But if there had been any discovery and relief it was Dr Livingstone who found and succoured Mr Stanley, as the latter was without supplies, whereas Dr Livingstone had large depots and stores at Ujiji, and was in a position to relieve the American on his reaching that place.'

The debate raged through the summer. The RGS and British press lined up to attack his integrity. Thanks to Bennett's tail-twisting, Stanley had no allies in Britain. On 12 July, Grant altered his allegiance to Stanley, saying to a friend, 'I see by *The Times* that Stanley has arrived with Livingstone's son at Aden in Suez – and feel much disappointed young Livingstone has left his father to his fate . . . no one believes Stanley found Livingstone.'

Sir Henry Rawlinson was proving to have an even sharper tongue, demeaning America and the *Herald* – 'our transatlantic cousins, among whom the science of advertising has reached a higher stage of development than in this benighted country' – while continuing to insist that Livingstone came to Stanley's aid, instead of it being the other way around. 'Dr Livingstone,' he said in late July, 'indeed, is in clover while Mr Stanley is nearly destitute.'

When Stanley finally arrived on British soil on 1 August, clinging to Livingstone's journal as proof as he stepped ashore in Dover, the British public was still unswayed. One newspaper, the *Echo*, even argued that the letters were written by a clairvoyant who channelled Livingstone's words, thoughts and handwriting.

The matter moved towards settlement on 2 August, when Stanley presented Tom Livingstone with his father's journals. As Oswell had already done, Tom announced the journals authentic. 'We have not the slightest reason to doubt that this is my father's journal, and I certify that the letters he has brought home are my father's letters, and no others.'

Earl Granville wrote a glowing thank-you letter to Stanley that same day. 'I cannot omit this opportunity of expressing to you my admiration of the qualities which have enabled you to achieve the object of your mission, and to attain a result which has been hailed with so much enthusiasm both in the United States and in this country.'

Despite that official blessing, and the international outpouring of interest, doubt about the journals' veracity lingered as the contents became public. The primary reason was Livingstone's writings about the women of Nyangwe. In an era where Victorian sexual mores meant that female masturbation was considered the root of lust (with clitoridectomy a popular remedy), and where it was never discussed that many upper-class men found their sexual satisfaction with prostitutes instead of their wives, Livingstone's journal entries about African women being beautiful and vivacious – an unthinkable notion at a time when the

English still regarded Africans as pagan savages – were considered proof that the journals were forgeries. Such a venerated missionary as Livingstone would never look at a woman – whether African or European – in that manner, it was considered.

Stanley seethed at the abuse, but endured it stoically, even as the truth about his childhood became public, and as Lewis Noe sold his tale of their Turkish imprisonment to the New York *Sun*. Stanley was shocked by the criticisms he was enduring, but felt impotent to speak out about them.

In New York, meanwhile, Bennett let Stanley suffer the slanders and accusations, knowing it would continue to keep Livingstone's name in the news. Stories about Africa had been appearing in the *Herald* throughout the summer, averaging one every four days. The term 'Dr Livingstone, I presume' first appeared in print in the 15 July 1872 edition, and soon became world famous. Throughout August, Bennett continued the Livingstone news cycle, focusing his attacks on the RGS for their myopia and anti-American feelings – ironically, the very feelings he had fostered.

Despite Bennett's taunts, British opinion slowly began turning in Stanley's favour. On 27 August, Granville wrote a letter that officially endorsed Stanley's accomplishment – and in a most grandiose fashion. 'I have great satisfaction in conveying to you, by command of the Queen,' Granville wrote, 'her Majesty's high appreciation of the prudence and zeal which you have displayed in opening a communication with Dr Livingstone, and relieving her Majesty from the anxiety which, in common with her subjects, she had felt in regard of that distinguished traveller.'

Stanley's transition from scoundrel to saviour was complete on 8 September 1872, when the bastard from Wales was formally introduced to the Queen of England. Sir Henry Rawlinson presented Henry Morton Stanley to Queen Victoria at Dunrobin Castle, making it clear to one and all that Stanley was the true discoverer of David Livingstone. 'The geographers as a body,' Rawlinson confided to Stanley, speaking of the RGS, 'rejoice in the honours you are receiving.'

Stanley's exploration pedigree reached its fruition in November 1872. He was paid ten thousand US dollars to write a book about his African travels. *How I Found Livingstone* answered all Stanley's critics (to the RGS's earlier proclamation that 'Livingstone was in clover', he responded in the book: 'May I ask, if you believe that . . . why you sent an expedition out to find him?'). It became an immediate bestseller. Henry Morton Stanley was, after a lifetime of well-intentioned mediocrity, a success.

V

HOMECOMING

Henry Morton Stanley, African explorer

© Hulton-Deutsch Collection/CORBIS

Dr David Livingstone, lion in repose

© Bettmann/CORBIS

THIRTY-NINE

CHITAMBO'S VILLAGE

JANUARY TO APRIL 1873
Near Lake Bangweolo

LIVINGSTONE RESTED IN TABORA UNTIL LATE AUGUST OF 1872. THE SUPPLIES Stanley had arranged reached him earlier in the month, and as Livingstone marched away from the Arab enclave, he led a fully stocked caravan for the first time since 1867. He travelled south-west, away from Mirambo and his ongoing war, around the southernmost tip of Lake Tanganyika, then into the highlands three hundred miles due west of Lake Nyassa to explore once again for the Source. Months passed. By January of 1873, the most miserable month of the rainy season, food was again short and his health again began to fail. He was skeletal. A crimson blossom on the seat of his threadbare trousers advertised bleeding haemorrhoids and chronic dysentery, adding humiliation to Livingstone's discomfort. The venerable Scot stepped off the trail to relieve himself so often his porters knew the curvature of his scrawny buttocks in detail.

Day by day, through means visible and concealed, the continent in which he felt most content whittled the world's greatest explorer down to a nub. Hundreds of miles from relief supplies, and with a second rescue a delirious fantasy, Livingstone was fated to die an anonymous death and be lowered into an anonymous wilderness grave, like Cook and Franklin before him. For the people back home, there would be curiosity about where his bones were turning to dust, but only for a time. That's the way it was with exploration. The curiosity would fade as his explorations were surpassed. Over time he would be forgotten. There was no romance in the dying, only the reality that it would be slow and painful. It would almost have been easier if Livingstone's lion attacker had finished what it started so many years before.

The prudent move would have been to turn east, towards the coast, and try to fall in with an Arab slave caravan heading for Zanzibar. Livingstone could have saved himself that way. The slavers would have food, and maybe even medicine, to fortify him for the six-month trek.

But Livingstone had come to Africa to find the Source of the Nile – he'd promised Murchison – and he was determined not to leave until he had solved mankind's last great geographical mystery. So instead of turning to the coast, Livingstone led his caravan west into the heart of Africa one last time, gambling he could pinpoint the Source and then flee to Zanzibar before his time ran out. Through his travels and through continuing interviews with local tribes, Livingstone was convinced the legendary Four Fountains of Herodotus were getting closer. Livingstone had already written the telegram he would wire to the Foreign Office. It lay in the watertight tin box holding his journals and letters. The only thing left was filling in the blanks. 'I have the pleasure of reporting to your Lordship that on the ____ I succeeded in reaching your remarkable fountains . . .'

Such a scenario, however, was not meant to be. Murchison was already dead, though Livingstone never knew it. And January was a treacherous month for him to gamble with his life. The first month of the year normally brought as much as forty inches of rain in that sub-equatorial belt, but January 1873 was the worst in memory, an exhausting continuum of cold and wet and clouds soaking feet and morale, bringing on chills and fever and misery in the healthiest of men. Even days that began with blue skies and puffy white clouds eventually blackened with storm, like a sudden act of sin consuming the clean soul of a believer.

The water poured down ceaselessly, flooding low-lying meadows and forests until they became chains of puddles and marshes and impromptu rivers that seemed to cover all of Central Africa. The only way to distinguish flood land from river was by the deceptive current that would suddenly knock a man off his feet. Minor depressions like elephant footprints were clotted with algae and muck until they became miniature swamps unto themselves.

Making matters worse was the lack of food. The ground was under-water, rendering foraging difficult. Game animals had run for higher ground. Livingstone's caravan numbered fifty-seven porters; his four faithful assistants Chuma, Susi, Gardner and Amoda; Halima, Amoda's wife, who cooked for Livingstone; and Ntoeka, Chuma's wife. There were others who had joined the caravan since Tabora, most notably a teenage boy, later distinctly remembered by African villagers but never mentioned in his journals by Livingstone. All the members of Livingstone's group, like the explorer, were starving. The porters were growing too weak to carry him or manage their bundles of cloth, beads and gear. They tramped through mile after mile of mud and decay and water, watching all the while for crocodiles and snakes.

But they pressed on. Throughout January, Livingstone and his men averaged just a mile and a half of travel daily. By the end of the month it was even less. Livingstone had grown too weak to walk. Chuma, with his broad shoulders and powerful legs, carried Livingstone on his shoulders, even through deep swamps.

'Rain, rain, rain, as if it never tired,' Livingstone wrote wearily in his journal on 23 January. And the next day: 'Went one and three-quarter hours' journey to a large stream through a drizzling rain. At least three hundred yards of deep water amongst sedges and sponges of one hundred yards. One part was neck deep for fifty yards and the water cold.'

The rains continued into February. Like the lion outside his camp one miserable evening 'that had wandered into this world of water and anthills and roared all night as if very much disgusted', Livingstone complained about the misery, even to God, but saw no easy way out of his predicament. In the end it was a simple choice. If he went home without finding the Source he would live out his days as a disgraced pauper. It was as simple as that. Livingstone pushed on for the Source, even after a massive colony of driver ants – carnivorous ants which travelled in swarms hundreds of thousands strong, capable of eating even large beasts – invaded his tent one night and bit him so extensively he had welts all over his body. Chuma and Susi saved his life by setting grass fires that smoked the ants from the camp, then spent hours plucking the remainder off Livingstone's body.

In early March, Livingstone and his men came upon an oasis of sorts when they discovered an abandoned settlement and the remains of a garden. They gorged on long-forgotten cassava and sweet potatoes before continuing their journey. Livingstone's strength returned after that impromptu starch feast, but not for long. Even in his pain, he wrote rapturous journal entries about Africa, like the day he wrote of the beautiful wildflowers blooming all around him. Vibrant hues of pink, blue, white and yellow burst forth 'in one whorl of blossoms'. He wrote of that beauty because it reminded him that God was near, just as he described the saturated lion, and the 'weird, unearthly voice' of a fish eagle. God's will had brought Livingstone to Africa in the first place, and in His presence Livingstone found strength.

Livingstone's birthday was 19 March. He celebrated in a swamp, sleeping in a hut choked with poisonous spiders. He waited for his men to purchase the canoes they would need to paddle onwards. Once, when the frustrating negotiations with the local chief renting the canoes, a man named Matipa, dragged on and on, Livingstone vented his rage by sitting up in bed and firing off round after round from his pistol. He would beat death, that was for sure. Through the kindness of strangers and enemies, he had done it over and over on the Source expedition. There was no reason to think he couldn't do it again if he had a little help. 'Can I hope for ultimate success? So many obstacles have arisen. Let not Satan prevail over me, Lord Jesus,' he prayed.

In a letter he'd received when Stanley sent the resupply caravan back to Tabora, his oldest daughter Agnes, who had graduated from her Paris boarding school and was living in London, had urged Livingstone to stay in Africa until he was done. 'Much as I wish you to come home,' she wrote, 'I would rather that you finished your work to your own satisfaction than merely returning to gratify me.'

Agnes was his favourite child, and he'd made a habit of telling her she was capable of achieving anything she set her mind to. Now she was doing the same for him. 'May blessing be on her,' Livingstone answered in his journal. 'And all the rest.'

His search expedition was seven years old. The rainy season was just ending. He had fought the ants of February. He had vented his rage and secured his canoes in March. He had crossed Lake Bangweolo with Chuma and Susi and his small caravan. He had observed, on 6 April, that the endless span of water south of Lake Bangweolo was not a seasonal flood, but the Nile itself 'enacting its inundations, even at its Source. The amount of water spread out over the country constantly excites my wonder – it is prodigious.'

Unbeknown to Livingstone, he would never discover the Source of the Nile. He was, in fact, almost six hundred miles due south of the Source. His death was now imminent. Not even a repeat of Stanley's exploits could save him. 'I am pale, bloodless and weak from bleeding profusely,' he wrote in early April. 'An artery gives off a copious stream, and takes away my strength. Oh, how I long to be permitted by the Over Power to finish my work.'

In addition to blood loss, anaemia, malaria, dysentery and hookworm, a blood clot the size of an apple had also formed in his abdomen. Livingstone didn't know it was there, but he could feel the pain – the slightest touch of a human hand on his lower back made him want to faint with agony. 'It is not all pleasure, this exploration,' he wrote on 19 April.

Livingstone planned to complete his discoveries within six or seven months of being resupplied at Tabora. But by the time he reached the village of a chief named Chitambo on 29 April 1873, the six months were up.

Like the lions of the animal kingdom, Livingstone had become a symbol of Africa. The male lion is a solitary presence, with meaty forearms designed for swatting, slashing and tearing. He looks docile and even affectionate as he sleeps the hot days away. But he has lethal speed, a taste for flesh and is always prepared to strike. It was an obvious choice for Murchison to call his African explorers lions. The comparisons between the unassuming men with their great accomplishments and the king of beasts were apt.

Livingstone thought too much was made of lions, however, and he lampooned their public mystique. 'The same feeling which has induced the modern painter to caricature the lion, has led the sentimentalist to consider the lion's roar the most terrific of all earthly sounds. We hear "the majestic roar of the king of beasts". It is, indeed, well calculated to inspire fear if you hear it in combination with the tremendously loud thunder of that country, on a night so pitchy dark that every flash of the intensely vivid lightning leaves you with the impression of stone blindness,' he wrote. 'But when you are in a comfortable wagon or house the case is very different, and you hear the roar of the lion without any awe or alarm. The silly ostrich makes a noise as loud, yet he was never feared by man. To talk of the majestic roar of the lion is mere majestic twaddle.'

Few men could make such a claim about lions, but Livingstone knew first-hand the terror of being in a lion's jaws. He had seen the animal up close, at its most vicious.

'In general,' Livingstone once described the way a lion killed prey, 'the lion seizes the animal he is attacking by the flank near the hind leg, or by the throat below the jaw. It is questionable whether he ever attempts to seize an animal by the withers. The flank is the most common point of attack, and that is the part he begins to feast on first. The natives and lions are very similar in their tastes in the selection of tit-bits: an eland may be seen disembowelled by a lion so completely that he scarcely seems cut up at all. The bowels and fatty parts form a full meal for even the largest lion.'

He even took a cocky attitude in his journals. 'One is more in danger of being run over when walking in the streets of London than he is of being devoured by lions in Africa, unless engaged in hunting the animal. Indeed, nothing I have seen or heard about lions would constitute a barrier in the way of men of ordinary courage or enterprise.

'Hunting a lion with dogs involved very little danger as compared with hunting the Indian tiger, because the dogs bring him out of cover and make him stand at bay, giving the hunter plenty of time for a deliberate shot.'

But lions taught him the most valuable lesson of his life. Each moment of the 1843 attack was unforgettable to Livingstone, from the instant he first laid eyes upon the lion 'just in the act of springing upon me' to the helplessness of watching the animal pounce and the horrible impact as the animal's incisors latched on to Livingstone's shoulder mid-flight before the two, intertwined, smashed to the ground, lion on top. 'Growling horribly close to my ear,' Livingstone wrote of what happened next, 'he shook me as a terrier dog does to a rat.'

Later in London, when asked what thoughts were running through his head during such a traumatic moment, Livingstone answered with a bit of black humour. 'I was thinking, with a feeling of disinterested curiosity, which part of me the brute would eat first.'

When the lion, who had one paw on the back of Livingstone's head, was shot by another hunter, Livingstone walked away from the tragedy afraid of nothing. Death held no sway over him. When John Kirk was asked what impressed him most about Livingstone, he mentioned his fearlessness. 'He did not know what fear was.'

'His absolute lack of any sense of fear,' Kirk told an interviewer years after his travels with Livingstone, 'amounted almost to a weakness. He would go into the most perilous positions without a tremor or a touch of hesitation. I never knew him to blench or show a sign of timorousness in any circumstance whatsoever.'

Through the years, what gave Livingstone pause was not fear, but regret. 'There are regrets,' he had written in 1862, 'which will follow me to my dying day.'

Lying in Chitambo's village, his primary regrets were family and indiscretion. His family ceased to exist as a unit when Livingstone sent them home in 1852 so he could attempt his walk across Africa. He cried as their ships sailed.

Parenting in Victorian England was not a hands-on activity. Children were expected to look after themselves and their younger siblings. When they were old enough, children were either sent away to boarding school or out to find a job. It was normal for fathers to work long hours and have limited contact with the children. Mothers spent an hour or two with the children each day, at most. So when Livingstone travelled for years at a time, there was never a question about him being a poor parent. Only cruel, abusive or drunkard men received such a label. Nevertheless, 'the act of orphanizing my children, which now becomes painfully clear, will be like tearing out my bowels, for they will all forget me', Livingstone wrote before his trans-Africa trek.

That his children had learned to do without him was pain enough. But Livingstone's infidelity was a breach of character. And there was one manifestation of this that remained fairly well concealed during Livingstone's lifetime. It may have occurred in the fiery Princess Manenko's village or in some other village during his many years in Africa, but Livingstone, it was later documented, fathered at least one African child. That son was the teenage boy who had joined the caravan some time after Tabora. 'He also had with him his son. He was a half-caste. The people said it was Bwana's son,' Chitambo's nephew later swore in a deposition, speaking of the day Livingstone entered his village. 'Bwana' was a term of respect. 'The people said it was Bwana's son. He was respected by the others as the son of a chief. I did not see the mother or any other woman with the Bwana's people.'

Chitambo wasn't the only villager who would swear to a subsequent generation of British travellers about Livingstone's son. Another African, Mumana, remembered that 'the Bwana had one son with him . . . his skin was quite white like a European child and his hair was fair'.

So as Livingstone lay in Chitambo's village, the boy was there too, having joined Livingstone between Stanley's departure from Tabora and Livingstone's arrival in the region surrounding Chitambo's village. Livingstone never wrote about the child. But the boy was sick and had been carried, like his father, and the locals would always remember the odd sight of the ill white father and his ill white son. They would speak of the respect accorded to Livingstone's son, and how Chuma and Susi had built a house of grass and sticks not only for Livingstone, but for the boy as well.

The night of 1 May 1873 would also be remembered vividly. In Chitambo's village, Chuma and Susi had made a small bed for Livingstone and arranged his mosquito netting, then left him alone for the night. Lying in the dark, his coming death was like an angel on his chest.

Livingstone woke between midnight and dawn. He slipped to the floor and got on his knees to pray. Chuma and Susi had gone to bed, as he'd instructed them.

It was 4 a.m. when they found him. He was still kneeling in prayer, but was pitched forward, with his face buried in the pillow as if he'd dozed while praying. David Livingstone, at the age of sixty, was dead.

FORTY

PALL MALL

MAY 1874
Chitambo's Village

CHUMA AND SUSI COULD HAVE SIMPLY BURIED LIVINGSTONE'S BODY NEAR Chitambo's village and left for the coast. It was the logical thing to do. But they knew he had longed to return to England before he died. Finishing the journey without him would have been inappropriate, so, embarking on one final exhausting journey with Livingstone, Chuma and Susi set out on a mission to carry his body back to England.

To preserve the explorer's remains, a tribesman named Farijala, who had once been a surgeon's servant in Zanzibar, made a single horizontal incision in Livingstone's abdomen, just above the pubic bone. The examining coroner in London would one day call Farijala's work 'ingeniously contrived', marvelling at how the uneducated tribesman was able to remove Livingstone's heart, lungs and abdominal organs through the small opening. As he did so, Farijala also removed the massive blood clot in Livingstone's intestine. Then, cradling the heart carefully, Farijala laid it in the precious tin box Livingstone once used to protect his journals. After handing the watertight box to Chuma and Susi, he shoved salt into Livingstone's empty chest cavity. Then, even as the remainder of Livingstone's body dried for two weeks in the sun, a hole was scraped from the ground at the base of a sprawling mpundu tree. The tin box was placed inside as prayers were read over the grave site. The dirt was placed back on top. His body would be returning to England, but Livingstone's heart would always remain in Africa.

The mummification of Livingstone's body continued. As it was dried, the legs were bent back at the knees to make him shorter and easier to carry. Blue and white striped calico was wrapped tightly around his corpse, followed by a protective cylinder of bark. Finally, the entire package was wrapped tightly in sailcloth, then slung from a pole. Two weeks after his death, Livingstone's body swaying between them, Chuma and Susi began the long march to Zanzibar with the rest of the caravan. A drummer boy marched at the front of the column. Livingstone's consular Union Jack snapped in the breeze. In all, seventy-nine porters made up the caravan. Many of them carried nothing more than Livingstone's books and papers.

Moving slowly, stopping frequently for weather and sickness, taking turns carrying Livingstone's body, the caravan reached Tabora in early November. The Royal Geographical Society, consumed by the sudden need to bring Livingstone back out of Africa, had sent yet another relief expedition to find him. This Third Livingstone Relief Expedition had seen one disaster after another. The usual litany of weather and malaria and geography had made their passage from Bagamoyo to Tabora miserable. Robert Moffatt, Livingstone's nephew, had been one of the expedition's four white men. He died of malaria. Another expedition member would commit suicide after a bout of dysentery drove him mad.

The only connection this discouraged, frazzled Third Livingstone Relief Expedition had with the African expeditions of previous searchers such as Burton, Speke, Grant and Stanley was the caravan leader – Sidi Mubarak Bombay. The grizzled veteran of three major expeditions in East Africa was going into Africa once again with yet another band of explorers.

The relief expedition was loitering in Tabora in November, trying to figure out its next move. As if by a miracle, Livingstone was suddenly brought into their midst. Chuma and Susi, however, had no intention of stopping or giving up the body of their beloved leader. After a rest of less than a week, the devoted porters marched from Tabora towards Bagamoyo. Two of the relief expedition members accompanied the body. The other, Lieutenant V. Lovett Cameron, continued for Ujiji, where Livingstone had cached letters and journals. He wouldn't stop his westward march until he got to the Atlantic, making Cameron the second British explorer to cross Africa.

Meanwhile, Chuma and Susi reached Bagamoyo in February 1874. When Chuma crossed to Zanzibar to formally present Kirk the news, he learned that the Consul was home in London on leave. Kirk's deputy, Royal Navy Captain W. F. Prideaux, ordered the warship HMS *Vulture* to pick up Livingstone's remains in Bagamoyo. Prideaux then dismissed Chuma, Susi and the rest of the caravan that had laboured for almost a year to carry Livingstone's body out of Africa. For Chuma and Susi, who had been with Livingstone throughout his search, and without whose assistance the journey would have been impossible, it was an abrupt and thankless end.

Meanwhile, Livingstone's body was placed in a proper coffin in Zanzibar, then he, his papers and his personal possessions were transferred to the steamship *Malwa*. By 16 April 1874, eight years and eighteen days after leaving England, Livingstone finally returned. England went into mourning as *Malwa* docked at Southampton to the thunder of a twenty-one-gun salute. A brass band played Handel's *Death March* as Livingstone's flag-draped coffin was transferred to a special train provided by Queen Victoria. The train carried Livingstone's body to London, where his remains were formally examined by Sir William Ferguson and five of Livingstone's friends. Kirk, ironically, was present, too. And while sun and salt and eleven hard months had rendered his face unrecognizable, the sight of his shattered left humerus was enough to convince all that this was truly Livingstone.

The body lay in state in the RGS Map Room on Friday, 17 April. 'Floor and walls were covered with black cloth,' *The Times* reported. 'And on all sides were memorials of the departed – his portraits taken at various periods of his career, his astronomical and drawing instruments, his charts in ink and pencil – the authentic records of his exploration – his chronometer, and other objects of unfading interest. Nor was the mournful darkness of the room unrelieved by graceful and tender devices. There were wreaths of amaranth and branches of palm.'

At half past noon on Saturday, 18 April 1874, a plumed hearse drawn by four horses pulled up at the Savile Row entrance to the RGS headquarters. Livingstone's polished oak coffin was carried out of the door and placed in the hearse. Then Livingstone's funeral procession made its way to Westminster Abbey. Twelve mourning carriages containing family, friends and RGS dignitaries travelled behind Livingstone. The Queen's royal carriage and the Prince of Wales's carriage followed next. A long line of personal carriages joined the procession. Houses along

Savile Row had their curtains drawn in respect, and shops along Piccadilly, Regent Street and Waterloo Place had one or two shutters raised in the customary sign of mourning. Thousands of onlookers lined the road in what would become one of Britain's largest ever displays of mourning. 'The crowd in Trafalgar Square was larger than at other and less advantageous vantage points,' *The Times* reported. 'But it was nowhere else so large as round the railings of Westminster Abbey.'

'Inside the Abbey an immense congregation had assembled by a little after twelve o'clock,' reported *The Times*. 'So dense was the throng of ticket holders that many who were able to pass into the building were unable to avail themselves of that right.'

Kirk was there. Grant, too. Even E. D. Young. And by appropriate coincidence, Stanley had just returned to England after an assignment covering the Ashantee War. Those men – all vital to the arc of Livingstone's search for the Source – would serve as four of the eight pallbearers. 'Such a gathering of sunburnt visages and far-travelled men was never seen before, and indeed, the list might be lengthened with the names of a hundred other famous travellers present, who listen with wistful looks around their great dead chieftain,' *The Times* noted.

The service proceeded with a minimum of pomp and fanfare. Then, to the strains of Handel, as the choir intoned, 'His body rests in peace, but his name liveth evermore,' Livingstone was buried. His final resting place was not anonymous and his accomplishments would not be forgotten. As the mourners filed out, they threw flowers and wreaths down into Livingstone's grave. 'Each of those present,' concluded *The Times*, 'takes a long parting glance at the great traveller's resting place, and at the oaken coffin buried in spring blossoms, and palms, and garlands wherein lies "as much as could die" of the good, great-hearted, loving, fearless and faithful David Livingstone.'

Stanley was among those taking a last, wistful look. Their time together had been just five short months, but his name and Livingstone's would be forever linked by history. Henry Morton Stanley, the drifter who fled Central City, Colorado, eight years before, striving to eke out a measure of adventure and success in his life, now knew both in spades – thanks in great part to Livingstone. 'When I had seen the coffin lowered into the grave, and heard the first handful of earth thrown over it,' Stanley wrote, 'I walked away sorrowing over the fate of David Livingstone.'

Stanley walked solemnly out of the great doors of Westminster Abbey into bright London sunshine, already charting yet another course in his life. He was successful, he was wealthy and he was famous, yet Stanley was preparing to throw it all away. He had made a promise to Livingstone in the heart of Africa – a promise to finish the explorer's work, and find the Source of the Nile. It was a promise Stanley intended to keep.

Henry Morton Stanley, the new lion, was going back into Africa.

EPILOGUE

THE SAGA OF STANLEY AND LIVINGSTONE SPARKED AN UNLIKELY TURNING point in history. Journalism's growing power, America's ascendance and Britain's eventual eclipse, one generation of explorers giving way to another, and the opening of Africa – all were either foreshadowed by or came about as a result of Livingstone's love affair with Africa and Stanley's unlikely march to find him.

Though the story's impact waned with every subsequent news cycle, author Joseph Conrad – who, as a child growing up in Poland, was so taken with Livingstone's adventures that he declared of Africa: 'When I grow up I shall go *there*' – gave Stanley and Livingstone literary immortality. Conrad called Stanley's search 'a newspaper stunt', and lamented that colonial 'empire builders suppress for me the memory of David Livingstone', but some of his biographers suggest Conrad's *Heart of Darkness* is based loosely on the New York *Herald* expedition. Stanley is Marlow; Livingstone is Kurtz. Ironically, it is that brilliant novel, not the journals of Livingstone or Stanley, which stands as the literary snapshot synonymous with nineteenth-century Africa.

David Livingstone's burial site lies in the centre of Westminster Abbey's nave, near the tomb of the Unknown Warrior. The stone reads: 'Brought by faithful hands over land and sea here rests David Livingstone, missionary, traveller, philanthropist, born March 19, 1813, at Blantyre, Lanarkshire, died May 1, 1873 at Chitambo's Village, Ulala. For 30 years his life was spent in an unwearied effort to evangelize the native races, to explore the undiscovered secrets, to abolish the desolating slave trade of Central Africa, where with his last words he wrote, "All I can add in my solitude is, may Heaven's rich blessing come down on every one, American, English, or Turk, who will help to heal this open sore of the world."'

Livingstone's death opened the floodgates to European exploration of Africa. Within a decade, history's infamous Scramble for Africa had begun. Europe's powers began a pell-mell dash to exploit the resources and peoples of the continent. By the Anglo-German Agreement of 1886, the Sultan of Zanzibar's influence was forever replaced by the two European nations. England took control of what is now Kenya, while Germany named their territory German East Africa. That is the land Stanley marched through on his journey to Livingstone. Nowadays the nation is known as Tanzania, and the railway tracks from Dar es Salaam to Kigoma roughly follow his path.

Germany's control of the region concluded at the end of the First World War. The British, who defeated the Germans in a major battle on the sands of Bagamoyo, effected total control of the region. In 1964, exactly one century after the Nile Duel, the British ended their colonial reign and the independent Republic of Tanzania was born.

Henry Morton Stanley's reportage defined his era: from the Civil War to the American Indian Wars to the British invasion of Abyssinia to Livingstone to the Scramble for Africa. By inserting himself into the story during the Livingstone search, he began a new tradition of first-person adventure journalism.

Though Stanley always swore he uttered the words 'Dr Livingstone, I presume?' the journal page pertaining to that specific moment was torn out, so there is nothing in Stanley's journals stating that he ever asked the question. It is possible that the missing page was an act of sabotage, likely perpetrated by a far-sighted collector. But if Stanley didn't make the statement, and tore out the page to cover his tracks, it would be in keeping with his character. He may have fabricated the quote when writing his *Herald* stories (he mentions the quote in two separate dispatches: the first was published 15 July 1872, the other 10 August 1872). However, what began as a self-professed attempt to sound eloquent became the journey's defining moment. The line would become the standard greeting for later generations of African explorers when encountering one another on the trail.

By the time Stanley returned to London, then America, 'Dr

Livingstone, I presume?' was so well known that recanting would have caused considerable loss of face and further corroborated the public perception created by the RGS and Bennett's rivals that the journalist's credibility was dubious. He continued using the quote in *How I Found Livingstone*. To the day he died, Stanley maintained he uttered the famous line.

More germane to the discussion are the heights to which Stanley soared after Livingstone died. Not only did he assume Livingstone's mantle of African explorer extraordinaire, he surpassed his mentor.

Stanley returned to Africa in 1874 to find the Source of the Nile. The expedition was funded jointly by James Gordon Bennett, Jr and the London *Daily Telegraph*. In one of the most incredible achievements in the history of exploration, he marched inland from Bagamoyo, travelled the circumference of Lake Victoria seeking confirmation of Speke's theories, continued his travels inland to circumnavigate Lake Tanganyika, then pushed even further inland to the Congo River, which he followed all the way to the Atlantic Ocean. His reputation later in life, however, was besmirched when Stanley was paid a substantial sum by the King of Belgium to colonize Western Africa. Leopold IV was a manipulative man who had long sought ways to expand the size of his tiny country in order to increase his personal wealth. With Stanley's help, the Belgian Congo came into being. Sadly, and contrary to Livingstone's legacy, Stanley would unwittingly help found one of the greatest slave-trading nations in history. Even after Stanley left Leopold's employ, the stench of that period hung about him.

Later in life he turned his back on America and lived out his days as a British citizen. He married one Dorothy Tennant, and successfully ran for Parliament. Stanley's legacy, however, could not shake the stigma of his association with slavery. When Stanley died from complications of a stroke and pleurisy on 10 May 1904, the funeral service was held in Westminster Abbey, just like Livingstone's. But the Dean of Westminster, the Reverend Joseph Armitage Robinson, refused to allow the interment of Stanley's remains in the cathedral. Instead, the body was cremated. The ashes were buried twenty-five miles south-west in Pirbright's village churchyard. A more fitting site would have been outside his house in Tabora, which still stands. Shaw's clearly marked grave lies just beyond its walls.

In 2002, almost a thousand of Stanley's artifacts from his African travels were discovered in a descendant's attic. These items, which included Stanley's annotated manuscript of *The Lake Regions of Central Africa*, his Winchester, his compass and a personally inscribed map of his Congo expedition from 1874 to 1878 were auctioned at Christie's on 23 September 2002. 'Never before,' a Christie's representative noted, 'has such a large collection of artifacts relating to one explorer been offered at auction.'

James Gordon Bennett and the *Herald* saw their heyday in the 1870s. In addition to Stanley finding Livingstone, Stanley tracing the path of the Congo and assorted other expeditions Bennett funded, the *Herald* had its second great scoop of the decade in July 1876. Acting on information wired to New York from, coincidentally, Fort McPherson, Nebraska, the *Herald* broke the story of the massacre of General George Custer and his cavalry at the Little Big Horn. That would be the end of Bennett's New York triumphs. He moved to Paris in 1877 after disgracing himself before New York society by drunkenly urinating in a fireplace during a formal dinner with his fiancée. By 1900 he was dividing his time between an apartment on the Champs Elysées and a mansion near Versailles, and owned a 301-foot yacht with a crew of one hundred. Bennett died in Paris on 14 May 1918. His body was interred in an unmarked mausoleum in the Cemetery of Passy. The New York *Herald* spawned a Paris edition, merged with the New York *Tribune*, and is known today as the *International Herald Tribune*.

Sidi Mubarak Bombay crossed Africa as Cameron's caravan leader between January 1874 and November 1875. Upon reaching Luanda, on the Atlantic coast, Bombay sailed home to Zanzibar. On 5 May 1876, just two months after his return, the Reverend W. Salter Price of the Church Missionary Society approached Bombay about leading a caravan into Uganda. Bombay accepted. But in August of that year, while concluding final preparations in Bagamoyo, word reached Bombay that the Royal Geographical Society was awarding him a lifetime pension as thanks for his many years of service. He immediately announced his retirement and returned to Zanzibar, where he died on 12 October 1885. Between 8 February 1857, when Burton and Speke plucked him from the obscurity of the Chokwe garrison, and the day he died, Bombay was a member of the Burton and Speke, Speke and Grant, Stanley, and Cameron expeditions. He travelled the Nile from Lake Victoria all the way to Cairo, and from Bagamoyo to the Atlantic coast. The former slave died as one of the most accomplished African travellers in history.

David Susi and James Chuma travelled to England shortly after Livingstone's funeral. Their fare was paid for by Livingstone's friend Horace Waller, who relied upon their insights and geographical expertise while compiling Livingstone's final journals for publication. At a Royal Geographical Society meeting on 1 June 1874, Chuma and Susi were presented with special medals by the Society. They returned to Africa in October of that year. The date of Susi's death is unknown, but Chuma died on 12 September 1882, at the mission hospital in Zanzibar.

John Kirk remained British Consul at Zanzibar until 1884. He endured a major investigation into his mishandling of Livingstone's relief supplies, and was exonerated of all charges of neglect. When the Zanzibar slave trade came to an end in the late 1870s, Kirk claimed credit for the accomplishment, and was knighted.

Sir Samuel White Baker left Gondokoro for England on 26 May 1873, just over three weeks after Livingstone's death. He died at home in Florence's arms on 30 December 1893.

E. D. Young returned to Eastern Africa in 1875, leading a group of missionaries sent by the Free Church Mission of Scotland to establish a new site known as the Livonstonia Mission, site of present-day Blantyre. He launched the first steamship ever to navigate Lake Nyassa. A warrant officer all his life, Young was officially bumped into a higher social standing when he was promoted to the rank of honorary lieutenant upon his retirement in June 1891.

F. R. Webb transferred from Zanzibar to become American Consul in New Zealand.

Buffalo Bill Cody and Wild Bill Hickok were invited to New York by James Gordon Bennett, Jr at the conclusion of their 1871 hunting trip. Cody, in particular, was the toast of the town. As a result of his newfound fame he abandoned life on the plains and became a successful and extremely wealthy entertainer, circus owner and movie producer. He owed that prosperity to a combination of dime-store novels about his exploits by writer Ned Buntline, and also to Bennett's ten-day journey across the plains. A series of business setbacks cost Cody his fortune. At the end of his life he was almost destitute. He died in Denver on 10 January 1917.

Hickok, who didn't share Cody's passion for New York, returned to the west after his visit. He became Mayor of Hays, Kansas, but was run out of town on a rail for trying to arrest George Custer's brother, Tom.

Hickok died on 2 August 1876 in Deadwood, South Dakota. He was shot in the back while playing cards in a saloon.

King of Wall Street and Bennett hunting companion **Leonard Jerome** was famous in his own right. It was his vivacious daughter Jenny, however, who left the greater mark on history. Named after an actress with whom Jerome was infatuated, Jenny Jerome was almost killed as a teenager when James Gordon Bennett, Jr crashed a coach in which she was riding. She was seventeen when her father went hunting buffalo in the American West. Three years later she married a member of British nobility, Lord Randolph Churchill. Their son Winston, born that year, would become Prime Minister of Great Britain during World War II.

In the days after Livingstone's death, there was still the matter of his children's financial security to be resolved. In September 1874, just five months after Livingstone's funeral, Agnes Livingstone discovered a legacy that might ironically have diminished her father's desire to find the Source (and therefore be found by Stanley) if he had known of it during his lifetime. As executor of his estate, Agnes was reviewing Livingstone's accounts when she discovered a forgotten sum of two thousand pounds still gathering interest in a local bank. Accounting for interest on that money, and from the posthumous publication of his Source journals, Livingstone left his children a nine-thousand-pound estate. They split it equally.

Livingstone's children led varied lives. **Tom** died in Egypt in 1876 at the age of twenty-seven. Cause of death was the blood and tissue affliction bilharzia, carried by parasitic trematode worms. The disease was contracted during his African childhood. **Oswell** moved to Trinidad, where he practised medicine until his death in 1892. **Anna**, Livingstone's youngest child, lived until 1893. Her son John became an African missionary. **Agnes**, Livingstone's oldest daughter and the child to whom he was closest, married A. L. Bruce, a wealthy Scottish brewery executive. She died in 1912 at the age of fifty-five, the mother of two sons and the owner of a coffee plantation near the Zambezi.

The Source of the Nile, that single element emanating from the earth, was a mystery which was eventually solved – albeit a century later. Stanley's later journeys suggested Lake Victoria as the Source, though it was not. The Source was also not the Lualaba River. And there were no Fountains of Herodotus. Rather, satellite photography would show that the Nile bubbles from the ground high in the mountains of Burundi, halfway between Lake Tanganyika and Lake Victoria. In their own unique ways, the theories of Burton, Speke, Baker and Livingstone were all partially correct.

ACKNOWLEDGEMENTS

IN THE BEGINNING, FOLLOWING THE PATH OF STANLEY AND LIVINGSTONE seemed a simple project. But over time, as it became clear through research that the story was not just about two men in Africa but about a worldwide series of events, I came to depend on a small army of friends and associates to help me access all the necessary resources. This book could not have been written without them.

In New York, I owe a huge debt to two very important individuals. The first is my incomparable editor, Jason Kaufman, for his vision, patience and perseverance. Jason, you're a genius. I salute you.

The second is my equally spectacular agent, Eric Simonoff. He is a man of great business savvy, wit and literary depth. This book could not have been written without him.

I'd also like to thank Bill Thomas at Random House, Miriam Abramowitz and the stellar Dorothy Vincent at Janklow and Nesbit.

In London, my greatest pleasure was exploring the Royal Geographical Society's archives and library. A particular thanks to Sarah Strong at the RGS for her tireless assistance in digging up the many documents relating to Stanley and Livingstone. Also, thanks to the British Library, where Stanley's original journals reside on microfilm. The staff at the House of Lords Archives and the British Newspaper Library were unfailingly helpful. Also in London, thanks to Simon Thorogood, Sally Gaminara and Susie Brumfitt.

In Washington, thanks to Judge Russell E. Train, whose private collection of Africana offered valuable insights into Livingstone.

In Kuala Lumpur, Phil Kennington was a treasure trove of arcane information on all things British. So many facts, so little space. Thanks for the insights on gin, Phil.

In Sydney, thanks to Graem Sims and Peter Gearin.

In San Francisco, thanks to Gordon Wright and to Austin Murphy.

In Tanzania, where the land outside the cities is still very similar to what Stanley and Livingstone travelled through, thanks to the people of Kigoma and Tabora, as well as the police commissioner of Sumbawanga.

In Johannesburg, thanks to the very knowledgeable Diana Madden, for taking hours from her busy schedule to transcribe Livingstone's letter to Seward.

In Los Angeles, special mention to Bill Baker and Dave Jenni, who traced Stanley's path through Tanzania with me. Also, thanks to Julie and Ian Joseph Baker, Vicki Butler, Matt Dugard, Jim Garfield, Sean Scott and Jeff Probst.

In Dallas, thanks to Cal Johnson.

In Coronado, a very special thanks to Sarah Harper at the Loew's Coronado. Also, a long overdue thanks to Marguerite Clark.

In Orange County, thanks to Denny Bellesi, Bub Kuns and J. P. Jones for the spiritual insights into Livingstone. Thanks also to Ron Allen, John Dybsky, Steve and Cathy Cullen, Cassie McKay, Diane Hunter and Vernie Jones.

All my love to Devin, Connor and Liam. Finally, and most important, love and thanks to Calene, my research assistant, travel companion and wife. Thanks for bashing on, regardless.

NOTES

FROM A RESEARCH POINT OF VIEW, STANLEY AND LIVINGSTONE'S ERA WAS IDEAL. THE days of nautical exploration had largely passed, and with them the sailor's crisp, mostly emotionless, journal entry. Stanley, Livingstone, Burton (and, to a lesser extent, Speke), Baker and Cameron wrote lengthy daily passages that provided a glimpse of the land around them and of their inner emotions. Livingstone's *Missionary Travels and Researches in South Africa, Zambezi Expedition of Dr David Livingstone* and *The Last Journals of Dr David Livingstone* allowed me to express Livingstone's feelings, thoughts and heartfelt prayers in his words. The same was true of Stanley's *How I Found Livingstone, My Early Travels and Adventures in America, Through the Dark Continent* and *The Autobiography of Henry Morton Stanley*. In Stanley's case, the emotions set forth in his books were often revised from his more honest journal entries. When given a choice between Stanley's public accounts and his private journals, I relied on the latter. In all chapters referencing Stanley or Livingstone, their own writing was the primary source. For this reason, I have used their spellings (for place names, tribes, etc.) in lieu of colloquial spellings.

Another great bastion of research was newspapers. Thanks to the proliferation of daily papers during the latter half of the nineteenth century, and also to Stanley's profession, it was possible to trace the story's arc through the pages of The Times of London, New York Herald, Bath Chronicle, New York Times, Manchester Guardian and assorted other publications.

The Royal Geographical Society has long been scrupulous about documenting its activities. Their various internal publications – records, proceedings, etc. – provided a wealth of information.

As for the distances between Stanley and Livingstone, those approximations are based on latitude and longitude notations from personal journals and on specific towns and villages on maps.

As with all writing, there is no substitute for first-person experience. So while I couldn't walk alongside Stanley or Livingstone, I could retrace their path and visit the places that were important to this story: London, New York, Paris, Denver, the East African coast, across Africa to Lake Tanganyika, Tabora and Ujiji.

The backbone of this book, then, is the compilation of journals, letters, newspapers and personal travels listed above. A more detailed reference to sources follows.

Prologue, Livingstone: Alan Moorehead's *The White Nile* (particularly for *baraka*), James Morris's brilliant *Heaven's Command*, Norman R. Bennett's *Arab Versus European* and *Studies in East African History*, *General History of Africa*, Wilfred Noyce's excellent and underrated *The Springs of Adventure*, Reginald Coupland's *The Exploitation of East Africa*, Phyllis Martin and Patrick O'Meara's *Africa* and Timothy Holmes's *Journey to Livingstone*.
Stanley: William Harlow Cook's description of his journey with Stanley is on file with the Royal Geographical Society, and provides a vivid account of their journey down the Platte. Further information was gleaned from Stanley biographies, of which two excellent books tower above the rest. The first is *Stanley: The Making of an African Explorer (1841–1877)*. The second is *Dark Safari: The Life Behind the Legend of Henry Morton Stanley*. Both were used as references for this chapter. Also, Davies's *Ten Days on the Plains* and Dee Brown's *The American West* and *Bury My Heart at Wounded Knee*. Norman R. Bennett's *Stanley's Despatches to the New York Herald*.

Chapter One: Because of the amount of erroneous published information on the Nile Duel, much of this chapter relies on eyewitness accounts via newspaper stories and Royal Geographical Society records in an attempt to set the record straight. The works on Speke and Burton listed in the bibliography (in particular, Edward Rice's thorough and readable *Captain Sir Richard Francis Burton: A Biography* and Alexander Maitland's *Speke*) were used extensively. *Heaven's Command*, *Journey to Livingstone*, *The White Nile*, H. G. Adam's *David Livingstone*, *Livingstone's Last Journey* by Reginald Coupland, Isabel Burton's *Life of Sir Richard Burton* and *To the Farthest Ends of the Earth* by Ian Cameron. Simpson's *Dark Companions* provided information on Bombay's life. As an aside, the 1989 Rob Rafelson film *Mountains of the Moon* is an entertaining, mostly accurate portrayal of Burton and Speke's battles.

Chapter Two: *David Livingstone* by C. S. Nicholls. Also, Adams, Coupland, Holmes.

Chapter Three: In addition to Stanley's accounts of his time in Turkey, McLynn, Bierman and Norman R. Bennett's *Stanley's Despatches to the New York Herald* all offer thorough investigations of that boondoggle. For information on the American West, Brown's *Bury My Heart at Wounded Knee* and *The American West*.

Chapter Four: The RGS Archives, which hold Young's original letters to Murchison and original Society orders, were invaluable. Of books, Young's *In Search of Livingstone* is the definitive tome, and goes into much more detail than his report to the Royal Geographical Society. For information on the Zulu, Morris's *Heaven's Command* was thorough and entertaining. Also, Coupland, Adams. Phil Kennington, formerly of the Royal Marines, provided invaluable insights into life on Her Majesty's yacht. Rawlinson's comments on Murchison's character are taken from his 1872 President's Address.

Chapter Five: McLynn, Bierman, Brown, the New York *Times*, Don Sietz's *The James Gordon Bennetts*, Allen Oliver's *New York, New York*, Mike Wallace and Edwin G. Burrows's *Gotham: A History of New York to 1898*, Richard O'Connor's *The Scandalous Mr Bennett*.

Chapter Six: Holmes, Nicholls, James Currey's *General History of Africa*, Robert Stock's *Africa South of the Sahara*, Coupland's *East Africa and Its Invaders*, John Spencer Trimingham's *Islam in East Africa*, Abdul Sheriff's *Slaves, Spices and Ivory in Zanzibar*, Stanley Engerman's *Slavery*, Martin and O'Meara's *Africa* and Robert A. Stafford's brilliant *Scientists of Empire: Sir Roderick Murchison, Scientific Exploration and Victorian Imperialism*.

Chapter Seven: McLynn, Bierman, Byron Farwell's *The Man Who Presumed*, Bennett's *Stanley's Despatches to the New York Herald*, Herman Melville's *Battle Pieces*, Bennett's *Studies in East African History* and Morris.

Chapter Eight: Holmes, Adams.

Chapter Nine: Stafford, Stephen Linwood's *A History of London*, Sally Mitchell's *Daily Life in Victorian England*, Patrick O'Brian's *Joseph Banks: A Life*, Tom Hiney's *On The Missionary Trail*, Morris, Cameron, Holmes, Moorehead. Also, Hugh Robert Mill's *The Record of the Royal Geographical*

Society, 1830–1930, for Rawlinson's obituary remarks on Murchison's character.

Chapter Ten: In addition to Livingstone's journals, Cameron's *Across Africa* was vital in providing physical descriptions of the land west of Lake Tanganyika: the Great Congo Forest, the rites of cannibalism in the Manyuema region and the odd body odour produced by those eating human flesh and animal carrion. Also, Holmes, Nicholls, Stafford, Adams, Daniel Liebowitz's *The Physician and the Slave Trade*.

Chapter Eleven: The primary source of all dialogue in the Stanley–Bennett encounter comes directly from Stanley's *How I Found Livingstone*. McLynn, Farwell, Moorehead, Coupland, Seitz, O'Connor. The staff at the Grand Hotel in Paris, which is still very much in business, were most helpful in confirming the exact location of Bennett's suite.

Chapter Twelve: *The Gladstone Diaries: With Cabinet Minutes and Prime Ministerial Correspondence* provides details of the extension of monies to Livingstone. Also, Stafford, David Babbington's *William Ewart Gladstone: Faith and Politics in Victorian England* and David Kynaston's *The Chancellor of the Exchequer*.

Chapter Thirteen: Stanley's original journals and *How I Found Livingstone* combine to portray Stanley's worries and fears. His original desire to follow the Rufiji instead of the caravan routes is seen in his journals. Also, Bennett's *Studies in East African History*, Liebowitz, Holmes, Bierman, McLynn.

Chapter Fourteen: Bennett's *Stanley's Despatches to the New York Herald*, McLynn, Bierman, Bennett's *Studies in East African History*, Liebowitz.

Chapter Fifteen: Oswell, Coupland, Holmes, Nicholls, Cameron. Livingstone's letter to Seward, dated November 1871, was purchased by the Brenthurst Library through Chas J. Sawyer at an auction at Christie's on 16 December 1991. At their request, it is cited thus: David Livingstone, Letter, MS.240/1f. The Brenthurst Library, Johannesburg.

Chapter Sixteen: Details of caravan life are best seen in Cameron, Bennett's *Despatches*, Rice. The Center for Disease Control provided the details about sleeping sickness and tse-tse. Dr Matthew Dugard and Dr Steven Cullen provided further insight.

Chapter Seventeen: It bears repeating that Stanley's thoughts and actions are all catalogued in his journals and *How I Found Livingstone*. Also, McLynn, Bierman. The CDC, Dugard and Cullen provided commentary on dysentery.

Chapter Eighteen: Granville's comments can be found in *Hansard's Parliamentary Debates*. The excellent *Encarta Encyclopedia* provided background on the war between France and Germany.

Chapter Nineteen: McLynn, Bierman, Brown, Holmes, Bennett's *Despatches*. The CDC provided information on elephantiasis. Stafford.

Chapter Twenty: Baker's *Ismaelia* provides a vivid recreation of life in Gondokoro, including records of conversations with passing travellers about Livingstone's possible location, and Florence Baker's tables listing the daily temperature and humidity. Also, Moorehead, Stafford, Holmes.

Chapter Twenty-one: Cameron, Holmes, Nicholls.

Chapter Twenty-two: McLynn, Bierman, Farwell. Stanley's early comments about Livingstone can be found in Bennett's *Despatches*. Stanley's sexual ambivalence is thoroughly catalogued in the various biographies.

Chapter Twenty-three: Stanley thoroughly documented his time in Ugogo, but Cameron's journals read like an anthropological odyssey, complete with drawings, vivid descriptions and various tales of the Wagogo. The CDC, for information on malaria.

Chapter Twenty-four: *The Proceedings of the Royal Geographical Society*, Cameron's *To the Ends of the Earth* and Mill's *Record*.

Chapter Twenty-five: Bennett's *East African History* and *Despatches*, McLynn, Bierman.

Chapter Twenty-six: McLynn, Bierman, Bennett's *Despatches*.

Chapter Twenty-seven: Livingstone's journal description of the massacre is vivid and horrific. He also wrote of the tragedy in a letter to Earl Granville, dated 14 November 1871. Also, Coupland, Holmes, Nicholls. Cameron, for his discussion of cannibalism.

Chapter Twenty-eight: McLynn, Bierman, Bennett's *Despatches*.

Chapter Twenty-nine: Bennett's *Despatches*, *Studies in East African History*, and *Arab Versus European*. McLynn, Bierman.

Chapter Thirty: I. F. Lockevon's original letter to Stanley is on file with the Royal Geographical Society. Davies's *Ten Days on the Plains*, Brown's *American West* and *Bury My Heart*, McLynn, O'Connor, Seitz. Weybright and Sell, Goodman and Leonard, for Buffalo Bill information. Bennett's *Despatches*.

Chapter Thirty-one: McLynn, Bierman, Snell-Blasford, Bennett's *Despatches*. The CDC website, for information on smallpox.

Chapter Thirty-two: Kirk's letter to Murchison, dated 25 September 1871. Kirk's letter to Earl Granville dated 22 September 1871. Bennett's *Despatches*. Bierman, McLynn.

Chapter Thirty-three: McLynn, Bierman, Farwell.

Chapter Thirty-four: Nicholls, Coupland, Holmes's *Letters and Documents* and *Journey to Livingstone*. Livingstone's letters to Granville.

Chapter Thirty-five: Bierman, McLynn, Bennett's *Despatches*, Oswell.

Chapter Thirty-six: Gladstone's *Diaries* are the most auspicious reference in this chapter. It's also worth noting, however, the attention Murchison's death received. Though largely overlooked in modern histories of the Victorian era, Murchison's accomplishments warranted an exhaustive obituary and his funeral a lengthy, detailed write-up in *The Times*. Burton's status in life can be found in his letter to *The Times*, as well as Rice. As for the revised date for Stanley's meeting with Livingstone, the source is François Bontinick's 'La date de la rencontre Stanley–Livingstone' from *Africa, Rivista trimestale di studi e documentazione dell'Istituto Italo-African 24*, as noted in McLynn.

Chapter Thirty-seven: Stanley and Livingstone's journals provide a thorough and insightful look at their time together. Further information can be found in Bierman, McLynn, Farwell. Bennett's *Despatches* is especially vital to this period, as are Seitz and O'Connor.

Chapter Thirty-eight: Bennett's *Despatches*, McLynn, Bierman, Liebowitz. The comments of Tom Livingstone, Granville, Queen Victoria and Rawlinson are included in the appendix of Stanley's *How I Found Livingstone*, in which he laid out his defence against his detractors.

Chapter Thirty-nine: The interviews of Chitambo and Mumana were conducted in October 1936. Their signed affidavits are on file with the Royal Geographical Society. Kirk's comments are taken from *David Livingstone: His Life and Letters. Daily Life in Victorian England* provided insights into parenthood. The general naughtiness of London society during that era can be found in Carey's *Eyewitness to History*. Dr Isaac Baker Brown's theories on clitoridectomies can be found in his *On the Curability of Certain Forms of Insanity, Epilepsy, Catalepsy and Hysteria in Females* (1866). It's worth noting that Brown's theories were later found to be repulsive. Brown himself went insane.

Chapter Forty: Cameron, Waller, Stanley, Coupland and *The Times* of London.

BIBLIOGRAPHY

Adams, H.G. *David Livingstone*. London, 1902.

Allen, Oliver E. *New York, New York*. New York, 1990.

Anstruther, Ian. *Dr Livingstone, I Presume*. New York, 1957.

Baker, Sir Samuel White. *Ismaelia*. London.

Bebbington, David. *William Ewart Gladstone, Faith and Politics in Victorian Britain*. Grand Rapids, 1993.

Bennett, Norman Robert. *Studies in East African History*. Boston, 1963.

Bennett, Norman Robert. *Stanley's Despatches to the New York Herald: 1871–1872, 1874–1877*. Boston, 1970.

Bennett, Norman Robert. *Arab Versus European*. New York, 1986.

Bierman, John. *Dark Safari: The Life Behind the Legend of Henry Morton Stanley*. Austin, 1990.

Blasford-Snell, John. *In the Steps of Stanley*. London, 1975.

Boorstin, Daniel J. *The Discoverers*. New York, 1983.

Brandon, Michael. *The Perfect Victorian Hero*. Edinburgh, 1982.

Brown, Dee. *Bury My Heart at Wounded Knee*. New York, 1970.

Brown, Dee. *The American West*. New York, 1994.

Burke, John. *An Illustrated History of England*. London, 1974.

Burrows, Edwin G. and Wallace, Mike. *Gotham: A History of New York City to 1898*. New York, 1999.

Burton, Isabel. *Life of Sir Richard Burton*.

Burton, Sir Richard. *The Lake Regions of Central Africa*. New York, 1961.

Cameron, Ian. *To the Farthest Ends of the Earth: The History of the Royal*

Geographical Society 1830–1980. London, 1980.

Cameron, Verney Lovett. *Across Africa.* London, 1877.

Clun, Harold P. *The Face of London.* London, 1962.

Conneally, Thomas. *American Scoundrel.* New York, 2002.

Coupland, Sir Reginald. *East Africa and its Invaders.* London, 1938.

Coupland, Sir Reginald. *The Exploitation of East Africa.* London, 1939.

Coupland, Sir Reginald. *Livingstone's Last Journey.* London, 1945.

Currey, James. *General History of Africa.* Paris, 1999.

Davidson, Basil. *Africa in History.* New York, 1966.

Davies, Henry E. *Ten Days on the Plains.* Dallas, 1985.

Dolman, Alfred. *In the Footsteps of Livingstone.* London, 1924.

Engerman, Stanley, et al. *Slavery.* Oxford, 2001.

Farwell, Byron. *The Man Who Presumed: A Biography of Henry M. Stanley.* New York, 1957.

Gladstone, William Ewart. *The Gladstone Diaries: With Cabinet Minutes and Prime Ministerial Correspondence.* Volumes VII and VIII. Oxford, 1982.

Hansard's Parliamentary Debates. Third series, volume 206. London, 1871.

Helly, Dorothy O. *Livingstone's Legacy.* Athens, Ohio, 1987.

Hiney, Tom. *On the Missionary Trail.* New York, 2000.

Hochschild, Adam. *King Leopold's Ghost.* New York, 1998.

Holmes, Timothy. *David Livingstone, Letters and Documents, 1841–1872.* London, 1990.

Holmes, Timothy. *Journey to Livingstone, Exploration of an Imperial Myth.* Edinburgh, 1993.

Hubbard Brothers. *Livingstone's Africa.* Saint Louis.

Inwood, Stephen. *A History of London.* New York, 1998.

Johnston, Sir Harry. *A History and Description of the British Empire in Africa.* London.

Kynaston, David. *The Chancellor of the Exchequer.* Suffolk, 1980.

Leonard, Elizabeth Jane and Goodman, Julia Cody. *Buffalo Bill: King of the Old West.* New York, 1955.

Liebowitz, Daniel. *The Physician and the Slave Trade.* New York, 1999.

Livingstone, David. *David Livingstone's Family Letters 1841–1856.* Volumes I and II. Edited by I. Schapera. London, 1959.

Livingstone, David. *Doctor Livingstone's Discoveries in South Central Africa from 1849 to 1856.* London, 1857.

Livingstone, David. *Missionary Travels and Researches in South Africa.* London, 1857.

Livingstone, David. *David Livingstone's Shire Journal 1861–1864.*

Livingstone, David. *Dispatches Addressed by David Livingstone, Her Majesty's Consul (Inner Africa), to the Secretary of State for Foreign Affairs, in 1870, 1871 and 1872 (com)*. London, 1872.

Livingstone, David and Stanley, Henry Morton. *Quest: The Story of Stanley and Livingstone Told in Their Own Words*. Edited by Sue Newson-Smith. London, 1978.

MacNair, James I. *Livingstone's Travels*. London, 1954.

Maitland, Alexander. *Speke and the Discovery of the Source of the Nile*. London, 1971.

Martin, Phyllis M. and O'Meara, Patrick. *Africa*. Bloomington, 1986.

Maurice, Albert. *H. M. Stanley: Unpublished Letters*. London, 1955.

McLynn, Frank. *Stanley: The Making of an African Explorer*. London, 1989.

Melville, Herman. *Battle Pieces*. New York, 1867.

Meyer, Bernard C. *Joseph Conrad: A Psychoanalytic Biography*. Princeton, 1987.

Mill, Hugh Robert. *The Record of the Royal Geographical Society, 1830–1930*. London, 1930.

Mitchell, Sally. *Daily Life in Victorian England*. Westport, Connecticut, 1996.

Monk, Reverend William. *Dr Livingstone's Cambridge Lectures*. London, 1858.

Montefore, Arthur. *H. M. Stanley, the African Explorer*. London.

Moorehead, Alan. *The White Nile*. New York, 1960.

Morris, James. *Heaven's Command: An Imperial Progress*. New York, 1973.

Murdoch, John G. *The Life and Explorations of David Livingstone, LL.D.* London.

National Portrait Gallery. *David Livingstone and the Victorian Encounter with Africa*. London, 1996.

Nicholls, C. S. *David Livingstone*. Gloucestershire, 1998.

Northcott, Cecil. *David Livingstone: His Triumph, Decline, and Fall*. London, 1957.

Noyce, Wilfrid. *The Springs of Adventure*. New York, 1958.

O'Brian, Patrick. *Joseph Banks: A Life*. Chicago, 1987.

O'Connor, Richard. *The Scandalous Mr Bennett*. New York, 1962.

Oliver, Roland and Atmore, Anthony. *Africa Since 1800*. Cambridge, 1967.

Ondaatje, Christopher. *Journey to the Source of the Nile*. New York, 1998.

Oswell, William Cotton. *The Last Diaries of Dr David Livingstone*. London, 1874.

Pakenham, Thomas. *The Scramble for Africa*. London, 1991.

Ransford, Oliver. *Livingstone*. London, 1978.

Rediker, Marcus. *Between the Devil and the Deep Blue Sea.* Cambridge, Massachusetts, 1987.

Reader, John. *Africa.* New York, 1997.

Rice, Edward. *Captain Sir Richard Francis Burton: A Biography.* 1990.

Rowley, Reverend Henry. *The Universities Mission to Central Africa.* London, 1867.

Russell, Don. *The Lives and Legends of Buffalo Bill.* Norman, Oklahoma, 1960.

Sheriff, Abdul. *Slaves, Spices and Ivory in Zanzibar.* London, 1987.

Seaver, George. *David Livingstone: His Life and Letters.* London, 1957.

Seitz, Don C. *The James Gordon Bennetts.* New York, 1928.

Sell, Henry Blackman and Victor Weybright. *Buffalo Bill and the Wild West.* New York, 1955.

Sheridan, General P. H. *The Posts in the Military Division of the Missouri.* Chicago, 1876.

Simpson, Donald. *Dark Companions: The African Contribution to the European Exploration of East Africa.* New York, 1976.

Speke, John H. *The Discovery of the Source of the Nile.* London, 1863.

Stafford, Robert A. *Scientist of Empire: Sir Roderick Murchison, Scientific Exploration and Victorian Imperialism.* Cambridge, 1989.

Stanley, Henry M. *My Early Travels and Adventures in America.* Lincoln.

Stanley, Henry M. *The Finding of Dr Livingstone.* London, 1873.

Stanley, Henry M. *How I Found Livingstone.* New York, 1874.

Stanley, Henry M. *Through the Dark Continent.* London, 1899.

Stanley, Henry M. *The Autobiography of Henry Morton Stanley.* 1909.

Stanley, Richard and Alan Neame. *The Exploration Diaries of H. M. Stanley.* London, 1961.

Sterling, Thomas. *Stanley's Way.* New York, 1866.

Stock, Robert. *Africa South of the Sahara.* New York, 1995.

Trimingham, John Spencer. *Islam in East Africa.* Oxford, 1965.

Waller, Horace. *The Last Journals of David Livingstone in Central Africa, from 1865 until His Death.* London, 1874.

Waller, J. P. R. *Zambezi Expedition of Dr David Livingstone.* Volumes I and II. London, 1956.

Wasserman, Jacob. *Bula Matari.* New York, 1933.

White, Andrea. *Joseph Conrad and the Adventure Tradition.* Cambridge, 1993.

Williamson, David. *National Portrait Gallery History of the Kings and Queens of England.* New York, 1998.

Young, E. D. *The Search for Livingstone*. London, 1868.
Zondervan Publishing. *The New International Version Study Bible*. Grand Rapids, 1995.

INDEX

NOTE: *people with surnames (family names) beginning with 'bin' appear under their first names, as used in the text; eg. Dugumbe bin Habib under D.*

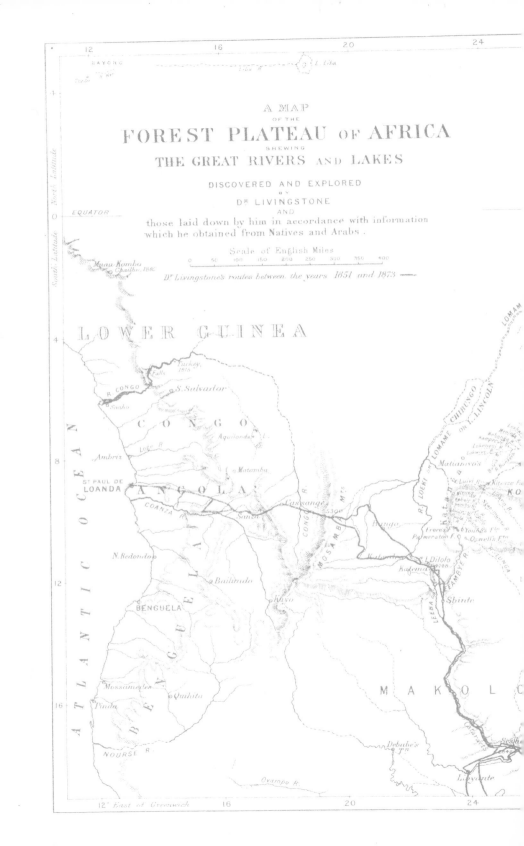

A MAP
OF THE
FOREST PLATEAU OF AFRICA
SHEWING
THE GREAT RIVERS AND LAKES

DISCOVERED AND EXPLORED
BY
DR LIVINGSTONE
AND
those laid down by him in accordance with information
which he obtained from Natives and Arabs.

Scale of English Miles

0   50   100   150   200   250   300   350   400

Dr Livingstone's routes between the years 1851 and 1873 ———